Identity
& *Intimacy*

Identity

& Intimacy

William
Kilpatrick,Ph.D.

A Delta Book

Published by
Dell Publishing Co., Inc.
1 Dag Hammarskjold Plaza
New York, New York 10017

Grateful acknowledgment is made for permission to use excerpts from the
following:

"A Man for All Seasons" by Robert Bolt: By permission of Random House,
Inc., and Heinemann Educational Books Ltd.

"As Time Goes By" by Herman Hupfeld: © 1931 Harms, Inc. Copyright
renewed. All Rights Reserved. Used by permission of Warner Bros. Music.
Reproduced by permission of Chappell & Co., Ltd., for British Common-
wealth (except Canada).

"In Bluebeard's Castle" by George Steiner: By permission of Yale University
Press and Faber and Faber Ltd.

Chapter 1 is based on an article which first appeared in *Adolescence* (Summer
1974, Vol. 9, 34) under the title "Identity: Continuity, Fidelity, and Future
Shock." Chapters 4 and 5 are based on an article which first appeared in
Adolescence (Summer 1971, Vol. 6, 22) under the title "McLuhan: Implications
for Adolescence." Chapter 7 is based on an article which first appeared in
Adolescence (Fall 1974, Vol. 8, 9) under the title "Identity: Youth and the
Dissolution of Culture." Chapter 10 is based on an article which first appeared
in *Adolescence* (Spring 1974, Vol. 9, 33) under the title "The Demythologizing
of Love." By permission of Libra Publishers, Inc.

Acknowledgments

I am deeply indebted to a number of people who provided both ideas and encouragement to me as I wrote. First, to Tony Chemasi for his many invaluable insights, suggestions, criticisms, and style improvements. Then to my brother, Robert Kilpatrick, who taught me how to organize a chapter, and insisted that I use English instead of jargon; to my editors, Nancy E. Gross and Deborah Takiff, who helped me bring order to a chaotic manuscript; to my colleague, John Dacey, for his support and suggestions; to Donald Chandler and Marleen Cenotti for their encouragement, but especially for their friendship; to Chuck Hopkins for his help in revising Chapter 2; and finally to Betsy Chisholm and Elena Vitug, who did most of the typing.

For
Guy,
Mark and Kathleen
and
My Mother

Contents

Introduction

The present era has been variously described as the age of liberation, the age of transformation, even the age of a new consciousness. At some future date, however, we may look back and discover that it was, in reality, the age during which we lost our identity, and with it, our ability to love.

We are on the verge of losing a certain conviction about life and love. That conviction can be illustrated by a song with which most Americans are familiar. Anyone who has seen the film *Casablanca* will not have forgotten its theme song and the memorable line from it which declares: "the fundamental things apply, as time goes by."[1] Ever since "Sam" played it again at Rick's Cafe in Casablanca, this romantic refrain has held a special fascination: somehow, those lyrics seem to capture the essence of all love songs. However difficult it may be to define love, there has always been a strong conviction that it ought to last. Shakespeare, for instance, observed that "Love's not Time's fool," that it "alters not with his brief hours and weeks." Admittedly, most of us get rather thick-tongued when speaking about matters of love. We stutter out our words, sounding more like William Budd than William Shakespeare. Still, we feel almost intuitively that love has something to do with constancy, that it ought to last no matter how much time goes by.

How feasible is a constant love today? To answer that question we have to consider the relationship between love and identity, because a constant love—one that does not alter with the passage of time—depends on an identity that does not alter. In a sense, identity is an even more "fundamental thing" than love. It stands behind love the way a bar of gold stands behind a federal reserve note: as a guarantee that our affections are legal tender, not counterfeit. The analogy is only partial, of course: the price of gold may rise and fall, but we tend to pride ourselves on the stability of our identity. It is this persistent sense of identity which allows us to make brash declarations of friendship and love such as, "You can count on me," or, "Trust me." It is a confidence that there is something durable about "me," something that doesn't fluctuate. Without that confidence our commitments remain half-hearted, and we hang back from love and friendship, afraid to let others trust us, or fearful that our tenuous sense of self may get lost in the tangle of another person's identity.

The connection between identity and love is further suggested by the way we respond when love goes on the rocks. If someone we love stops loving us, we suspect that some massive alteration in their identity has occurred: "You've become a stranger," we say. "You're not the person I fell in love with." Or even, "How could I have ever loved *you!*" Perhaps it is experiences of this kind that cause us to feel about identity the same way we feel about love: that, however difficult to define, it too ought to last. In keeping with that spirit it would be pleasant to conclude this introduction with some comfortable reassurance that, even today, "the fundamental things apply . . ."

But do they? During the past decade or so, new models of identity have surfaced in Western culture, and along with them, new patterns of intimacy. These new patterns force a reconsideration of our musical analogy. For instance, when two lovers woo, do they still say "I love you"? Or are they more likely to say, "I'm really not ready for an involvement at this stage of my life." And if I'm not, why not? Because "we're always growing and changing, aren't we? It doesn't make sense to get too committed if our feelings may change." Other variations of contemporary love language go something like this: "I have to be free to grow, and I want you to be free, too." Or, more simply, "I really don't know who I am yet."

This unromantic newspeak may be admirable in its honesty,

and it is in some ways more realistic than declarations of undying love, but it can also be used as a deceptive manipulation. My interest, however, is not to anatomize the sincerity of modern love talk. Of more interest, I believe, is this: behind such now-commonplace statements there lies a new and radically different philosophy of identity.

Our current inability to sustain relationships or responsibilities is the result of a largely unnoticed but nevertheless remarkable transformation in our sense of self stemming from that philosophy. The prevailing theme of this transformation is a reverent faith in what we may call the fluid self. It has become the dominant cultural orthodoxy of our day.

This book attempts to explain the development of this new identity and to explore its consequences for intimacy. It is, at the same time, a defense of a more traditional concept of identity. Let me outline that traditional view and contrast to it some recent trends.

Identity is, first of all, a conviction of self-sameness—a bridge over the discontinuities which invariably creep or crash into our lives. It is the link between the child of seven and that same person at seventeen; between that seventeen-year-old and the seventy-year-old self to come. It is, in brief, a sense of personal history. A sure way to rob a person of identity is to take away his history. This loss of history explains the confusion of the amnesia victim, as well as the docility of the brainwashed prisoner. These are extreme cases, but it is well to remember that the eradication of the past can be effected on an extreme scale. It happened to millions of European Jews who were reduced to numbers in concentration and extermination camps. They were shorn of their pasts just as effectively as they were stripped of their clothes and possessions; and many lost their identity long before they lost their life. In Stalin's Russia, one of the first steps toward creating a new Soviet identity was to rewrite the history books; and Soviet citizens with an eye toward survival were forced to reconstruct their personal history to accord with the official revision. Conversely, identity—the identity of one individual or of a whole people—can be strengthened by finding links to the true past. In our own country, the creation of a new Black identity has been accompanied by attempts to recover Black history, much of which had been "lost, stolen or strayed."[2]

John Dos Passos once wrote: "a sense of continuity with generations gone before can stretch like a lifeline across the scary present."[3] What Dos Passos said of men in general can be applied as well to men in particular. In our individual lives the sense of continuous identity is a lifeline across times of personal crisis. In the concentration camps, those who managed to counteract the process of identity disintegration made a conscious effort to keep the past alive. I think in particular of the Austrian psychiatrist Victor Frankl, who from 1942 to 1945 was imprisoned in Nazi concentration camps, Dachau and Auschwitz among them. Most of his family, including his wife, died in the camps or gas chambers. Joseph Fabry tells how Frankl "gathered around him a group of inmates who were, as he was himself, enthusiastic rock-climbers. They met every two weeks, and at every meeting one of them had to talk about some of his rock-climbing exploits in the Alps. Engrossed in listening, in their own memories, and their hope of seeing their mountains again, they were, for moments at least, able to rise above their hopeless situation."[4]

The story vividly illustrates the importance of continuity. It also points to two other factors that sustain identity. One of these is the presence of other people who have shared our past or who at least can affirm our memory of the past. An identity cannot stand alone—not for long. We need others to bear witness to our personal history, others who are willing to take note of our passage. They give to us something we cannot always give to ourselves: the assurance that our history has been and is being recorded. Those who specialize in crushing the human spirit understand this well enough. They can destroy an identity simply by depriving a man of any contact with his fellows. Isolation is as effective as torture in making men malleable to the whim of their captors. Without others to confirm his self-worth, a man soon comes to doubt that he has any.

Frankl's efforts to keep hope alive illustrate another factor crucial to identity: the future. He not only prodded his fellow inmates to recall past achievements; he challenged them to consider future tasks still waiting for them—future tasks which promised that their present existence was not meaningless. For one prisoner the future might lie in a child still alive somewhere; for another it might mean completing a manuscript; for another man, his family and profession wiped out, it might mean a chance merely to return again to the challenge of the Alps.

The courage with which we can tackle the future, however, depends a great deal on the strength of our present identity, and that in turn evolves out of our links to the past. The sense of continuity—the "lifeline" of which Dos Passos spoke—both secures us to our roots and allows us to strike more boldly into the future. Rock-climbing, Frankl's passion, happens to provide an apt analogy. The leader of a rock-climbing expedition is the one who takes the most chances, for there is no one above him to stop his fall. To protect himself he hammers pitons (metal spikes) into cracks along the rocks' surface as he edges up the cliff. To these he attaches metal clips called carabiners, passing his rope through the carabiners as he goes up. If he should slip, his fall can be stopped from below by a second climber who holds his rope. The leader will only fall as far below his last-placed carabiner as he has climbed above it; pitons and carabiners form a chain of safety to the climber below. The more of these links there are, the more confidently the leader can ascend. And confidence is the climber's main asset; without it knees begin to shake, and toes begin to slip. A good climber may be daring, his moves sometimes breathtaking, but he is not foolish; below him stretches a lifeline to the place he began.

Up to this point I have laid great stress on the importance of continuity. A healthy identity, however, requires more than a sense of continuity with one's past self. We are always growing, changing, rethinking—or we ought to be. A twenty-year-old can't get along with the self-definition he had at age ten. And by the time he reaches forty, he'll have had to make several more redefinitions. If he doesn't, he's simply not being true to his experience of life. Identity is not a static established achievement but a dynamic and continuous process of consolidation and reorganization. It is a synthesis of many interests and choices into a unique and distinctive style—but a synthesis that never stops. A healthy identity, then, maintains a balance between continuity and change. Just here, however, is where the present identity confusion lies. If I place much emphasis on continuity, it is because that balance has been upset to the point where the element of continuity is in danger of being neglected. Already the absence of any regard for continuity is unmistakably evident in current psychologies and in current life-styles.

Let me make one final point. Identity is also built on choices and commitments. It is partly by committing ourselves to others or to causes or to passions that our self develops. As identity develops, the urge to share it grows more insistent. Yet by giving ourselves over to the things and people that matter to us we get back a fuller identity in return. Conversely, a major obstacle to achieving identity is the temptation to avoid choices and postpone decisions. Hackneyed as the thought may be, we do, in fact, identify ourselves by what we choose to do and by the people we choose to be with. In Walt Whitman's poem "Native Moments" we find a striking example of just such an identity decision when he resolves to align himself with his true comrades: the rude, the coarse, the homosexual, the outcast.

> *I will play a part no longer, why should I exile myself*
> *from my companions?*
> *O you shunn'd persons, I at least do not shun you,*
> *I come forthwith in your midst, I will be your poet,*
> *I will be more to you than to any of the rest.*[5]

No doubt there are many today (as there were many in Whitman's day) who would consider this a negative identity. But for Whitman it was a positive step toward defining the self he emphatically wished to be.

What I have sketched above is a view of identity that generally accords with that worked out by Erik Erikson, and also by certain existential psychologists, notably Victor Frankl and Rollo May. Erikson, in particular, has called attention to the importance of individual identity, defined it in a roundabout sort of way (which is really the best way), and suggested the dangers of its absence. After his now classic studies the inquiry into the problem of identity seemed almost a closed case. But certain new "evidence" demands that the investigation be reopened—and promptly. This new evidence can be classified under three distinct but sometimes overlapping trends: one cultural, one psychological, one philosophical. Together, these three trends pose a distinct threat to the kind of identity outlined above.

The first trend encompasses a variety of demographic and technical changes summed up by Alvin Toffler under the heading "future shock." The consequences of future shock were foretold years ago by the poet Yeats when he wrote: "Things fall apart; the centre cannot hold." In a hastily evolving society we are subjected to rapidly accelerating centrifugal forces which tug at the center—our sense of identity. And it becomes increasingly difficult to hold on to a continuous sense of self. The lifeline to our past self frays and finally snaps.

The second trend seems to be a response to the predicament of rapid change: instead of resisting change we should flow with it. This is the approach advocated by the Human Potential Movement—easily the most important and influential school in contemporary psychology. Its answer to social acceleration is an identity that is adaptable, flexible, even fluid. Rather than cling to an unchanging rocklike identity, we should launch ourselves into the swirling stream of change.

This is a new definition of identity: identity not as a persistent sense of self but as a completely fluid process.

The third trend is the most radical, for it seeks to do away entirely with the notion of individual identity. It is difficult to fix a precise label to this movement, but the type of thinking that inspires it is well represented by theorists like Marshall McLuhan and Norman O. Brown, and by certain Eastern mystics. To their way of thinking, the cultivation of individual identity constitutes a heresy against the essential unity of all persons. What they recommend instead is a supraidentity: a union of all individual identities into one human identity.

These three trends are closely related. Human potentialism is an attempt to cope with the rapid change and increased mobility of future shock. In turn, we find that those immersed in the Human Potential life-style often undergo a subtle sea change which causes them to flow in an Easterly direction. In fact, the river down which they float sometimes appears to be that very river by which Siddhartha sat while he meditated on the oneness of all creatures.

The spokesmen for these currents of change are not modest. They promise a metamorphosis that will remake Western man in a new identity—one more adaptable than the traditional identity to the stresses of twentieth-century living. Moreover, the new philosophies hold out the promise that the freshly created person will be more loving, more capable of intimacy than ever before. So far these ideas have been accepted rather uncritically, not only by growing numbers of the general public, but also by a sizable segment of professional psychologists and counselors. While the Eastern brand of nonidentity is still somewhat suspect, the Human Potential view is by now almost sacrosanct. The majority of psychologists are comfortably unaware that there is any incompatibility between the model of identity proposed by the Human Potential Movement and that proposed by Erikson. More seriously, there are few who recognize that the much praised fluid identity is more likely to destroy the capacity for intimacy than to enhance it. Yet much of the current restlessness about relationships—the inability to satiate needs for sex or intimacy, the endless quest for fresh partners and ever more variety, the cry for "madder music and for stronger wine"[6]—can be traced to the wholehearted and unquestioning adoption of this new style of identity.

In Part One of this book I wish to consider the ways in which rapid social change affects identity. Even without the advent of new psychological and philosophical trends, the uprootedness and mobility which now prevail in our society are of themselves enough to undermine the stoutest identity. We must ask ourselves, What does it mean to grow up in a society where almost everything is disposable, rentable, or impermanent? Clothes, toys, books, appliances—use them, then throw them away. Tools, skis, furniture, apartments, automobiles—rent them for a day, a week, a year. And is there a subtle transition from the disposable object to the disposable friendship? How many friends, neighbors, and lovers have come and gone? How willingly will we commit ourself next time? How much will we hold back?

Identity builds on choices and commitments and on the ability to stick to them. But future shock, since it accustoms us to constant mobility and novelty, undercuts our capacity for fidelity and our willingness to commit; it deprives us of a sense of continuity and leaves us vulnerable to identity confusion. Moreover, rapid change makes self-definition almost impossible. It is painful to define one's self in any one way when so many alternative ways are available. But the effect of this surfeit of choices is to keep us in a perpetual traffic jam of anxiety: in a hurry to get somewhere in life, but fearful that we have chosen the slow lane, fearful that those in the other lanes will soon be whizzing by us, wondering if we ought not make a change before it's too late.

Part Two is an attempt to analyze the Human Potential psychology and its impact on identity. The unceasing motion of modern society raises a very simple and basic question:

"Can I keep up?" To this question the Human Potential Movement has answered, in effect, "You can if you keep loose." The Human Potential key to surviving change is to loosen our deep instincts for growth. And growth implies continual redefinitions of the self. Because the world, and our experience of it, is constantly changing, our identity needs constant revision. So the healthy self is the self-in-process; the healthy individual is the one with the jazz musician's ability to improvise as he goes along.

The idea has considerable merit, but it has been pushed to extremes. Perhaps the popularizers have been more to blame than the theorists. Perhaps there has been a tendency for them to select some aspects of the theory and neglect other, balancing elements. So popular has the Human Potential philosophy become, so much a part of the air we breathe, that many who subscribe to it are unaware both of the movement's existence and its theoretical foundation. Those theoretical underpinnings are embedded in the work of two psychologists, Carl Rogers and Abraham Maslow. And since Rogers' theory of personality is less complicated, it has come to predominate while Maslow has increasingly been relegated to the status of founding father—respected but unheeded. Which is too bad, because Maslow often cautioned against the dangers that self-actualization is heir to.

It appears now that the dangers have been embraced rather than avoided. If anything, it has been a matter of excess: of taking things too far. The Human Potential emphasis on "the here-and-now" is, for example, a good antidote to our tendency to postpone life's vital encounters—to measure out our lives in coffee spoons, Prufrock-style. But an exclusive emphasis on the present moment plays havoc with a sense of continuous identity. The celebration of the present lapses into the cultivation of short-term spontaneity and the neglect of long-term commitment.

This reluctance to commit is intensified by the movement's understanding of the self as *pure* process. Since identity is constantly shifting and turning, one really can't afford to get involved in lasting commitments. And since the stress is laid on floating and flowing with one's instinctual self, the importance of willing and choosing is likewise undermined. The choices necessary for growth in identity do not get made. While the Human Potentialists may describe this ideal fluid self in terms of a gently meandering stream, it begins to appear that a more appropriate metaphor might be that of a snake shedding its skin. Just as a snake worms out of its old skin when that becomes too small and scaly, we are supposed to wriggle out of our old identities and relationships when they begin to hamper our freedom of movement.

Finally, though it purports to be interested in the improvement of human relations, the Human Potential Movement provides no basis for lasting relationships. It proclaims, on the contrary, that the self exists as a free-floating entity unbounded by space, time, or relationships; and it encourages its devotees to believe that life's true meaning is to be found in self-actualization rather than in commitment to others.

Every psychological theory which doesn't die gets translated into everyday use. It gets popularized. And eventually it molds both attitudes and life-styles. The theories of Rogers and Maslow, as freely rendered by the Human Potential Movement, have indeed affected our lives, but they have also lost a lot in translation. What we end up with is a concept of identity in which the elements of continuity and choice have been distilled out. It is a heady brew, capable of inducing a powerful euphoria, but eventually there comes a morning after, and the inevitable hangover.

In Part Three I discuss the impact on identity of a phenomenon which, for want of a better term, I will call "the new tribalism." Individual identity is a Western preoccupation—an attempt to answer some of the pressing questions of human existence: "Who am I?", "Where do I fit in?", "What shall I do with my life?" But in tribal societies, where these questions are answered almost before they are asked, individual identity is not an urgent concern. By and large, primitive people do not go to the trouble of defining themselves apart from the tribe.

The tribal man does not have an identity he can call his own. Now, certain voices in the West have taken up the tribal chant and mingled it with an Eastern litany. Sparked by the ascendance of electric media and abetted by the speculations of Marshall McLuhan and Norman O. Brown, a new tribal-mystical philosophy of self has taken hold among some segments of our population.

As McLuhan and Brown see it, identity is the ultimate inconvenience: the final barrier between you and me and everyone else. It's the insulating wire that keeps us from participating in the electromagnetic field of tribal oneness. To the question, How can I keep up with change? McLuhan/Brown answer in effect: "Forget you're an 'I.' Salvation lies not in individual identity but in a collective one; not in self-definition but in undifferentiated union." And along with their speculations on identity goes an interesting proposal for a nonindividual, "polymorphous" sexuality which will supposedly free us from the shackles of possessive sex. Once again, there is a healthy element in all this: a reminder of our common humanity, an invitation to community. But the negation of identity involved in the McLuhan/Brown creed is no basis for community and much less a basis for personal relationships. It is, for instance, hard to imagine how one can identify with the Universal Human Self when one has no understanding of one's own self, or how an individual can love everyone without first loving someone. It is possible, of course, to have a love for mankind in the abstract without loving any particular person. But who wants to be loved in the abstract?

Another main ingredient in this blend of tribalism and mysticism is the "here-and-now" philosophy of life, or "Dionysian madness" as Brown prefers to call it. Once again, it's the old story of the New Man who needs no connections to the past or future. And, once again, the negation of the past or future can be a very dangerous game. But this time it appears to be catching on.

The McLuhan/Brown philosophy is, together with the Human Potential Movement, part of a general cultural drift that is coming to be called the transformation. The transformation, according to its apologists, will supplant the future-oriented, responsibility-ridden, inhibited culture to which we have grown accustomed in the West and replace it with a more free and natural and, therefore, more human society.

This may be so. No one would deny that some kind of transition is under way; but what the transformationists envision looks suspiciously like one of those baby/bathwater situations. What is particularly disconcerting is that the babies at issue will be real rather than metaphorical.

One of my concerns is that the transformation will, in the process of purging the "repressive" culture, also eradicate the type of identity that grows out of that older milieu. For, despite its faults, the "old" culture generates certain virtues—individuality, introspection, concern for privacy, commitment to the future—which in turn contribute to a sense of personal identity.

If that is lost, what will replace it? What the transformationists have in mind is an identity based on the tribal model—a bit more primitive than what we have now, perhaps, but more natural, more liberating, they say. In that case, one must ask, what happens to fluidity? What ensures fluidity in our society is a long childhood and adolescent moratorium: a time to think, grow, and experiment. The moratorium in turn depends on adults who are willing to provide it—adults who are future-oriented, individually committed, and even somewhat self-denying. In tribal societies, however, there is little sense of individual responsibility, not much orientation to the future, and no fluidity. What holds things together is a strong bond of community and kinship. But the chances of achieving such solidarity in our culture are slim, especially if the Human Potential philosophy takes hold, for that philosophy is dedicated not to community but to self-growth. What idea of a community it does have is woefully limited to the model of the weekend encounter group—and that is perceived chiefly as a vehicle for massaging individual egos. The truth is that people engrossed in their own self-actualization simply don't have much time or inclination for maintaining community or kinship ties. Yet this pattern of self-absorption is now being widely accepted as the prototype for a better society.

With the old sense of continuity and future commitment gone, and with the new spirit of fluidity triumphant, the question then arises, Who's going to mind the children? And who is going to provide them with a moratorium? Already, according to psychologist Urie Bronfenbrenner, an increasing number of divorced parents are fighting over the right not to have custody;[7] and much of the current attitude of child avoidance can be summed up in a recent issue of *Esquire* devoted to the topic "Do Americans Suddenly Hate Kids?"[8] Only an adult with a secure sense of identity and a sense of commitment— the two are closely linked—can guarantee to children an equal chance for the good times we now propose to grab for ourselves. Human advancement, by which I understand a better chance for all to pursue happiness, requires a prolonged and dependent childhood. But implicit in the transformation of identity are some forces that will tunnel under this childhood moratorium and leave no supports in place of the solid earth that will be removed. The irony is that fluidity itself will then be threatened, for only an identity-secure adult can guarantee to a child the protective environment in which to experiment with fluidity. Adult identity, not fluidity, is the best guarantee that our children also will be fully human.

Part Four attempts to answer the question, Where does the new look in identity lead? In particular, what happens to that fundamental thing called love? In subsequent chapters I will explore the relationship between identity and love more thoroughly, but for the moment, I think the essence can be summed up this way: First, we can't give a self that we don't have. Without a secure sense of identity we aren't capable of the self-abandon sexual love calls for or the self-giving other forms of love require. Second, and equally important, a love that lasts needs an identity that lasts. Because of the bond which unites the two, any major transformation in identity will produce marked changes in patterns of love. Such a transformation in identity—subtle but sweeping—is already well under way. What then happens to love? Already there is a tendency to talk about "intimate" relations rather than "love" relations. And the word "intimacy" has begun to take on a connotation of lovemaking without love. "Intimacy," furthermore, has acquired a connotation of brevity, whereas "love" implies constancy. Since it is brevity, not constancy, that characterizes so many of today's relationships, "intimacy" has become the word of choice.

The shift in vocabulary is only a reflection of an actual shift. As I see it, widespread acceptance of the new versions of identity has two negative effects on intimacy. It has, first of all, just about killed romance. Except for a few brief nostalgic revivals here and there, the whole notion of romantic love seems to have fallen victim to the new wisdom. Romance simply does not thrive in the soil of nonexclusive relationships that has been so carefully cultivated by the transformationists. Romance, moreover, is a passion, and passions demand commitment, and commitment does not square with the prevalent keep-loose ethic.

Romance has always, it is true, been tainted with a hint of madness, and those who wish for its quick demise do have some justification. In many ways, however, romance seems to be a prelude to a more mature love. This brings me to my second negative conclusion: that the transformation in identity will eventuate in a diminished capacity for love in any form. That conclusion may sound rather sensational (in my imagination I picture some tabloid with the headline "Psychologist Predicts Death of Love"), but it also seems inescapable. We seem to be drifting into a loveless condition. The blame is due partly to mobility (people on the run don't have time for involvement), partly to Human Potentialism (keep loose, don't limit yourself to one person), and partly to the Eastern influence (universal love is better than individual love).

Loving intimacy has become difficult because identity achievement has become difficult. Without a continuous sense of self, we are forced to take a tentative, noncommittal approach to relationships. And faced with the current emphasis on fluidity and self-actualization we are made to feel like fools if we settle for less than the intimacy in abundance which is supposedly our due. Psychologists do not necessarily create the conditions which undermine intimacy but they can contribute to them by constantly reminding us of potentials unactualized and impulses denied. Too often they play the advertisers' role, creating a need where none existed. The other day I happened to pick up and read through a paperback which exemplifies the trend. The book was written by a psychiatrist obviously imbued with the Human Potential outlook. In large part it played variations on the following theme: feel free to move out of a relationship once it becomes sluggish; and don't feel guilty, because lasting and exclusive relationships between any two people are not practical. Why not? Because, "from the person they once were they become someone else."[9]

This is the type of thinking that upsets the balance between continuity and change so essential to identity. Moreover, it creates a self-fulfilling prophecy that guarantees intimacy won't last. When we enter a relationship with the attitude that identity can't last—that there is nothing essential or persistent about the self—then we won't make the emotional investment that a lasting relationship requires; and we will ensure that the relationship does in time become sluggish.

Behavioral scientists and their popularizers seem intent on modernizing our attitude toward love. Love is to be redeveloped along the lines suggested by the newest psychological theories. While one can only applaud the interjection of a little psychological realism into our love relationships, it is hard to escape the uneasy feeling that the redevelopment in store for us is akin to the method of the urban "experts" who redevelop a city block by razing it and paving it over for a parking lot.

It was my intention in undertaking this inquiry to remain as objective as possible, but I found that I could not avoid expressing preferences and passing judgments. Those who are looking for complete objectivity will have to turn to textbooks and academic journals for enlightenment, though even here they will have to proceed carefully. I found also that the presentation has taken the form of variations on a theme rather than a logical step-by-step progression of ideas. This is due partly, I believe, to the fact that I started out somewhat on the opposite side of the issue from the one I ended up on. Some of the distinctions and similarities dividing and uniting the various theories became apparent to me only as a result of the writing process. Many of my opinions were worked out as I went along. And, although I take the Human Potential theorists to task in this book, I do not think they will begrudge me the fluidity which allowed me to travel from their end of the spectrum to a point rather distant from it.

In any event the Human Potential Movement (not, by the way, an official organization, but a loose coalition of like-minded people) does not lack for supporters. Neither does the New Tribalism. Every day the ranks of the self-actualizers and the self-transcenders swell with new converts. Every day the capacity for commitment and true intimacy is sapped in the name of warmth and closeness. If this is the world we are to live in for the immediate future, then it is well we should know all we can concerning its nature and motivations.

Part one
The Trauma of Change

1

Identity in a Temporary Society

*A*T the parochial grammar school I attended we were taught that it was wrong to have impure thoughts. It was in fact a sin. This caused a lot of trouble for us because on the one hand we took our religion seriously and on the other we kept having impure thoughts. When confession time came each week it was always a problem deciding how many of these thoughts to admit to. I decided on three. Somehow three seemed like a good number—about what the normal Catholic boy should have, I guessed. Besides, I didn't want to scandalize the priest by letting him know the actual count.

In our school a good person was defined by the nuns as being, among other things, pure and chaste in thought, word and deed; as being, so it seemed, asexual. And we, if we wanted to be good (which we did) were supposed to define ourselves in the same way. In our self-definition there was no place for sexuality. But it was hard being "good." One constantly had to contend with desires that were inconsistent with one's narrowly defined self. The environment was full of temptations—magazine racks and tight sweaters—and one had either to compulsively restrict one's activities ("avoiding the near occasion of sin," as the church called it) or resort to obsessive rituals such as reciting "ejaculations" at three-second intervals. These were brief spurts of prayer designed to keep Satan at a distance, but the very thought of that word was enough to set off a new chain of impure speculations. It was a vicious circle.

Most of us, as time went on, learned to redefine ourselves on a larger scale and to admit the sexual part of our humanity which had, of course, been there all along. It was a process of letting in more reality, of widening the boundaries of self to take account of life's variety. One could, as it turned out, have impure thoughts and still be a good Catholic. It was only necessary either to broaden the definition of "good" or else restrict the meaning of "impure."

I don't recall how my own growth up from parochialism in this respect occurred. It may have been occasioned by the reading of an enlightened pamphlet in a darkened church. Or it may have been some absolution-weary priest, tired of shriving a child's daydreams, who gave me new perspectives on the nature of evil. More probably the change happened gradually through a process of reflection. At any rate I felt no great dislocation from my scrupulous past—only a little older and wiser. Whatever new definitions of the self I arrived at, there was always a continuity with what I had been, a solid sense of sameness winding through my life, a wide unbreakable ribbon tying it all together. After all, despite the changes, everything in my life was still there. For thirteen years, the same house with the same wisteria vine climbing to the roof, changing as I did, only in growing larger and stronger; the same neighborhood, the same friends, the weekly visits to aunts and uncles, cousins, and grandparents—all giving reassuring testimony to that essential continuity with my past.

Since the pace of change was slower in those days, continuity was not so difficult to achieve. But today the situation is different. In a constantly changing society, a sense of personal continuity becomes extremely important. In such a context it is necessary to redefine oneself many times, for rapid change creates sharp discontinuities which must be bridged in order to retain a unified sense of self. This sense of self, composed in large part of the experience of continuity, is what we call identity.

The Formation of Identity

A child doesn't have an identity so much as a collection of identifications. He identifies with his mother and father or with some aspect of their personalities, perhaps rejecting other aspects. As he grows he makes identifications with brothers and sisters, playmates, grandparents, folk heroes, athletes, and other figures; some more significant, some less so. These identifications may be transient, partial, unrealistic, even contradictory. Added together, they do not form a coherent or consistent sense of identity, but this is not yet a problem for the child.

For the adolescent it *is* a problem—the main problem. His body is growing rapidly and changing. His mind is becoming capable of high-level abstraction. He becomes acutely aware of possibilities. He begins to worry about his future. The adult world he is about to enter seems at odds with his dependent childhood. This internal revolution creates in him a need to pull his life together into a coherent unity. He needs to believe that the person he was as a child has persisted despite the changes—or else what was his childhood for? He has to find connections between the person he was and the person he anticipates he will be. If he is not quite the same as he was yesterday he would like to trace the history of that transformation; to find the links that bind past self to present self. In short, he seeks to create an identity that will bridge all the discontinuities of puberty.

Identity is not created all at once, nor is it ever really completed, but it takes shape gradually out of the successive identifications of childhood and those newly formed. These are slowly integrated into a new configuration which is both a coherent and unique whole. It is not an easy task. Consciously and unconsciously the growing child must somehow reconcile the identifications he has made with figures as diverse as his aging grandfather and the hero of the last movie he has seen. Out of the bag of partial identifications which he carries from his earliest years and out of the future toward which he aspires, he must synthesize a unique self he can call his own.

The Essential Self

It is only our sense of continuity that allows us to tolerate the contradictions and inconsistencies of such a process. A sense of continuity reassures us that despite the redefinitions we have made, there still persists an essential self. We may not be able to locate this bedrock foundation precisely, but without the sense that it exists, without the conviction that something essential endures, our identity would seem an insubstantial thing.

This is the self to which we believe we must be true; which we would prefer on the whole to keep faith with. And it is upon this core self that others rely when they trust us or take us at our word. Our self is their guarantee of fidelity; the part of us that can be held responsible. It is possible to retreat from many things we hold dear. Principles can be compromised and ideals sacrificed without completely losing our integrity. We can draw lines and redraw them if necessary and still retain our self-respect. But there is a point at which we must draw a line and stand fast, for beyond that point lies something indispensable. That something is the essence of what we mean by identity or the self.

Exactly where that point is we can never say. Certainly it differs from person to person. But when the self reveals itself it leaves no doubt that such a place exists. The life of Thomas More provides a point of reference. In it we can find the place at which one man located his sense of self. As a loyal subject of King Henry VIII, More was expected to sign an oath approving of the king's marriage to Anne Boleyn; as Lord Chancellor of the Realm and as a man who held the admiration of the populace, his assent was all the more crucial to Henry.

More refused the oath. Not out of any sense of propriety or priggishness, but because it required him to swear to something he considered untrue, something that constituted a denial of God's revelation as he understood it. To consent to the oath would be to deny his faith.

As represented in Robert Bolt's play *A Man for All Seasons,* More comes under increasing pressure to sign. One by one his friends give in until Thomas is left alone against the king. To one of these friends he proclaims in defense of his dangerous obstinacy: "I will not give in because I oppose it—I do—not my pride, not my spleen, nor any other of my appetites but I do—*I!*"[1]

For his disloyalty More is imprisoned in the Tower. But in the face of continued interrogation and the king's growing impatience he remains unmoved. Finally, More's family comes to him to plead that he sign the oath. Their appeals to his affection are matched only by More's appeal to his integrity. To his daughter he says:

> "When a man takes an oath, Meg, he's holding his own self in his own hands. Like water. [*He cups his hands*] And if he opens his fingers *then*—he needn't hope to find himself again. Some men aren't capable of this, but I'd be loathe to think your father one of them."[2]

The rest of the story is well known. More is made to stand trial, and on the basis of trumped-up charges is sentenced to death and executed.

In his preface to the play, Bolt provides an explanation for More's behavior in what must stand as one of the finest statements on the ultimate meaning of identity:

> He knew where he began and left off, what area of himself he could yield to the encroachments of his enemies, and what to the encroachments of those he loved. It was a substantial area in both cases, for he had a proper sense of fear and was a busy lover. Since he was a clever man and a great lawyer he was able to retire from those areas in wonderfully good order, but at length he was asked to retreat from that final area where he located his self. And there this supple,

humorous, unassuming and sophisticated person set like metal, was overtaken by an absolutely primitive rigor, and could no more be budged than a cliff.[3]

The perjured testimony which finally sends More to the gallows is given by one Richard Rich. In the career of Rich we see an opposite process at work—the dissolution of identity. In fact we can almost pinpoint the precise point at which it is abandoned. Rich is a young man who is anxious to enter into the world of affairs—at any price, as it turns out. What little sense of identity he has, threatens to be engulfed by his ambition. Yet one can see possibilities in this young man. He is a reflective person who admires More's integrity, and behind his adolescent intensity there glimmers the possibility of loyalty and courage. We detect in him an attempt, however feeble, to cling to whatever verities he has been schooled in; to find some continuity with a past that was more plain and honest than the cunning deceits of the courts and chambers through which he now moves.

But finally these possibilities never develop. The lure of power and money is too great. At one point in the play More has been given a silver goblet which he belatedly realizes to be a bribe. Rather than be influenced by it, he gives the goblet to Rich. Later Rich is being questioned by Thomas Cromwell, who is seeking some kind of damning evidence against More. Since Cromwell is a powerful man, Rich stands to gain considerably by revealing what he knows. In his extended dialogue with Cromwell we can trace the disintegration of a self. Cromwell has just asked Rich if he believes he would never repeat anything said in friendship:

RICH: Yes!
CROMWELL: No, but seriously.
RICH: Why, yes!
CROMWELL: *(not sinister, but rather as a kindly teacher with a promising pupil)* Rich; seriously.
RICH: *(pauses, then bitterly)* It would depend on what I was offered.

He is offered a position as Collector of Revenues for the Diocese of York. Then Cromwell questions Rich about the silver goblet.

> CROMWELL: Where did he [More] get it? *(No reply. Rich puts the cup down.)* It was a gift from a litigant, a woman, wasn't it?
> RICH: Yes.
> CROMWELL: Which court? Chancery? *(restrains Rich from filling his glass)* No, don't get drunk. In which court was this litigant's case?
> RICH: Court of Requests.
> CROMWELL: There, that wasn't too painful, was it?
> RICH: *(laughing a little and a little rueful)* No!
> CROMWELL: That's all there is. And you'll find it easier next time.[4]

"Court of Requests." A simple enough statement. Yet at that point Rich has abdicated his self. After this the man no longer has a self to commit. His word has no guarantee. Sensing this inner hollowness More can say to him: "Richard, you couldn't answer for yourself even so far as tonight."[5]

We would not want to say that Rich can never again get back his identity. That possibility always remains, we must suppose, until the final moment. It would be a damaged identity, of course, but the possibility for repentance and renewal always exists. But Rich, as it turns out, never gets his back. By the end of the play his personality has hardened into a mask, and behind the mask there is nothing. Nothing has persisted in him but his ambition.

The self that persists, the self upon which others rely and upon which we found our identity—that self is now threatened from several directions. Any society produces more Richard Riches than Thomas Mores, but our present American culture is now far more conducive to the production of people like Rich than it has ever been. It is not the type of society that provides a solid sense of identity; and it is upon identity that ethics are built.

Rarely is anyone called upon to make the type of heroic

self-definition that Thomas More made, and the encroachments upon our identity are more subtle than those that Rich suffered; but in less obvious ways there are forces at work that threaten to undermine that something in us which we feel ought to persist. This chapter and the ones that follow will examine these forces.

An oath is not nearly so sacred as it once was, and we would now prefer that men, as Bolt puts it, "guarantee their statements with, say, cash, rather than with themselves."[6] Nevertheless there is an anxiety that pervades our sense of self: a fear that underneath the many roles we play there is nothing. If we cannot identify with More, and if we are loath to find in ourselves the deceitfulness of a Richard Rich, there is yet another metaphor for us. It can be found in Ibsen's play *Peer Gynt*, where Peer, seated among a field of onions, imagines his personality to be no different from an onion. The layers he peels off one by one represent the roles he has played in life, but after all are peeled away there is nothing left:

> "There's a most surprising lot of layers! Are we never coming to the kernel? [*Pulls all that's left to pieces*] There isn't one! To the innermost bit it's nothing but layers, smaller and smaller. Nature's a joker!"[7]

It's a cruel joke that leaves a man with no core of identity. But it would appear that just such a joke is being played on a growing number of individuals in our society. The jokester in this case is not nature but a culture that accelerates social and technological change at a dizzying pace.

Identity in a Changing World

The work of Erik Erikson provides the most useful recent discussion of identity, and one which makes sense in human terms, for Erikson makes allowance for the ambiguities and uncertainties of life, for the possibility of this going wrong and that going right. It is Erikson who stressed the importance of continuity in the formation of identity, and it is to Erikson that we owe our understanding of how identity is synthesized out of many childhood identifications. As Erikson describes it, identity emerges out of a dialectic between the need for continuity and the need for experimentation. Identity formation leads in the direction of a new self-delineation, yet it is also an "accrued confidence" that one retains an "inner sameness." With this confidence it is possible to take the chances with one's identity that true intimacy requires. Erikson has become the preeminent theorist of identity, and this perhaps most of all because his is a theory made to fit men rather than one they are fitted into.

But theories, like selves, need occasionally to be redefined in light of new realities, and certain new realities would seem to require a rethinking of our ideas about this fundamental process of identity formation. There is the possibility that these new realities are not realities at all, of course, but only new myths. But since men live as much by myths as realities, we are still forced to consider the usefulness of our traditional explanations. I would not suggest that Erikson's explanation is no longer useful (it is extremely useful) but that the model of health it presents no longer reflects the norm. As social realities change, a theory can become more and more a statement of the way things should be than the way they are, and this, I believe, is what has happened to Erikson's criteria of health. For Erikson, a healthy identity is one that is open to change and redefinition, but above all is rooted in an historical, traceable past, so that through all there runs an invigorating "sense of sameness,"[8]—what I have been calling "continuity."

This healthy sense of sameness is increasingly difficult to come by as we approach the last quarter of the twentieth century. To illustrate let us juxtapose Erikson's definition of identity with a statement from Toffler's (1970) *Future Shock.* First, Erikson:

> Ego identity . . . is an awareness of the fact that there is a self-sameness and continuity to the ego's synthesizing meth-

ods, *the style of one's individuality,* and that this style coincides with the sameness and continuity of one's *meaning for significant others* in the immediate community.[9]

Contrast to this a statement from Toffler's book:

> What remains? What is there of "self" or "personality" in the sense of a continuous, durable internal structure? For some, the answer is very little. For they are no longer dealing in "self" but in what might be called "serial selves."[10]

"They" are for the most part the affluent and highly mobile elite most involved in the accelerated pace of change that produces future shock. But since "they" are soon to be followed by the rest of us, it seems worth investigating this matter of "serial selves" and the sharp contrast it opposes to Erikson's definition of identity.

Continuity and Change

Identity—the type Erikson has in mind—requires a threefold continuity: a continuity of significant others; a continuity with one's past self; a continuity with one's anticipated future self. At all three levels the phenomenon of chronic change acts to disrupt these continuities.

It is imperative that our sense of identity be reinforced by significant others. We need their reassurance that despite the transformations we have undergone something essential remains. What are we after all but social creatures? Even Thomas More, who had stood alone against all, at the last begs his family for their understanding. An identity is a fragile thing when it stands by itself. It is strengthened when we feel that others recognize in us that self-sameness which we recognize in ourselves.

Identity achievement then would seem to require a continuity of significant others in our lives to confirm our links to our past selves. One of the problems of a future-shocked society, however, is the absence of such continuity. Friends and neighbors come and go with alarming rapidity. They change, and we change, and "those who knew us in some previous incarnation," as Toffler puts it, have a difficult time recognizing us. They do little to reinforce our sense of sameness.

Mobility and transience combine to create a society of nomads. Incessant moving is the norm. Who still lives in the house of his birth? In the house of his childhood? Even for the young the answer is that practically no one does. The house of my own youth no longer exists. In its place stands a modern apartment building. The backyard in which I discovered praying mantis and morning glory is now a paved parking lot. The phrase "you can't go home again" takes on for us a physical as well as psychological meaning. And even when we can return to a physical site, what strangers will we find at the door? Among the statistics Toffler cites is that one out of five Americans changes his address each year. Over half the listings in the 1969 Washington, D.C., phonebook, he tells us, were different from the year before.

No one, it seems, can be counted on to stay in one place. The aunts, uncles and grandparents who once lived across the street now live across the city or across the country. By and large we are left with only the stripped-down, streamlined nuclear family to fill the role of "significant others." And even here there is a growing lack of continuity. The nuclear family is coming apart. An increasing number of children must adjust to the fact that parents, like friends and neighbors, can come and go. Serial marriage—a succession of temporary marriages —is already an established although unofficial pattern. Those parents who do stay together increasingly shift the burden of child rearing to schools and day care centers. Annual rituals through which families could confer a unique sense of belonging to an ongoing tradition have largely been taken over by mass commercialism. The organization of our activities for Thanksgiving week is now in the hands of *TV Guide*. Little chance for identity confirmation here: the family is caught up in the same winds of change that buffet individual lives. As a result, we all have a vague feeling of truly belonging nowhere and to no one.

It is not only the continuity of our meaning to others that is threatened. We also have increasing difficulty in recognizing our own past selves. This would seem to be especially true in the matter of rapidly changing values. To a high degree our identity—our sense of continuity—is bound up with our sense of right and wrong. The world may change, we feel, but if we hold fast to our ethical moorings we can still retain a sense of our place in it. But what happens to identity when our values turn over almost as rapidly as fashions in dress? What does it mean for identity when, for instance, the Catholic who yesterday opposed birth control today accepts abortion and tomorrow may embrace euthanasia and test-tube reproduction? What does it mean for personal continuity to continually redraw the moral line at which one will make his or her stand? According to some of the sex researchers (e.g., Gilbert Bartell, 1971),[11] it is not unusual for a suburban woman to move from chastity through monogamy to adultery and on to group sex and lesbianism in a half-dozen years or less. My intent is not to pass judgment on any of these activities, only to point out that the more lines we erase, the harder it becomes to trace the genealogy of our morals or the lineage of our identity.

But it is precisely such historical acts that constitute the process of identity formation. This is why the adolescent whose main developmental task is identity formation becomes so concerned with questions of his personal lineage, descent, and legitimacy. The biological discontinuities of puberty prompt him to find connections with his past; the integration of his past and present identities demands that he take an historical perspective. It is the point of *Future Shock*, however, that the current diversity of life-styles and the rate at which we move through them makes such integration increasingly improbable. Erikson himself, anticipating this possibility, states that "the integration of infantile part-identities and fragmentary roles can be interfered with by . . . rapid social evolution or technological change."[12] In a similar vein, Kenneth Keniston sees contemporary youth as suffering from "historical dislocation," which he describes as "the inability to find connections with the past and future" and as "the feeling of unrelatedness, of being adrift, of not being able to 'catch hold' of anything or anyone in our rapidly changing society."[13] He sees this dislocation as being due on the one hand to the difficulty of synthesizing the many irreconcilable identities our society proffers, and on the other to an inability of youth to identify with their parents because their parents have been "outdated" by rapid change.

To the youth Keniston studied, parents are seen as simply irrelevant. To identify with them is to choose obsolescence. Although they may be the only link to their children's past, the children simply cannot relate to them. The ever-present generation gap is widened by the factors of transience, mobility, novelty, and diversity that Toffler describes and analyzes in *Future Shock*. When change accelerates beyond a certain point it is difficult to retain a sense of continuity with one's past; the past seems increasingly distant and beside the point.

The same holds true for the future. Endless change makes the future unpredictable. That which we thought to be stable and permanent rapidly becomes obsolescent. In the face of accelerating social and technological innovations it is difficult to anticipate the future or plan for it. We turn instead to the present, the only time we can be sure of. If the past is irrelevant and the future enigmatic, the present is more certain.

When the past loses its significance and the future becomes unknowable, when those on whom we rely to confirm our identity depart our lives, and when we have been forced to play many successive parts, we may begin to wonder, like Peer Gynt, if there is any center. Chronic change undermines our sense of the persistence of something essential in us. It separates us from our identity as effectively as Cromwell unburdened Rich of his.

Even as basic a touchstone as our sense of physical identity may soon be undermined by rapid advances in the field of medicine. Our sense of identity is reinforced on a physical level by the simple fact of bodily continuity. Allowing for normal wear and tear and cell replacement, we recognize ourselves as being of our own flesh and blood. But even now, Teflon and Dacron and metal are replacing skin and bones. And the heart we were born with may have to be discarded along the way in favor of a "new" one. What happens to an individual's sense of uniqueness or continuity when faced with the knowledge that his body is a system of interchangeable parts? The speed with which we enter the future is measured by the fact that questions like this find us totally unprepared.

Fidelity

The sense of continuity is not the only quality to be threatened by accelerated change. Erikson observed that at each stage of development a capacity or "virtue" emerges in the individual to help him meet the crisis of that stage. An important step in the crisis of identity formation is the development of a capacity for what he terms "fidelity." Fidelity is faithfulness, loyalty, commitment. In large part the adolescent quest for identity is a search for something to which one can commit one's newly developing sense of identity. Through fidelity, moreover, one can cultivate those long-term relationships that give continuity to one's sense of self. Our fidelity is our guarantee that there is something solid about our identity—something which endures. "Without the development of a capacity for fidelity," says Erikson, "the individual will either have what we call a weak ego, or look for a deviant group to be faithful to." And elsewhere in stronger terms he asserts, "Fidelity . . . must not, in the crisis of youth, fail its time of ascendance if human adaptation is to remain intact."[14]

Once again, if we juxtapose to this some statements from Toffler we find a sharp contrast. It is Toffler's contention that most of our relationships are characterized by transience. This is especially true of our relationships to things and places but is becoming increasingly true of our relationships to people. Our attitude toward things that are disposable, rentable, and impermanent may begin to color our attitude toward people. Although we are very much attached to material goods in general, there is no longer the tradition of specific attachment to a specific thing which prevailed when goods were less abundant and things were made to last. All this is preparation for a world in which our attachments to people become equally tenuous; in which we feel driven to experience the latest model friend, lover, or spouse. "The logical end of the direction in which we are now travelling," writes Toffler, "is a society based on a system of temporary encounters."[15] Here Toffler is speaking not only of our transient relations to acquaintances, colleagues, and neighbors but also of friendship, love, and marriage bonds. The traditional ideal for marriage has been that of shared growth. This pattern, says Toffler, has been difficult to achieve even in stable societies, but people no longer change at the same rate or in the same direction. The best we can hope for is the system of serial marriages mentioned earlier.

In a world of disposable goods, easily replaced, we probably should not wonder that people also come to seem disposable. And our vaunted mobility only intensifies the feeling that it is wiser if we do not get too attached. Commitment to others is difficult enough in a stable society because it entails not only the risk of rejection but also the risk of involvement. People who move around a great deal are even more reluctant to commit themselves to friends, colleagues, or communities. Why invest the energy when one is going to move on? Why get involved?

The Risks of Fidelity

Moreover, fidelity carries with it the risk of what Keniston calls "damaging commitment to false life styles or goals."[16] To understand the meaning of this risk it is necessary to understand that identity and fidelity have a mutually supportive relationship; they do not develop apart from each other. Identity generates the capacity for fidelity, which in turn generates a stronger sense of identity. The more tenuous one's hold on his identity, the less likely he is to risk losing it in a relationship with another. He fears that the price of commitment may be the absorption of his self into another's. But without commitment or intimacy there is no further growth for him. Conversely, the anxieties of identity diffusion may propel an individual to find any identity, no matter how premature and limiting, in an effort to have done with it. He may seek an end to anxiety in a hasty and confining marriage or in narrow commitment to some group or cause. The "true believer," as Eric Hoffer points out, is only too willing to have his uncertain sense of self welded to some ideological superstructure.

The danger of being welded or wedded to false life-styles or to the wrong persons makes fidelity risky in the best of circumstances. In a world characterized by mobility, novelty, faddishness, transience, and temporality where there are many competing life-styles and persons, and little time to examine or decide, the risk is multiplied enormously.

Not only is fidelity difficult in such a world, but the job of synthesizing identifications also becomes highly problematic. The more variegated a society, the more identities it offers, and the harder it is to pull them together into a coherent unity. When an individual fails to achieve an integration of past and current identifications he falls victim to what Erikson calls identity confusion: an inability to feel that one is all together, a feeling of not fitting in, of not knowing who one is or what one wants to do, of trying on many roles and settling for none.

Erikson sees the resolution of the identity crisis in the achievement of a ratio between a sense of coherence and a sense of identity confusion, with the balance tipped in favor of the former. But in a future-shocked society the ratio is reversed. If Toffler's assessment of cultural change is correct, then the balance has been tipped the other way. Identity confusion, not coherence, has become the prevailing norm.

It is true that the human race has an impressive record of adaptability. But to adapt is not to thrive or prosper. We cannot be too sanguine about the benefits of adapting to a society where identity confusion is not redeemed by a sense of continuity. Toffler is not unaware of the danger that is posed to our identity in an accelerating society. There are, he asserts, definite limits to the amount of change that the human organism can cope with. The higher the level of change, the greater the likelihood of illness, both physical and mental. The more change is accelerated, the more we run the risk of being thrown into a state of shock.

I do not mean to imply that the future-shock problem is the main difficulty for identity formation. It is one of several problems that .necessitate a rethinking of our traditional ideas about the achievement of identity. In this chapter I have merely tried to draw attention to the discrepancy that exists between a major theory of development and a widely accepted description of current social change. What the one requires, the other refuses.

A New Formulation

There is another alternative to the apprehensive analysis I have sketched. That is to reject the root assumption that it is healthy for a person to develop a firm and coherent identity. Perhaps in a chronically changing society it is more a burden than a blessing to attempt to maintain our sense of personal continuity. Perhaps what we call "identity confusion" is in reality the best adaptation we can make. The phenomenon of future shock invites us to consider an entirely different concept of identity from the one we have been assuming.

A new concept of identity consistent with high mobility and all that mobility implies is in fact already at hand. The extreme form of this new identity is proclaimed in a recent book by F. M. Esfandiary.[17] In this book, *Up-Wingers*, Esfandiary claims that fixed identity is now outmoded. The modern individual, he says, is characterized by a fluid identity—a continual sense of motion and process. It is this fluidity rather than "total permanent commitments" that confers identity on the modern man. In the next breath—it is a breathless book in the sense that Mr. Esfandiary, in his hurry to get through with it, can only pant out his ideas in short gasps much like a sprinter after a race—he christens this new form of identity "nonidentity." It is a truthful description. What he describes, though ever so briefly, is no identity at all. Not in the sense that we have become accustomed to; not in the sense that Erikson painstakingly conveys in *Childhood and Society*. Yet this new formulation represents a definite and growing school of thought. It is in fact only the most recent expression of a drastic revision in the Western concept of the self—a revision that gains daily in popularity. It is to this revised view of self that I would next like to turn my attention.

Part two
Fluid Identity

2

The Self-in-Process

WHAT kind of identity is called for in a future-shocked society—that is, under conditions of mobility, transiency, and disposability? Is it healthy to maintain a durational identity in such a fluid world? Or should we try to cultivate a more flexible one? Shall we emphasize tentativeness, or shall we stress commitment? The first approach is advocated by the Human Potential Movement, the second by Erikson and certain Existentialists. At first glance the Human Potential approach seems more compatible with a rapidly changing society. It places a much-needed emphasis on growth, fluidity, and frequent redefinitions of the self.

The other side of the identity issue is represented by theorists like Erik Erikson, Victor Frankl, and Rollo May, who stress choice, fidelity, continuity, and self-definition. The type of slowly consolidated identity which they advocate is more difficult to come by in a fast-paced society and may even prove a handicap. But it can also serve as an antidote to the ills of too-rapid change. Moreover, Erikson's theory of identity contains a built-in system of checks and balances, which the Human Potential Movement does not have.

The connections between identity, choice, commitment,

and self-definition, on which this latter school insists, can be illustrated in the life of Søren Kierkegaard, who is well known as the father of Existentialism. What is less well known is that Kierkegaard longed to be a real father: to have children, a home, a domestic life. And everything he wanted was represented in the person of the girl he loved and was engaged to marry, seventeen-year-old Regina Olsen.

But Kierkegaard broke the engagement, thereby renouncing the simple hearthside pleasures for which he yearned. He took up instead a life of solitude and feverish work, pouring out his passions on paper. For the next dozen or so years he fought a lonely battle against the established church and the established philosophy of his day. At forty-two, exhausted by his struggle, he died.

Why did he do it? From our post-Freudian vantage point it would be all too simple to speculate about dark neurotic cellars of the mind. There are probably at least a few analytic pigeonholes we could stuff Kierkegaard into if we were so disposed. But it would be wrong to do so. Kierkegaard himself tells us why he did what he did, and there is no reason not to take him at his word. He renounced Regina because he had another commitment—a mission that he alone could accomplish, a task to which marriage and children would prove an insurmountable obstacle. That task was to assert, as against the churchmen and philosophers, the finitude and concreteness of individual human beings and in so doing to show the world what it meant to be a true Christian. Kierkegaard loved Regina and continued to love her after he renounced her, but he could not allow her to suffer the scorn and ostracism to which he knew he would be exposed. He could not draw her into his own melancholy, and above all he could not let her weaken his resolve to carry out his mission.[1] With Hamlet, that other melancholy Dane, he might well have said: "The time is out of joint; O cursed spite, that ever I was born to set it right!"

If anyone ever understood what it means to choose, it was Kierkegaard. For where does a man come to grips with his self? In the either/or of choice, replies Kierkegaard. It is the point at which a man gives up what he *could* be and chooses what he *will* be. Every choice implies a renunciation: to choose one thing is to lose something else. But a man must choose, must commit himself; otherwise he remains only possibilities. By his choices, painful as they must be, a man defines himself. In choosing between Regina and his vocation, Kierkegaard was creating his identity, though at the moment he chose there was no way of knowing whether the possibility he had chosen to actualize was the right one. There was no certainty, nothing to guarantee his choice, no way to tell whether the path to which he had committed himself was not a dead end. Nevertheless he wagered because he wished to be someone. It is through choice that an individual actually creates a self, and the ability to choose is essential to identity formation.

The Refusal of Choice

It is precisely this that contemporary man finds so difficult to do. He does not want to choose. He does not want to give up any of the possibilities. Indeed, he wants to taste all possibilities without ever having to choose among them. He looks about him at the many attractive identities from which to choose and fears that any exercise of choice will limit him to something less than his appetite for variety demands. The media show him more possibilities than he ever dreamed of, with new ones appearing daily on the horizon. Television makes him feel that he is missing out on these possibilities, so does the press when it devotes an article to the latest life-style, and the polls of his neighbors' sex practices only add to his feeling of being left out and left behind. So he goes dashing about hoping to partake of all these possibilities, choosing none of them. He wishes to postpone commitment until a more convenient time—that is to say, indefinitely.

But in postponing commitment the modern man or woman also postpones the development of identity, for identity, as Kierkegaard demonstrated, is created by the choices we make. It is experienced in the commitment, not in the potential.

The plight of being unable to choose, and the identity crisis that can result, is poignantly illustrated in Sylvia Plath's novel *The Bell Jar*. The narrator, Esther, uses the metaphor of a fig tree to symbolize the possibilities that life holds for her. The green boughs of the tree branch out in many directions and at the top of each branch is a "fat purple fig." One fig represents a happy home and children, another a career as an editor. Another is a brilliant professor, and yet another is a famous poet. There are figs which represent travel and adventure, a bevy of lovers, even an olympic crew champion:

> I saw myself sitting in the crotch of this fig tree, starving to death, just because I couldn't make up my mind which of these figs I would choose. I wanted each and every one of them, but choosing one meant losing all the rest, and, as I sat there, unable to decide, the figs began to wrinkle and go black, and, one by one, they plopped to the ground at my feet.[2]

As we have seen, sociological factors like mobility and novelty have led to this unwillingness to choose. A swiftly changing society offers a great diversity of choices and life-styles as possibilities rapidly succeed and replace one another. Corresponding to this outward flux is an incessant inward motion of constantly shifting tastes, desires, and attitudes. This, it is argued, is the reason why friendships no longer last, nor do marriages. Since people change at different rates and in different directions, it is hopeless to expect that any two people can grow together for more than a few years. Their commitment to one another must remain tentative lest their options shrivel up. He gets into massage, organic gardening, and back-to-nature; she turns to theater and to dining out. On one point they both agree: their own self-actualization is paramount and when their relationship becomes an impediment to that, then it is time to part company.

The popularity of such ideas as "self-actualization" and "self-fulfillment" points toward another source of the reluctance to choose. The psychological justification for the refusal of commitment finds its expression in the writings of those who, like Esfandiary, are pushing for a fluid concept of identity.

The Human Potential Movement

Actually, Esfandiary is only repeating a theme which the psychologist Carl Rogers has been developing for the past thirty years. Together with the writings of Abraham Maslow, Rogers' many books and articles constitute the basis of Humanistic Psychology and what has come to be known as the Human Potential Movement. The Human Potential Movement has made significant inroads not only in psychology but also in religion, business, industry, education, recreation, the arts, child rearing, marriage, and that more amorphous category called life-styles. Almost imperceptibly, Rogers' vocabulary, once confined to the clinic, has been appropriated for use by larger and larger segments of the general culture. Teachers speak glibly of "child-centered" classrooms; teachers are, in fact, no longer teachers but "facilitators." Factory foremen seek "nondirective" ways of relating to their subordinates, while liberated housewives are kept busy "actualizing" themselves without neglecting the growth of their children's "self-concept." This is reminiscent of the way, twenty years before, Erikson's terms "identity," "identity crisis," and "moratorium" filtered into general usage, although for some reason—perhaps because he didn't promise as much—Erikson's concepts never had the power of generating mass movements.

I first became interested in Rogers' theory of personality growth about a dozen years ago; not until several years later did I encounter Erikson's *Childhood and Society.* I admired both systems and for a long time the two coexisted peacefully in my mind. But as I gained a better insight into Erikson's work, this initial harmony began to fade. It occurred to me that I had never seen any reference to Rogers in Erikson's writings or any reference to Erikson in Rogers'. Could it be that there was no compatibility in their thought? Upon reflection I concluded that instead of compatibility there was a split; and that this split, far from being a subject for the mandarin speculations of psychologists, reflected philosophical and historical divisions of great consequence.

The division mainly concerns what we understand by the term self. Perhaps the best way to describe the point at issue is to take Heraclitus' famous question and apply it to the self. "Can you step twice into the same river?" becomes for us, "Will the person I am today be the same person tomorrow?" Or to twist Polonius' aphorism into a question: "Is there a self to be true to?"

These are philosophical as well as psychological questions, but it should be obvious by now that the psychologists have long since taken over the job of the philosophers. When the modern man seeks a justification for his actions or a path to follow he does not turn to philosophers or, for that matter, to theologians; for the ultimate answers he turns rather to authorities like Abraham Maslow, Fritz Perls, and Eric Berne.

And Carl Rogers. The attraction of Rogers' ideas lies in the fact that they confirm a tendency already present in us. The phenomenon of future shock has prepared us to seek a definition of the self more congenial to the flux of modern society. Rogers provides it. "At its best," he writes, "life is a flowing, changing process in which nothing is fixed."[3] Health consists in flowing with this stream, being whatever thoughts and feelings are flowing through one now, and recognizing that these will be constantly changing. The important thing is to be aware of what is going on inside; not necessarily to do anything about it, but to admit to awareness more and more of the flux and flow of the total self (or, to use Rogers' terminology, "the organismic self"). It is not really necessary to do anything because one can trust one's self. Human nature is good, constructive, self-enhancing, self-actualizing—if only it can be freed from the unnecessary boundaries we impose. Lie back and float in the stream of it. It may be scary but it's basically safe. Trust yourself. Be yourself.

Rogers' theory of personality is the story of Dorian Gray in reverse: our inner self, if only it could be exposed, would prove to be far lovelier than the self-portrait we mistake for the real us. The trouble with most of us, by Rogers' account, is that over the years we build up a static self-definition which ignores the ebbing and flowing of our real self. Our real self is the pulsating sum of all our experiences, thoughts, desires, bodily sensations—a stream of consciousness and unconsciousness. But the stream keeps getting dammed up by this narrow definition we impose on ourselves, and this is unfortunate, says Rogers, because our definition of self is largely derived from parents and society. We buy somebody else's definition of what we should be and then spend our life trying to cram our own unique experience into this procrustean bed. As Rogers sees it, an unhealthy person has a narrow self-definition derived from others. He excludes much of the "data" of his life from awareness and spends much of his energy defending his narrowly defined self against experiences which are inconsistent with it rather than enlarging it to admit them.

A healthy person, on the other hand, would fit Walt Whitman's self-description:

> *Do I contradict myself?*
> *Very well then I contradict myself,*
> *(I am large, I contain multitudes)*

His self-definition is big enough to admit the whole of his fluid experience. Health and liberation come by way of continually expanding the self-definition—freeing it to change with changing realities.

Having had to redefine myself several times over the last thirty-four years I can attest to the essential wisdom of Rogers' scheme. For example, my conception of parenthood was hopelessly unreal—derived, in part I believe, from listening to radio programs of the *Ozzie and Harriet* genre during my teens. During those years I decided that I would be the type of parent that Ozzie Nelson was. After all, he never spanked his children, never yelled at them, never even raised his voice to them. When David and Ricky went astray it was always out of good intentions gone awry, and a short heart-to-heart talk between father and sons would soon put things right. Ozzie was both father and pal, and I determined to be like him when I had children of my own. Aided and abetted by some idealistic books on child raising which I later read, and possibly fostered by certain Rousseauian assumptions about human nature, these notions began to coalesce into a self-concept. I knew the type of parent I would be before I even became one. It was all defined in my head. It would be easy—just as it was easy for the radio parents. Unfortunately, the self-concept I was developing wasn't much more realistic than my plans at a younger age for modeling my life after the Lone Ranger.

Eventually I became a father and the narrowness of my parental self-definition was soon revealed. As it turned out, I was nothing like Ozzie and in no way did my children resemble David and Ricky. If anything, they were more like the Katzenjammer Kids. Unlike Ozzie, I found myself losing patience with them, scolding them, even spanking them. I can write about this now in a light vein, but at the time I felt quite guilty. I wasn't living up to the picture I had of myself as perfect parent. Some of the things I did were quite inconsistent with my self-definition and it was making me anxious. But the more anxious I became, the more impatient I was. It was a vicious circle. Eventually I had to scrap the radio-parent self-definition and exchange it for one big enough to admit a little more of life's ambivalence. I decided that one could occasionally lose patience, scold, and spank and still be a good parent.

The redefinition helped considerably. I stopped feeling anxious and guilty and began feeling a lot more comfortable about the responsibilities of parenthood now that I was working out of my own definition instead of the network scriptwriter's. I believe that I even found less occasion to scold and spank.

Situations like my own are, I believe, not uncommon in this society: men trying to fit themselves into the procrustean definition of manhood presented in the movies and denying their real selves in the process; women trying to mold their lives into the image of femininity proffered on TV commercials, and losing contact with their inner experiences; children growing up into their parents' expectations without ever discovering their own wants; people everywhere, distorting or disowning their fluid experience of life for the sake of culturally ordained interpretations of experience. As society becomes more changeable, so does our experience of life. Under these conditions, as Rogers says, it's a mistake to get caught in a too narrow identity. Better to keep a little loose. Human beings should always be in the process of becoming more than they are. It's not in our nature to settle into a static identity.

Perils of Potentialism

All this is to the good if it frees people from unnecessary and neurotic rigidities. But there are certain liabilities that can be incurred by following this line of thinking too enthusiastically and too uncritically. For in elaborating this process view of the self, Rogers is also providing encouragement to the growing number of those who refuse to commit themselves in any way to anyone.

This noncommittal attitude is buoyed up by Rogers' view of the self as an automatically unfolding process. Although Rogers (who paradoxically claims to be influenced by Kierkegaard) is unwilling to admit it, such a view of human nature must lead to a debasement of will and to a debilitation of choice. Rogers' essential determinism is evident in his penchant for the word "organism." Organism, meaning a member of the animal or vegetable kingdom, is a biological term used to designate the preprogrammed workings of creatures as diverse as amoebas and aardvarks. But Rogers consistently applies the term to human beings as though people were like roses unfolding out of buds. This is why Rogers is limited to defining volition as "simply the subjective following of a harmonious balance of organismic direction."[4]

In doing so he manages to avoid the existential question of either/or choices; what he recommends instead is a passive participation in the "wisdom" of the organism. This, of course, is a far cry from Kierkegaard's understanding of choice, and, if it is not quite the ethics of the vegetable garden, it is certainly no basis for commitment either. The existentialist point of view is (in general) that an individual's identity is constructed on the choices and commitments he makes. But Rogers is not interested in determining the self, only in experiencing it. Hence, in his many books and articles, we find an emphasis on floating and flowing rather than choice, on awareness rather than action. It is the psychology of the passive tense: the philosophy of laissez-faire applied to psychology. One can almost hear Jefferson's voice in the background admonishing, "the less government, the better."

The organism, says Rogers, is regulated by its own "thermostatic controls." Why interfere with it? The overlay of social conditioning often acts to prevent us from getting in touch with these deep instincts, but if we can just ignore society and leave matters to the "rationality" of the organism we will become more fully ourselves.

If the self is understood as an automatically unfolding process, however, there is little incentive to create it, or to define it one way rather than another. The emphasis shifts instead to experiencing it in all its flux and flow. Choice yields to sensation. Getting in touch with one's feelings is somehow supposed to solve the problem of choice.

Identity also suffers in such a scheme. Self-definition, since it might erect barriers between the self and its openness to experience, is avoided. And commitments which might lead to self-definition are, likewise, shunned. Whatever identity one has becomes experimental: a loosely worn overcoat, easily shuffled off if the weather changes.

Despite its drawbacks, however, the notion of fluidity seems to have an overwhelming appeal. The Rogerian view is increasing in popularity. Although few people outside of psychology and education have a real familiarity with Rogers' theories, his basic ideas are filtering into general acceptance, thanks to the phenomenal growth of the Human Potential Movement. By 1970, there were some 220 institutions throughout the United States devoted in full or in part to training people in the ways of growth.[5] The movement has spread to Europe, Australia, Southeast Asia, Africa, and South America. Even fleets of Norwegian fishermen have been sensitized by HPM type encounters. The Rogerian philosophy of self which the movement espouses has become, in its popularized form, the new conventional wisdom. The notion that one must keep one's identity fluid and one's options open is now common coin. No one wants to limit himself or allow others to have a claim on him. Everyone wants to remain "open to experience," to "increase awareness," to "get in touch with feelings," "to be themselves." But behind these high-sounding catchwords there often yawns a basic emptiness, the emptiness of Peer Gynt in the onion patch. There is, to use an old-fashioned phrase, nothing solid about these people who are so intent on their self-actualization. Beneath the surface sincerity they exude, one detects a void. What is missing is a self that can with some assurance be depended on. Where it does exist it is most likely the vestige of an earlier training, for the Human Potential creed does not foster the consistency and continuity that make for dependability or commitment. When this horticultural view of man is finally translated into everyday language, it appears as the ultimate excuse for avoiding involvement or self-definition.

Tentativeness is fine as a partial or temporary approach to life. It keeps us open to change and helps us avoid the dangers of too hasty commitment or too narrow self-definition. However, the longer this tentative approach is prolonged, the more likely it is to harden into a character state: the tentative approach to everything and everyone. If tentativeness or fluidity is not tempered with a sense of continuity, fidelity, or commitment, it becomes in the end a very cold and calculating stance. Sooner or later the tentative person will find himself incapable of involvement or commitment. His approach to life has become strictly experimental. Other people become instruments: occasions for his self-growth—though after a point the question of growth-in-what-directions is hardly raised.

The question of direction is a crucial one for identity. Abraham Maslow is the Human Potential theorist who comes closest to confronting the issue. But in the end he appears to tiptoe around it. Maslow developed a theory of motivation that puts great stress on self-actualization. Providing that their needs for food, security, sex, and love are regularly satisfied, people automatically become motivated by a need to actualize themselves, that is, to fulfill their potentialities, to become everything they can become. Like Rogers, Maslow tends to lapse into horticultural imagery. He assumes a preexisting inner core of self with all sorts of latent possibilities that will simply unfold, given the right climate and soil. And since Maslow, along with Rogers, has a basically Rousseauian view of human nature, he hardly questions in what direction the growth will go. He simply assumes it will go "forward." In Maslow we find the same unswerving faith that Rogers puts in the wisdom of the organism. His is a philosophy of self-discovery rather than of self-creation—a "passive-receptive" acceptance of one's basic instincts and deep feelings.[6]

The Existential Viewpoint

The trouble with this view is that self-actualization becomes an end in itself, becomes, in fact, the ultimate purpose. And that, according to the Viennese psychiatrist Victor Frankl, is a self-contradiction:

> A concept such as self-actualization, or self-realization, is not a sufficient ground for a motivational theory. This is mainly due to the fact that self-actualization, like power and pleasure, also belongs to that class of phenomena which can only be obtained as a side effect and are thwarted precisely to the degree to which they are made a matter of direct intention. Self-actualization is a good thing; however, I maintain that man can only actualize himself to the extent to which he fulfills meaning. Then self-actualization occurs spontaneously; it is contravened when it is made an end in itself.[7]

To find meaning in life, Frankl asserts, an individual has to go outside himself, for it is only in commitment to others that real self-actualization can be found. The same is true for identity. A person finds identity "to the extent to which he commits himself to something beyond himself, to a cause greater than himself."[8]

It is worth pausing here to look more closely at Frankl's concept of motivation because it poses a much-needed counterbalance to the Human Potential Movement. It is, in a sense, a theory born out of desperation—the type of desperation an individual experiences when his life collapses about him. But despite the degradation and suffering of his years in concentration camps, Frankl was able to retain dignity and meaning in his life. "He who has a why to live can bear with almost any how," wrote Nietzsche, and in the camps Frankl discovered the reality of that statement. For Frankl in the prison camp, the one thing that gave meaning to his life was the image of his wife, somehow more real and vivid in his mind than the reality of his prisoner's existence. He did not know whether his wife was alive or dead but he felt he experienced the truth of the Biblical message "Set me like a seal upon thy heart, love is as strong as death." Frankl recalls: "In the consciousness of every single being somebody was present and at hand, somehow 'there' as the thou of the most intimate dialogue. For many it was the first, last and ultimate Thou: God. But whoever occupied this position, the important thing was to ask, *What does he expect of me . . . ?*"[9] It is not surprising that Frankl often asks his patients, struggling with their sufferings, "For whose sake do you do so?"

After his release from the camps, when Frankl went back to the practice of psychiatry, he found that many of his patients were afflicted not with neurosis of the usual kind but with an essential lack of meaning in their lives. Man, in Frankl's view, is a being characterized by self-transcendence, by his reaching out for meaning and purpose. Where this sense of purpose is missing, a vacuum forms which no amount of self-actualization can fill. The meaning that a person has to fulfill is something beyond himself; it is never just himself.

A similar theme is expressed by Rollo May in *Love and Will*.[10] Love cannot be separated from will, and the human will is always stretching out, pointing to something or someone beyond itself. It is this directionality, this moving out to specific causes or people that makes life meaningful and makes love personal. According to May, meaning is always a matter of commitment. And, as with Kierkegaard, commitment is "always a leap and risk." Without commitment individuals sink into apathy. The important question to ask oneself, says May, is simply, "Does something or some person matter to me?" The essential idea that inspires both May and Frankl can be summed up in a statement by the philosopher Karl Jaspers: "What man is, he becomes through that cause which he had made his own."

The Problem of Direction

The theory of self-actualization, because it fails to grapple with questions of meanings, values, and directionality, is an incomplete explanation of human motivation. We can't realize all our potentialities, because in realizing one potential we cancel others out. A man may have the potential to be an architect, a lawyer, or a minister—but actualizing any one of these is fairly certain to cancel out the others. Which of his values determines his choice? A man may have the potential for loving many women but he cannot marry many women, nor carry on many simultaneous love affairs (except on the most superficial level). Whom does he choose? What makes her more meaningful than the others?

Identity, as I have said before, is experienced in the commitment, not the potential. To simply endorse actualization is to leave too many questions unanswered. Are all potentialities born equal, or are some more meaningful than others? Out of the many directions available, which one should I move in?

The Human Potential Movement does not give very satisfactory answers to these questions.

Admittedly, Maslow himself has reservations about his own scheme. He sees problems that Rogers does not. At one point he freely admits, "A problem we psychologists have been ducking is the problem of responsibilities, and necessarily tied in with it, the concept of courage and of will in the personality." Again Maslow states: "Self-actualization is meaningless without reference to a currently active future life." He adds, "We need a validated, usable system of human values that we can believe in and devote ourselves to (be willing to die for)."[11] One gets the feeling when reading Maslow that he was trying to cover all bases; that he was latching on to every virtuous trait known to man since Adam and equating it with self-actualization. Will, direction, and choice are good things, Maslow insists, but he is hard pressed to explain exactly how they fit into his theory of self-actualization. The best he can offer is the observation that in the self-actualizing person such dichotomies as fluidity and commitment are somehow resolved. Nevertheless, he did try. He was looking for a link between the European Existentialist emphasis on choice and the American emphasis on biology.

The Human Potential Movement would do well to take a second look at Maslow and the uneasiness he felt with directionless self-actualization. Especially in his later years, Maslow became increasingly interested in the problems of values and choice in psychology. The Human Potential Movement, if it is to avoid deterioration into mere self-indulgence, needs to raise this same sort of questions. But right now it seems more interested in experiencing the self than in defining it in the light of values. The Rogerian branch of the Human Potential River flows more smoothly, and for the moment that is the one that most people in the movement have elected to explore.

Erikson

If this is the direction the Human Potential Movement is heading in, then its leaders ought at least to cease claiming Kierkegaard as a spiritual father, for, on the subject of choice and identity, Kierkegaard's thinking is very different from theirs. Kierkegaard did not abdicate his painful choices to the "harmonious balance of organismic direction." He was not one to float in the flowing rivers of a self devoid of will. Kierkegaard wagered. He knowingly and willingly cut himself off from cherished possibilities for the sake of a commitment. He chose what he became. Let us not pretend that the Human Potential Movement follows in his footsteps.

If we were to look for a contemporary American psychologist whose work embodies the spirit of Kierkegaard we would look not to Rogers or Maslow but to Erikson, who like Kierkegaard was born in Denmark. It is no coincidence that Robert Coles' intellectual biography of Erikson[12] begins with a discussion of Søren Kierkegaard, for Erikson like Kierkegaard is deeply concerned with the necessity of choosing. At the center of his theory is the thesis that an individual life is a series of stages, one building upon another. At each of these stages there is a clash between two polarities—an either/or situation in which development must go one way or the other. The eight stages which Erikson reluctantly formulated—reluctantly because he feared the simplification an outline might convey—are:

1. trust vs. mistrust (infant)
2. autonomy vs. shame and doubt (toddler)
3. initiative vs. guilt (preschool)
4. industry vs. inferiority (school years)
5. identity vs. identity confusion (adolescent)
6. intimacy vs. isolation (young adult)
7. generativity vs. self-absorption (adult)
8. integrity vs. despair (maturity)[13]

The specific character of each individual's crisis will be determined by many factors: biology, sex, social conditions, parental and peer influences, cultural pressures, and so on. There is an element of mutuality involved in growth as well: the father who helps his adolescent son achieve a sense of identity is in turn being helped by his son to achieve a sense of generativity rather than self-absorption; the young couple in love are helping each other to develop a sense of intimacy rather than isolation. However, no crisis is ever fully resolved. A crisis of trust or a crisis of identity may reoccur at any time in life. But successful resolution of an earlier crisis will ease the way for mastery in subsequent struggles.

In all this growth through crisis, except perhaps at the earliest stages, despite the press of biological and cultural factors, and despite the outcome of previous crises, one's development is always to some extent in one's own hands. Identity is more than a product of forces; it develops, as well, as the result of a series of decisions.

The necessity of choosing becomes particularly apparent at the adolescent stage. This is the crisis of identity and identity confusion. More than anything else, identity confusion involves an inability to choose. One of the classic literary portrayals of this is the character of Biff Loman, the son in *Death of a Salesman*. Biff, still an adolescent at thirty-four, has been brought up by his father to believe that a world of unlimited possibilities lies in his future. But Biff, who has had "twenty or thirty different kinds of jobs," and has made the least of his opportunities, is beginning to feel that he is not getting anywhere. To his brother he says:

> "I'm mixed up very bad. Maybe I oughta get married. Maybe I oughta get stuck into something. Maybe that's my trouble. I'm like a boy. I'm not married. I'm not in business, I just —I'm like a boy."[14]

Biff is gradually realizing that among all the possibilities of life he must begin to choose and select. But his inability to decide persists:

LINDA: *(His mother)* Are you home to stay now?
BIFF: I don't know. I want to look around, see what's doin'.
LINDA: Biff, you can't look around all your life, can you?
BIFF: I just can't take hold, Mom. I can't take hold of some kind of life.[15]

His dilemma is such a common experience that it needs no explication. The only difference, as we have seen, is that now this kind of confusion is often raised to the level of a virtue.

The difficulty in choosing comes with the adolescent's growing realization that more and more his choices are becoming irreversible. A child who has made a bad move in a game of checkers may ask if he can "take it back," and, more often than not, we let him. To some extent we do the same for adolescents. To the end that a youngster may find a proper identity, society provides what Erikson calls a "psycho-social moratorium": a delay of adult commitments during which the adolescent is free to try on and reject any number of roles. But the day when the moratorium ends comes closer, and with it comes an awareness that some choices must be lived with. The child sees no reason why he cannot at some future time be simultaneously fireman, President, sports star, and adventurer. The adolescent grudgingly gives up some of his childhood dreams so that he may pursue others. This recognition that one's decisions may be irretrievable brings both a sense of personal history and a reluctance to commit. Robert Coles puts the matter very well:

> He [the adolescent] finds himself at a loss, and he fears that the world is breathing hard down his back . . . ready to restrict him, type him, define him, and thus close him off from any number of possibilities he still finds attractive. He wants "out," he wants to be away, he wants time to think and decide and only later act.[16]

Luckily, at this stage of development youth is endowed with a saving capacity for fidelity. Otherwise the burden of making up one's mind might be too great. It is this quality of fidelity, this drive to show the world or the beloved what faithfulness really is, that makes choice bearable, makes it almost a necessity. What is an identity for—if not to be given in love or to a cause? In large part youth is set off from other generations by its passionate loyalty to friends and its burning devotion to causes. The sometimes reckless bravery of the young stems from their conviction that valor in the service of fidelity is the better part of prudence.

We have in our literature a figure, half-adult and half-adolescent, in whom can be seen both the energy of fidelity and the danger of false commitment. Hamlet's pledge of fidelity to his friend Horatio is, in its intensity, characteristic of youth's eagerness to choose and then to commit to that special chosen one, one's own very special self:

> *"Since my dear soul was mistress of her choice*
> *And could of men distinguish, her election*
> *Hath sealed thee for herself; for thou hast been*
> *As one in suffering all, that suffers nothing,*
> *A man that fortune buffets and rewards*
> *Hast ta'en with equal thanks; and bless'd are those*
> *Whose blood and judgment are so co-mingled*
> *That they are not a pipe for fortune's finger*
> *To sound what stop she pleases. Give me that man*
> *That is not passion's slave, and I will wear him*
> *In my heart's core, ay in my heart of heart*
> *As I do thee."*[17]

Sadly, as Erikson points out in commenting on this passage, Hamlet's words outstrip his deeds and in the end he is confirmed in a negative identity—that of a madman. The role of madman is at first just that: a role at which Hamlet playacts, a method by which he seeks to cut through the duplicities that surround him. Like many young people he tries on different identities in search of the one that is his. His purpose: "By indirection [to] find direction out." But the world is ever ready to "restrict him, type him, define him," and Hamlet is confirmed in his experimental madness as some contemporary youths are confirmed in their experimental delinquency by angry adults and zealous courts. Hamlet's temporary defense against identity confusion becomes his final role in life: the mad avenger of his father's death—fidelity at its deadliest.[18]

In light of society's proclivity to typecast, it is little wonder that youth wish to leave their options open for as long as possible and to prolong their moratorium to the nth degree before committing themselves to a role and status which may be binding, which may be altogether the wrong one. It is likely that this noncommittal state of affairs would go on forever did there not exist within each one that strength of devotion so eloquently stated in Hamlet's speech to his friend. This is that quality of loyalty which, when it exists in our friends, is our guarantee "that they are not a pipe for fortune's finger to sound what stop she pleases."

Fidelity carries with it the danger of commitment to madness, motorcycle gangs, or murderous ideologies, but without it there would be no courage to remain faithful to the choices by which a positive self is built. Without it, also, there would be little hope for achieving intimacy or the relationships that are built on intimacy. In Erikson's scheme, identity comes before intimacy. The rationale for this arrangement is that only the achievement of a reasonably consolidated identity permits us to "face the fear of ego loss in situations which call for self-abandon."[19] Until one knows who or what one is, how can he share that self with another? But an identity doesn't develop in a vacuum. A young person can't postpone relationships until his identity is developed. That would be like a middle-aged man postponing exercise until he's in shape. It's a two-way street. Intimacy requires identity, but identity is in turn strengthened by intimacy. Until we risk a relationship, identity remains tentative and formless; but each new relationship forces us to define ourselves a little more clearly.

The risk lies in making the wrong choices. The old saw about identifying yourself by the company you keep has a lot of truth in it. To some extent we do become like the company we keep, and inevitably we give over a portion of our autonomy to that company. Friends and loved ones do limit us.

We are not necessarily the worse for having this focus in our lives but it is an inescapable fact. Not everyone can articulate the dangers of intimacy but everyone senses them. One common reaction, especially among the young, is to declare a moratorium on closeness. Until they are surer of their identity, some young persons shy away from intimacy or else find a substitute in brief encounters. The danger here is that an excessively prolonged deferment of intimacy may lead either to isolation or to a permanent state of tentativeness. On the other hand some young persons, as a defense against identity confusion, may seek a close and even confining relationship. They want security above all else. Because they define themselves almost exclusively by their relationship, they have little life outside it. And they tend to be overly possessive out of fear that in losing their love object they will lose the only identity they have. It is not so much a relationship that they have but a fixation; one underdeveloped self fixed upon another in symbiotic attachment. As in most of development, growth in intimacy is a matter of charting a course which, with a little luck, will avoid both Scylla and Charybdis.

The Uncommitted

What is becoming increasingly apparent, however, is that the choices and the decisions necessary for growth in intimacy and identity are not being made. As evidence of this trend we have Kenneth Keniston's in-depth study of Harvard students in the early sixties which culminated in the publication of *The Uncommitted.*[20] Relying on self-reports, interviews, autobiographies, and projective tests, Keniston provides us with a detailed picture of uncommitted and alienated youth.

As Keniston describes them, these young men are reluctant to have their freedom circumscribed in any way. Yet their basic attitude is not one of self-assertion but of passivity. They would rather be done to than do, would rather be seduced by women than vice versa. As children these men were the objects of unusual maternal solicitude. They all came from a highly gratifying early environment and all were reluctant to leave it. The adult world, because it requires choosing from among possibilities and settling on a limited identity, is exceedingly unattractive to them. Theirs is not merely a moratorium on commitment but a fixed refusal of it. About these young men there hangs an almost cherished mantle of isolation. They would rather isolate themselves than lose themselves, and it is because they fear the latter that they shun involvement with causes or persons. They somehow perceive that their relationship with their mothers has limited them, and they are not going to let that happen again. Commitment is for them a form of submission. It involves the acceptance of boundaries, restrictions, and responsibilities they are not ready for. Their main project in life seems to be a diffuse quest for sensate experience of all kinds. It is a search that is more in the mind than in reality, for they cannot usually muster the elemental decisiveness for plunging into the realms of sentience. It is the possibilities rather than any reality of their life which they wish to keep inviolate. And since commitment might entail a limitation on these possibilities, it is all the more to be avoided. Paradoxically, alongside their actual withdrawal is a recurrent fantasy of fusion, experienced as a desire to merge with all others and with nature in a quasi-mystical state of undifferentiated oneness best expressed in Eastern religious and philosophical traditions. Evidently, the well-defined self, which these students have been avoiding all along, might prove a barrier to that complete union for which they unconsciously yearn.

The alienated that Keniston wrote about in 1965 were not happy men, nor were they representative. They were an elite, and they were confused and disturbed by their lack of a sense of self. The syndrome Keniston described is now far more widespread and there is now a much more willing acceptance of the uncommitted status. What was anguish for the alienated of the early sixties has been raised to the state of high art or, more precisely, to the state of high behavioral science in the seventies. For them tentativeness was a protective reaction; for us it has become an article of faith.

The Endless Moratorium

The current popularity of the tentative approach is a direct result of accelerated change. In a fast-paced, complex, and unsettled society, identity formation becomes difficult for most, impossible for some. One way to react to multiple and competing options is to turn to a cult of simplicity. Whether in the form of a literal-minded "Jesus movement," a Krishna cult, or a vegetarian commune, there are always prepackaged identities available that lay claim to being the Way by which complexity will be ordered and the rough ways made smooth. But a more usual reaction to future shock is the route of the prolonged moratorium. As a society becomes more complex there is a tendency for this breathing period to lengthen. The United States, with an economy based on change, turnover, and innumerable choices, now extends this moratorium into the third decade for some of its promising youth. A large number of other youth have decided to similarly prolong their own adolescence without any official sanction. The widespread postponement of marital, parental, and career commitments in America is indicative of how difficult the task of self-defini-tion has become of late. It is not only youth who are involved in these delaying tactics. Many adults are attempting a second adolescence, a chance to try out those possibilities they missed the first time around. After all, the major reason youth is envied and emulated in our culture is the feeling that young people represent possibilities that have not yet closed up. If, in climbing onto the youth bandwagon, adults often "take back" their original commitments to spouses, children, and careers, it is only in the service of that higher cause called self-actualization.

What it comes down to is this: adolescence, which used to be a staging area for the assault on adulthood, has now become a sanctuary that adolescents don't want to leave, and that adults want to reenter. The adolescent moratorium, though, is a tricky business. End it too quickly and you stunt your growth; keep it up too long and you never come to grips with yourself. A nice illustration of the dangers on both ends is provided in the successful film about teenagers, *American Graffiti*. John, the drag-strip king, has just about come to the end of his moratorium. His self has already been defined in many ways, yet because of this definition he has a style and character about him which the others do not possess. But we sense that there will be no further development for John. Whether through his own fault or society's, we feel that his identity has been shaped too quickly and too narrowly. Another character in the film, Kurt, is at the opposite pole. His moratorium has only just begun. Kurt is all fluidity. He adapts with equal ease to the role of hoodlum or to that of scholarship recipient. He doesn't really know where he's at, and because of this he lacks John's integrity. Nevertheless, we don't worry about him. He's going off to college—plenty of time to find himself. We sense somehow that Kurt's moratorium will go on for a long time but will result eventually in a life richer and more complex than the one that awaits John.

Shifting Into Fluid Drive

This is what the Human Potential philosophy promises: endless moratorium, endless youth, endless fluidity. And this is why it is so appealing to a fluid and changing society. As I have tried to indicate, the Rogerian version of identity is more compatible to this type of society and is more easily attainable than is the slowly consolidated identity Erikson describes. It may be that in the face of innumerable decisions and under the weight of choosing from a diversity of appealing but often incompatible life-styles, it has become impossible to build a strong, clearly defined identity which coheres over time. It may be that the only rational alternative is to forgo continuity and give one's self over to a continual process of change and continual redefinition, unrestricted by the boundaries that people and places provide.

Although I do not believe that this is the answer, many people apparently do. There is every indication that the Rogerian concept of identity as process is supplanting Erikson's more fixed concept. It is not a cheerful prospect. Not that our identity can't stand a measure of fluidity. Fluidity and adaptability are necessary for people to deal with a changing future; and any theory of identity that emphasizes commitment must be tempered with an awareness of how difficult commitment has become under the new conditions. Still, there is a delicate balance at issue: the balance between tentativeness and commitment, between fluidity and decision. No one wants to be confined in the wrong identity, but if we want any identity we do have to make choices. By endorsing a directionless self-actualization and a too-fluid fluidity at the expense of continuity and direction, the Human Potential Movement threatens to obliterate what little identity we have left as individuals.

3

The Temporary Self

SEVERAL years ago I participated in a sensitivity group which met twice a week for about six weeks. It was the fourth meeting, and I was being briefed on what had transpired during the previous session, which I had missed. The intense young man who was doing the briefing was somewhat annoyed at me for having been absent on that occasion and told me so (our group had two prime rules: regular attendance and complete honesty). Then he came to the heart of the matter:

> "Last week we all told what was most important in our lives. Do you have something that is most important to you?"
> "Yes," I replied.
> "What is it?"
> "It's none of your business."

It wasn't my intention to be so blunt, but since honesty was the order of the day I rose to the occasion and told him what I felt. He was truly shocked, as though I had violated some ancient code—as though I didn't have the right to withhold information from the group. I can't remember what was said after that; all I recall is the look of complete incomprehension that covered his face.

Relationships: The Historical Dimension

I mention this incident because it illustrates a prevalent intellectual trend of much importance: the tendency to deny the historical dimension of relationships. "What was most important to me," had I revealed it, would not have raised any eyebrows. It was nothing esoteric, just personal. The reason I did not tell him was that I did not know him. Three sessions were not enough to build up the kind of mutual trust I wanted before casting my pearls in the open. Jane Howard describes a similar feeling in her account of a year spent travelling from one encounter group to another. After it was all over she observed that none of the many people she encountered came to be really important to her or she to them. But her experience did make her realize the importance of continuity:

> I have come to esteem history as a component of friendships. In my case at least friendships are not igneous but sedimentary. Mine usually take a year, sometimes several, before they ripen, and I am not persuaded that behavioral science can hasten this process.[1]

The behavioral sciences, however, are attempting to hasten this process. American psychologists, especially those in the Human Potential Movement, have grown impatient with time and history; like my antagonist in the sensitivity group they seem intent on cutting out the historical dimension of relationships. This they do, not out of any mischievous iconoclasm, but simply out of the conviction that there is no need to waste time, that, in brief, identity can flourish apart from continuity. Once again it helps to clarify the trend if we contrast Carl Rogers with Erik Erikson. We can start with the simple observation that Erikson is a biographer (Gandhi, Luther, Jefferson) as well as a psychologist. He is fascinated with history because he feels that the formation of identity is very much an historical process. I am not talking here about a psychoanalytic archeologist digging in the sands of his patient's past, intent only on uncovering the artifacts of the first six years. That would imply a passive view of man as a product of forces outside his control. Erikson's sense of history is more dynamic than that. Not only does history make us, but we make it. Few of us make it on the grand scale of a Gandhi or Luther although all of us are involved in the history of our times; but just as decisively as they, whether by our acts or omissions, we have a hand in shaping our personal histories. Our life is a history that is slowly made and felt by others as we in turn feel the impact of others' lives on us. Moreover, we construct our identities not only out of the past but out of the present and future as well. Our identity is made up of every hour of every day we ever spend, and also out of the future that we want or fear: that future will, after all, determine the choices we make now. It is this sense of continuity that gives our identity its quality of permanence so that, in Erikson's words, it comes to be experienced as "an irreversible historical fact."[2]

Rogers, on the other hand, is not particularly interested in history, either social or personal. It is difficult to imagine him tracing the development of a Gandhi or a Luther, or for that matter, one of his own clients. In fact, he advises would-be counselors not to take case histories or to read existing ones. The same unconcern over personal history is shared by others in the Human Potential Movement—Michael Murphy, George Bach, and Bernard Gunther, to name a few. What they are interested in, as any participant in an encounter group will attest, is the here-and-now. "What are you feeling now?" the group leader invariably asks. To talk about the past or the future is considered a "cop-out," a way of avoiding present confrontation. Unlike Freudian psychologists, the Human Potential people have little interest in descriptions of early life or reports of family background or past conflict. The present moment is of supreme concern, and for this reason the vocabulary of the encounter groups is laced with terms like "immediacy," "spontaneity," and "the here-and-now." The purpose of this emphasis is to enable the group participant to get in touch with what he really feels and to open himself to whatever experiences are coursing through him at this moment. Life is a stream of consciousness, an "awareness continuum," as Fritz Perls called it. The encounter group member is not to take heed of the morrow but to be fully alive in the present. Thus the encounter experience is a process of stripping away the props the past and future provide until the pure self stands naked in the pulsating light of the present. It is meant to be a rebirth of the self, and many claim that it is.

This remarkable doctrine finds a ready welcome among those who have already been disposed by the rapid passage of events to see their past as irrelevant and their future as unpredictable. A rapidly evolving society, because it does not allow us to find connections with the past or look to the future, induces an alteration in the sense of time: we orient ourselves to the present moment and to whatever intensity can be extracted from it. It is this collapse of the time continuum that the Human Potential philosophy taps into. Rogers, for instance, expresses a widespread sentiment when he asks of himself, "Can I meet this other individual as a person who is in the process of *becoming*, or will I be bound by his past and by my past?"[3]

Reading this we are no longer in the time-bound world of yesterdays and tomorrows. Rather we are in the world of free-floating selves who, in the process of becoming more fully human, are freed from the historical dimension of personality. In this world we are not to be tied to our past or shackled to the future. In Maslow's words, "The person now becomes more a pure psyche and less a thing of the world living under the laws of the world."[4] It is a concept admirably suited to the future-shocked man who, since his body is no longer much confined by space and time, sees no reason that his identity should be.

Given the difficulty of maintaining a continuous sense of identity in these hurried times, it was inevitable that this view should catch on. Moreover, the appeal of the here-and-now philosophy is doubled by its promise of a breakthrough to relationships that are more authentic because less hampered by worn-out roles or binding expectations. Proponents of this opinion argue that the main reason love turns sour is that it is confined and cramped by past promises and future expectations instead of being allowed to breathe freely in the present. Encounter groups operate on the premise that people everywhere are hungry for intimacy, but often go without it not only because they lack trust in others but also because they fear the binding nature of intimacy. One function these groups perform, then, is to teach people to hurry up the process of intimacy by bypassing the circuitous route of small talk and gradual familiarity by which trust is usually built. They teach also that a liberated intimacy need not be binding. The short road to this type of intimacy goes by way of immediate self-disclosure and even immediate physical contact (groups are replete with touching exercises). This requires trust, of course, but that is what the group is for—it's a community of trust and acceptance. If you let yourself go, either physically or emotionally, the group will catch you.

Intimacy and Time

Unfortunately, the two most beguiling promises the Human Potential Movement holds out—intimacy and community—are undermined by its emphasis on the present. For once you have cut out past and future, you have removed the basis for human relationships, which is commitment over time, and you are left with the capacity only for intimacy and community of the most transitory nature. Never in history has a community been built on so little as the Human Potential people now propose to build: namely, free-floating and mobile selves devoid of religious, family, regional, political, or vocational ties and uncommitted to anything but the here-and-now.

Most Americans find precious little sense of community or intimacy, and it is understandable if they seek these in the encounters that the Human Potential people provide. What better setting could there be for learning to get along with others than a small group in which all facades and pretenses are dropped and in which emotions flow freely? The encounter group's emphasis on shared honesty and self-disclosure seems the proper preparation for intimacy. Its trust-building exercises, such as falling backward into the arms of the group or being led on a blindfolded gallop through the woods, would appear to be good practice for the trust on which a community depends. The encounter groups cater to this need for a sense of contact and closeness. They do not hesitate to promise deep relationships and full communication. And they do deliver something that often gives the illusion of meaningful relationships.

That something is an intense emotional experience. It is something that most Americans, numbed by the exigencies of living in a technocratic society, are in need of, but it should not be confused with real intimacy or community. These demand time, and time is something that encounter groups are short on. The current Esalen-type experiences originated from the T-group, a much longer process that extended over a period of weeks or months and that concentrated on specific issues. But the newer groups don't make much of an effort to stay together. Increasingly, the trend is toward weekend or even twelve-hour marathons as the chief mode of encountering. What these groups offer, in keeping with their here-and-now philosophy, is an intense but momentary experience. Such experiences can be valid and important, but they should not be confused with lasting relationships.

Significant relationships are those that we have with persons who give meaning to our lives. More often than not, they are significant because we have built up over the months or over the years a bond of mutual trust and commitment. With such people it is good that we share our emotions and disclose our innermost feelings. In encounter groups, however, there is a pressure to "spill your guts" at the earliest opportunity to those whose only significance lies in the electric intensity of the moment. This type of self-disclosure can easily cheapen into an exercise in emotional exhibitionism and lead to a consequent feeling that one's inner life has been devalued by overexposure. A recent and extensive study of encounter groups indicates that few of the participants demonstrated any behavioral or attitudinal changes, but that among those who did, the change was more likely to be in a negative than in a positive direction.[5] This study is all the more telling because the researchers who conducted it are all committed to the group method of changing behavior. The authors of the study suggest that the negative effects of the group may be attributed to the high expectations of some of the participants. These high hopes often center on finding lasting friendships or even love. For those who hold these optimistic anticipations, the group experience can prove quite disillusioning.

Although the Human Potential Movement promises growth in interpersonal relationships, it cannot make good on that promise. The reason it doesn't work is that the extreme orientation to the present that underlies it serves to undermine faithfulness, loyalty, and familiarity—all of which take time. Trust and intimacy, which are at the heart of the Human Potential idea, depend on continuity, which is not there at all. One simply can't place much trust in those whose sense of commitment does not extend beyond the immediate moment. One can, it is true, fall backward into their arms, and one can count on them to provide temporary emotional support in a group situation designed for that purpose. If, indeed, the present-oriented philosophy of the Human Potential Movement were confined to group encounters as a special arena for the exploration of interpersonal feelings, then one could only wish it well. What has happened, however, is that it has become the paradigm for all intimate relationships.

One sees this in the sudden growth of a number of foreshortened phenomena such as swingers clubs, singles weekends, participatory theater, and various other devices for getting close quickly without getting committed. One sees it in the emergence of a new style of sexuality in which the act of intercourse precedes other forms of intimacy. One sees it also in the compulsion to start off a relationship not with declarations of affection but with elaborate qualifications about keeping it casual. The essence of such relationships is best described not in poetry or in ballads but in those labels we see printed on dairy products: "This item good only until date stamped."

An extreme case of uncluttered intimacy is the relationship between the man and woman in the film *Last Tango in Paris*. The film is really a parable for the wish to deny the historical dimension of a relationship—and since that wish is now so widespread, the film can be taken as a parable for the modern condition. By coincidence a man and a woman find themselves together in a vacant Paris apartment. Almost immediately he initiates a sexual relationship, but from the start he refuses to reveal his name or to hear hers. He wants to know nothing about her past, her parents, her background, nothing that could identify her. The apartment itself is shuttered off from the rest of the world, suspended in time and space, and completely without context. The desk clerk doesn't know who lives in the building, doesn't know their names, only knows that they come and go. Outside, elevated trains pass each other at high speeds leaving no trace of their passage, symbolizing the brief encounters which mark human lives.

The makers of this film could have done no better than they did in choosing Marlon Brando to play the lead part. Brando has always been good at portraying a type of personality too big to be constricted in a role and too tentative to be predictable. As the film critic Pauline Kael has observed of him, "Brando represented a contemporary version of the free American."[6] In *Last Tango*, Brando is a man who is determined not to be bound by any past or by any outside reality. He says in effect: "I am what I am right now, which is all that matters. Who I was in the past or who I am outside this context is beside the point." There is a certain awesome recklessness to this moment-to-moment identity. It is not an historical self he creates but a biological self, pulsing, throbbing, expanding, contracting—a raw self fresh-born at every second. And his relationship with the girl has the same unexpected quality of being newly created at each moment. One doesn't know where it is going; it can only be experienced as it happens.

Mortality

The term "self-in-process" is, I suppose, a rather curious scientific way of describing such a person, but Brando's portrayal does serve to illustrate how that particular concept of identity must eventuate in a denial of the time span. Living moment to moment is just the logical expression of a self that disowns the past. Even though the time span is denied, however, it is still there. The intensity of the relationship between Brando and the girl is merely an index of the intensity which both, despite themselves, bring with them from the past. The film is not misleading on this point: it will not let the two lovers extricate their present from their past. What is misleading is the currently popular view that deep and intense relationships can flourish in an uncluttered present. It's the other way around, really; the present gets much of its intensity from past associations and future anticipations. If each moment were fresh, without any history, then each moment would fall flat. A man who lived purely in the present would have the affectlessness of an amnesia victim.

Something of this can be seen in Tolstoy's story "The Death of Ivan Ilyich." Ivan Ilyich is any one of us; an average fellow, mildly successful, generally unobtrusive, he is caught up in the cogs of society with little time or inclination to reflect on the pointlessness of life. He suffers a fall but his injury seems a minor one, a pain in his side. The pain grows more insistent and he travels from doctor to doctor only to find that they are unable to diagnose his malady or treat it. Gradually, his condition worsens and suddenly Ilyich is faced with the awful reality that he is going to die. Not just anyone, but him—Ivan Ilyich:

> The syllogism he had learned from Kiezewetter's Logic:
> Caius is a man, men are mortal, therefore Caius is mortal,
> always seemed to him correct as applied to Caius, but cer-
> tainly not as applied to himself. That Caius—man in the
> abstract—was mortal, was perfectly correct, but he was not
> Caius, not an abstract man, but a creature quite separate
> from all others.[7]

The realization that he is going to die causes Ilyich to experience his daily life with an intensity he had never known; he
only begins to appreciate the present when he is forced to
consider his whole life span. Without that perspective his life
would have remained a series of dull moments, one succeed-
ing another.

The Tragic Sense in Love

Rollo May makes a similar point in noting that the love affairs
of the immortal gods on Mount Olympus do not stir us. Because the gods live in an eternal present, their passions are
insipid; it is only when a mortal enters the picture that we are
moved. May makes a profound comment on the nature of true
intimacy in observing that "Love is not only enriched by our
sense of mortality but constituted by it."[8] This is not a morbid
statement but merely an acknowledgment that there is a tragic
sense in love that comes from the awareness that the ones we
love are vulnerable to death. And because they are vulnerable
to death and the ravages of time we love them all the more;
the tragic sense both heightens and deepens our love. The
only way to avoid this tragic sense is to remove the time element from love, to resolve not to commit yourself beyond the
moment (it is this tragic element that Brando is trying to avoid
in *Last Tango*: his wife has just killed herself), but in doing this
you also remove the intensity of love which the tragic sense
gives. C. S. Lewis writes that "the event of falling in love is of
such a nature that we are right to reject as intolerable the idea
that it should be transitory. In one high bound it has over-

leaped the massive wall of our selfhood; it has made appetite itself altruistic, tossed personal happiness aside as a triviality and planted the interests of another in the center of our being."[9] Transitoriness is acceptable only when we refuse to make that kind of leap. "Eros," wrote the Greek poet Hesiod, "breaks the limbs' strength";[10] it is understandable, even reasonable, to want to avoid getting involved in that type of love. It is safer, maybe even psychologically healthy (if one wants to be healthy only on a psychological level), to take a tentative approach to intimacy. But true intimacy is never safe; it does not make calculations, it does not hold anything in reserve; it makes foolish—almost impossible—declarations, and it invariably involves us in much more than we bargained for. Faced with that prospect it is no wonder that many go looking for a more manageable form of intimacy: they want to avoid the tragi-historical dimension of the relationship, they want to live in the present, and they want to be able to move out of the relationship at a moment's notice. But it is a mistake to claim that such relationships are a giving of the self when they are essentially a withholding of the self. The fact that such relationships may be marked by a high degree of self-disclosure should not fool us. Self-disclosure itself is not the measure of the depth of a relationship. In fact it is quite easy to disclose oneself to strangers and casual acquaintances whom one is not likely to see again or with whom there is no real danger of commitment.

Time and Meaning

Again, it is usually a mistake to call these short-lived relationships "meaningful." Meaningfulness implies lastingness. In the here-and-now, which can be merely a succession of dreary moments, meaning is not always apparent. But meaning does become apparent in considering the historical dimension: the commitments that one has made and kept, the joys that one has stored up, the loyalties and loves that one has built and maintained despite hardship and change, the future to which one aspires. Meaningfulness, like identity, is slowly accrued and often it is only time which reveals it.

A poignant illustration is provided in Victor Frankl's account of a mother who, in the wake of her son's death, attempted suicide. An older son, a cripple, prevented her. The woman was now participating in a psychodrama. Frankl asks another young woman in the group to project herself into the future, to her deathbed, and then to look back on a life that had been childless but "full of financial success and social prestige." Looking back from the vantage point of an old woman of eighty, she can find no meaning to that life. Frankl then turns to the mother and asks her to do the same, only looking back on her own life. This is her reply:

> "I wished to have children and this wish has been granted to me; one boy died, the other, however, the crippled one, would have been sent to an institution if I had not taken over his care. Though he is crippled and helpless, he is after all my boy. And so I have made a fuller life possible for him; I have made a better human being out of my son."

At this point Frankl records, "There was an outburst of tears and crying." The mother continues:

> "As for myself, I can look back peacefully on my life; for I can say my life was full of meaning, and I have tried hard to fulfill it; I have done my best—I have done the best for my son. My life was no failure!"[11]

Almost invariably the meanings Frankl helps his clients discover take the form of commitments and fidelities that persist despite change and hardship. But for this very reason, a meaning must involve more than an experience of the immediate present. It necessarily extends also into the past and the future.

Time and Commitment

The leaders and innovators of the Human Potential Movement may be very committed people (though I doubt that their psychological assumptions are the source of that responsibility), but there are elements in the Human Potential theory that lend themselves all too readily to those who are seeking a shortcut to intimacy and to those who feel burdened by choices and obligations. Instead of encouraging real relationships, the process view of identity fosters an inability to sustain them. The reasoning behind this reluctance to get involved, when translated into the vernacular, runs something like this: "I can't commit myself if I don't know who I'll be tomorrow. It wouldn't be fair to me or you." But couched in this sweet reasonableness may be a justification for taking leave of responsibilities to spouse, children, friends, and finally society. A process cannot be held responsible. Only a person is liable for his decisions. If that is not the way Rogers and his colleagues meant it, that is the way their doctrine is increasingly being interpreted by those who would like to leave all their options open. Their identity is not an "irreversible historical fact"; rather it is shot through with tentativeness; it is not much of a base from which to move on to that stage which Erikson calls generativity, the care and nurture of other people's growth.

American communes, which usually share the present-oriented assumptions of the Human Potential Movement, provide a case in point. Writing in *Commentary,* Sonya Rudikoff makes the point that the life of communes is embarrassingly short; that relationships are marked by a lessening, not a strengthening, of personal obligations; and that where children are present, "the adult's responsibility for the children is capricious, willful, sporadic, unpredictable, indeed the very type of chaotic life."[12] The original idea behind group rearing of children was that responsibility would be shared among many. But among people whose life is built on a philosophy of self-actualization, and whose motto is "don't lay your trip on me," the concept of "each one takes responsibility" apparently degenerates to "no one takes responsibility." Those communal societies that *do* work, like the Amish communities or the Kibbutz, have no such philosophy of self-actualization.

Rudikoff says that what chiefly distinguishes the American "youth" commune from the successful Israeli Kibbutz is the failure of the former to establish schools, that is, to look to the future. Through schools, however informal, the ideas upon which the communes are founded could be continued and passed on, as well as the lessons of successes and failures. But American communards are not much interested in who comes after them and the reason for this, Rudikoff asserts, is that in their self-absorption and in their concern for the "cherished immediacy," they cultivate attitudes that are indifferent to thoughts of the future.

Identity demands time. And the capacities and relationships that flow from identity—trust, commitment, friendship, love, generativity—also demand time. They suffer in a present-oriented climate. The Human Potential philosophy, however, is short on time; or more accurately, it's down on time. Its followers concentrate on the here-and-now, on the present unfolding of the self. But a philosophy or psychology of self that negates the time factor does not promote the capacities and relationships mentioned above. Trust and commitment depend on continuing identity; they are not inspired by a self that remains always in process. A self-in-process can't be committed beyond the next redefinition of self—and that may simply mean the next change in feeling. If the Human Potential philosophy fails to break out of the confines of the present, it will undermine its own avowed purpose of fostering meaningful relationships. A philosophy oriented purely to the present leads only in the direction of an endless cycle of instant but ephemeral intimacies. If we do not wish to travel that route, then it is time to renew the idea that identity has a historical dimension.

Part three
Beyond Identity

4

Not-So-Distant Drums

*I*F the Human Potential Movement advocates the loosening of identity, other, more radical thinkers suggest getting rid of it altogether. One of these is Marshall McLuhan, who was a solid but prosaic English scholar until, as John Leonard puts it, "he lay down with the Mechanical Bride and they performed all sorts of unnatural acts."[1] Out of this liaison between the professor and popular culture sprang a full-grown theory of massive cultural change. If McLuhan is correct, or even close, in his assessment of this change, then we are on the threshold—perhaps already in the midst—of an identity crisis of epic proportions.

The transition from the print age to the electric age—from eye culture to ear culture—that McLuhan elaborates challenges our traditional notion of identity. The advent of McLuhan's electronic world may, in fact, signal the end of the search for personal identity. His analogy, comparing this new culture to the tribal state, suggests that if any identity survives, it will be corporate rather than individual. Identity conceived in terms of unique self-definition or personal meaning will be hard to come by in the global village.

Understanding McLuhan

McLuhan, like Lewis Mumford, has a media interpretation of history. Man creates media but then, in the McLuhan version of Genesis, media turn around and recreate man in their own image and likeness. Thus the punning title of one McLuhan book: *The Medium Is the Massage.* Media knead us, punch us, work us over, shape us up. Eventually we become like them. We take on their characteristics. Different character types go with different media. McLuhan explains the present cultural transformation in terms of the decline of print media and the rise of electric media. Mechanical media like print and the clock combined to create a climate favorable to introspection, individualism, privacy, and a future-orientation; electric media now reverse this process and foster a present-oriented, communal type.

The print age made its debut in the fifteenth century with the invention of movable type. And it wasn't long, says McLuhan, before Western Europeans began to acquire the characteristics of that medium. The essential structure of print lies in its linear, fragmented, and sequential nature. A box full of lead type is just alphabet soup: bits and pieces that don't make sense until they are strung out in a line according to a certain sequence. Western man, his senses monopolized by print, began to perceive the world in a linear, fragmented, and sequential way. He chopped up life into bits and pieces of thought— a jumble of classifications and categories—and then put it all into sequence as if to say, "Let me get this straight." Like a typographer composing a line of print, Western man was composing his line of reasoning. The form of print became the form of his perception. It was not even necessary that one read a great deal, for the technology of print soon shaped every aspect of life. McLuhan believes that the linear, sequential frame of mind accounts for phenomena as diverse as assembly lines, job specialization, and graded schools.

Print also upset the balance of the five senses. Under the

influence of print the visual sense came to predominate over the other four. The resulting eye culture led to detachment: people who live in an eye culture don't get involved because they're always stepping back to get things in perspective. The shift to the eye culture broke the oral-aural bond which had held tribes together, and we became a collection of shifty-eyed individualists.

Like print, which cuts people away from the oral bond, the clock cuts them off from the rhythmic time of nature. And like print, the clock breaks life into fragments.

> *Noble machine with toothed wheels*
> *Lacerates the day and divides it in hours—*
> *Speeds on the course of the fleeing century*[2]

Already in the seventeenth century the poet Ciro di Pers recognized that the clock was a machine that not only recorded time but controlled it, parceled it out in miserly measure, and demanded it back in great quantities. Also, it was becoming apparent that those who served this machine became like it. In the clock as well as the printing press the awesome power of media to shape men in their own image is revealed. In Newton's time the clock was already a metaphor for the Universe; God was conceived of as the Great Clockmaker who had wound up the mechanism and then left the scene. By the nineteenth century the clock metaphor could be applied also to men, whose lives and habits had become as regular as clockwork. What Weber called the Protestant ethic, what Riesman called the inner-directed character, was born amidst a clatter of gears and a whir of wheels.

"The acceptance of such fragmenting of life into minutes and hours was unthinkable," writes McLuhan, "save in highly literate communities."[3] But once accepted, the clock served to strengthen those habits of mind which print had already fostered. Before the clock became commonplace the visually oriented man was prepared to put a visual interpretation on time. Time was something that had to be seen in perspective: a sequence of events that stretch out behind and ahead. The clock encouraged this linear and fragmented way of thinking. It broke up time into equal units and ticked it off in a straight line, in a never-ending progression. Only in this time-conscious frame of reference could the idea of progress flourish. If the whole idea of pressing forward from one point to another which we call progress now seems so natural to us, it is only because we tick to that same linear beat.

Progress depended, of course, on industrialization, but industrialization was in turn bound to the clock. "The clock, not the steam engine," wrote Mumford, "is the key machine of the industrial age."[4] It kept both machines and the workers who tended them in synchronization, but the effect on the workers was a kind of spiritual devastation, as Chaplin's brilliant film *Modern Times* demonstrated: anyone who has seen it cannot forget the comic but classic portrayal of the little man mesmerized by the rhythm of the machines.

The internalization of the machine is nowhere more evident than it is with the clock. Once confined to factory walls, timepieces were eventually chained to vests and strapped to wrists as ever-present reminders of time's claim on mind and body. Men would rise, work, eat, and sleep to their measured beat. Man's guts and bones, his very soul, would vibrate to the tempo of clock time.

But now, says McLuhan, we are entering into the postmechanical era—the electric age. The electric media—TV, stereos, computers—have broken the monopoly of print and its extension of the visual sense, and have freed us from the monotony of clock time. If print and other mechanical media brought us out of the tribe, electricity returns us to it. By extending all the senses and by banishing sequence, the electric media turn the print-fragmented world into a global village.

McLuhan's argument runs something like this: Tribal man took part in a collective existence, tied together with his fellows by an oral bond. Information was picked up through all the senses but it was particularly important to remain within earshot of others. The lack of other forms of communication necessitated a close and interdependent society. However, with the coming of the alphabet and later of print, it became possible to give and receive information in isolation from the community. One could go off alone with one's book. The written word and especially print thus gave impetus to individualism.

One effect of print is, then, to detribalize. Electric media reverse this process, says McLuhan. They refurbish the four senses that print had neglected, so that the electric-age man begins to perceive the world in the same way as did tribal man. Unlike print, which is specialist and fragmenting, electricity is nonspecialist and all enveloping. Electric sound, electric light, and electric communication can surround us as print cannot. Electric communications and especially electric sound are the new tribal drums that recreate the oral-aural bond. Instead of dividing one man from another as the sword of print does, electricity casts him into a tribal web of interdependence, this time on a global scale. Moreover, since electricity is instantaneous, since there is no time lapse between the throwing of the switch and the illumination of the bulb, we begin to experience life in its simultaneity rather than its sequence, much as does the primitive.

In the new electric age, says McLuhan, the virtues of print-oriented man—privacy, individualism, specialization—are falling into disrepute. As a result of "electric implosion," neo-tribal man is in the ascendancy. The characteristics of neo-tribal or "postliterate" man are similar in several respects to preliterate tribal man. McLuhan quotes with approval J. C. Carothers' description of tribal man:

> . . . a [tribal] man comes to regard himself as a rather insignificant part of a much larger organism—the family and the clan—and not as an independent, self-reliant unit; personal initiative and ambition are permitted little outlet; and a meaningful integration of a man's experience on individual, personal lines is not achieved.[5]

McLuhan's message, in plain language, is that we are reverting—or progressing—to something like this primitive mode: the entire human family scaled into a single world tribe by electricity. This message, when examined closely, has enormous implications for the process of identity formation. If media have the immense shaping power that McLuhan assigns to them, then the conversion to the tribalizing media will create a new type of person for whom the sense of individual identity will be of little relevance or value.

The Rise of the Print Culture: Its Effect on Identity

What character changes are entailed in a shift from a print to an electric culture? The ascendance of print (when I speak of the print culture I include clocks and other mechanical media) brought with it certain habits of character which have lasted to this day. It helped shape persons who were future-oriented, introspective, individualistic, and private.

1. *Future orientation.* Americans and, to a lesser extent, Europeans have a paradoxical attitude toward time. They save it but don't spend it. The simple fact is that most of us are ingrained with a deep reverence for the future; we keep saving for it—not just our money but our lives also. When we are young we tell ourselves that we will really start to live as soon as we finish our education, but in the meantime we work like demons to make the grade. After graduation we tell ourselves that we will really start to live as soon as we get a little job security. In the meantime we've married and had children and life has to be postponed until the children are grown. When they are grown we tell ourselves that we will really start to live—to do the things we've always wanted to do—as soon as we retire. But when we retire we discover that we no longer have the enthusiasm or energy to do the things we've always wanted to do. Having postponed life for so long, we forget how to live it. Even if all we have in mind is a little leisure, we find that we've

been wound up to operate at a tempo too fast for the workless world we now enter.

This tendency to live for the future at the expense of the present is an example of the way in which our attitudes have been massaged by the powerful and insidious hands of media. When time is conceived as a line stretching out to the horizon and marked off by equidistant points, it follows that the purpose of life has to do with reaching points or goals along that line. With his eagle vision the linear man sees far ahead along that line of sight. Too far. His sense of perspective misleads him into thinking that future rewards will always justify present deferments. In pursuit of that future he is all too willing to postpone living. Increasingly he lives in the future because print and the clock have conspired to deprive him of the present.

That is the dark side of the future perspective. It has a good side too. A future perspective makes it possible for an individual to make and keep long-range commitments and to pursue meaningful goals. It can make one reliable and it can give one a sense of continuity. Furthermore, it brings with it a sense that one's life is not determined; that one can by his choices affect the future and even mold it—an expectation that does wonders for one's identity. For a sense of self, as Rollo May has suggested, the conviction that "I can make it so" and "I will make it so" is as important as "cogito ergo sum."[6]

2. *Introspection.* In 1598 King Henry IV of France granted religious liberty to his Protestant subjects through the Edict of Nantes. It was no coincidence that upon the revocation of this grant almost a hundred years later, French watchmakers, most of whom were Protestant, emigrated to Calvinist Geneva. It was a setting congenial both to their conscience and their precise temperament. Calvinism was quick to take advantage of the new clock consciousness. Life on earth was short; not a minute was to be wasted in idleness or leisure. God was to be served, and the way to serve Him was by constant vigilance

against sloth, by tireless self-examination, by rigorous disciplining of the flesh, and by work.

Once time is broken up into visible, uniform segments it is hard to avoid the question of its most efficient use: "Am I making the best of my time or am I wasting it?" It is perhaps no coincidence that the word "watch" has both visual and time connotations. The good Calvinist was always standing watch, one eye on the clock and the other on his character. As it turned out, this merger of Calvinism and clockwork served not only God, but also industry, for the factory system would soon require the same inner restraint that Jehovah demanded.

The clock was not the only instrument that caused men to search their souls. From Gutenberg on down, an extraordinary amount of type has been set in the service of character development. And to meet the high standards set down in innumerable tracts, books, and pamphlets, one had to be engaged in a constant program of self-examination and self-improvement. The goal was to develop a self as good as the models in print: a self characterized by restraint, discipline, and control. So print not only extended the visual sense, it exercised the inward eye as well. The print-oriented man looked out at the world with new eyes but he also looked within. Here we have the beginnings of that quality of "inwardness" which by the twentieth century would be thought indispensable to identity development.

But though introspection is often the high road to scrupulosity and a top-heavy superego, it is also the road to self-definition and identity. Reflection gives an individual life a certain clarity and richness. Moreover, introspection, by providing an alternative to the cultural definition of events, is one of the foundations of autonomy—a way of differentiating ourselves from the mass. Finally and most importantly it is the source of individuation.

3. *Individualism.* If print fosters introspection, introspection leads to individualism. Tribal people who do not have a well-developed sense of individuality do not trouble themselves with self-examination or character building. Only those who

consider themselves uniquely different imagine that they have a self worth developing along unique lines. As said before, print contributes to the spirit of individualism; a print culture inevitably confers on its members what David Riesman has called "inner-direction." We can take Protestantism as one proof of the individuating power of print. It was born with Luther about the same year that Gutenberg started mass-producing Bibles. Unlike the Catholic Church, which relied as much on oral tradition as it did on scripture, Protestantism insisted on the sole authority of the written word in matters of doctrine. The slogans of the Reformation were "justification by faith" and "Scripture alone"; and Gutenberg's invention provided ample opportunity to be alone with scripture. But, without the oral bond which made of the Catholic Church one vast community, it was inevitable that in the privacy of their studies different men would interpret that word in different ways. Protestantism became not only the religion of the individual conscience but the religion of a hundred individual variations.

The advent of individualism was hardly an unqualified boon to civilization. There was a blatantly selfish side to the spirit of individuality, which took nourishment from a narrow Calvinism and a grasping capitalism. The emphasis on individualism was readily perverted to the suggestion that each person ought to be his own keeper, owed nothing to his fellows, and should press his advantage to the full. Poverty and misfortune were no longer looked upon as the result of circumstances but were seen to reflect a lack of will. Misery and malnutrition were God's punishment for a lack of moral fiber. Worldly success was a sign of His pleasure. "God punishes the wicked and prospers the good," wrote Jonathan Edwards in the late seventeenth century. When in the nineteenth century this brand of religious and economic individualism blended with the Darwinian notion of survival of the fittest, the way was cleared for robber barons and captains of industry—men who were captains not only of their own fate but masters of the souls of millions.

That was and still is the ugly side of individualism: the white underbelly which has to be exposed over and over again. But it's well to remember the benefits that can come with it: a sense of the personal, a respect for others as being worthwhile in themselves, fidelity, personal responsibility, the possibility of creating an identity rather than submitting to one.

4. *Privacy.* According to McLuhan a visual orientation creates a concern for privacy and private parts.[7] He believes it was visual specialization that originally led to notions of indecency and pornography and that the shift to an ear culture will lead us back out, which indeed it appears to be doing. For the visually oriented person the sin is in the seeing. Therefore sex is something to be done in private, in the darkness, or between the sheets; something to read about between the covers of a book. That the high premium we now place on privacy is a modern development is evident in the journal of Heroard, the court physician to the same Henry IV who granted the Edict of Nantes. During the first years of the seventeenth century Heroard kept a careful diary of Louis XIII's childhood. The details of Louis' sexual education are particularly intriguing, since they present a marked contrast to contemporary notions of decency, especially in regard to children. The behavior of the young Louis and the adults around him might strike the modern reader as somewhat bawdy. Here are some excerpts from the diary as they appear in Philip Aries' book *Centuries of Childhood:*

At age one: "He laughed uproariously when his nanny waggled his cock with her fingers." Among his favorite pastimes, "he has everyone kiss his cock." At age five: "Put to bed, he asks to play, plays with Mademoiselle Mercier, calls me [Heroard], saying that Mercier has a cunt as big as that, showing his two fists, and that there's a lot of water inside."[8]

According to Aries, the whole notion of childhood as a separate and protected stage of life did not come until later. But in reviewing the same documents, the historian David Hunt[9] notes that even among the court there were those who encouraged the Dauphin in decency of language and behavior.

Among these was Heroard himself: he did not seem to share the enthusiasm of the other attendants for Louis' sexual antics. Hunt attributes the doctor's concern with modesty to an insightful grasp of the dangers of Oedipal attachments. It is interesting, however, to speculate on another possibility—the fact that the doctor was obviously one of the most literate members of the king's retinue, a man who not only kept a meticulous journal but was capable of switching from French to Latin when describing particularly embarrassing scenes. Perhaps he was displaying the reflexive reticence of a visually oriented man. Hunt notes that it was also the custom in France at that time for children and adults to sleep in the same room, often in the same bed, and not much was thought about it. Not, he observes, until certain religious pamphleteers began to attack the practice. The interesting point to be noted in all this is not that there were crusaders for decency in those days but that the standard of privacy is first raised among the literate and print-oriented: the writers of tracts and the keepers of journals.

In the sixteenth and seventeenth centuries increasing exposure to the high standards of print, when combined with the Calvinist demand for self-examination, led inevitably to a desire for privacy. The new spirit of bourgeois individualism required a time and a place to be by oneself and to sort out one's thoughts. Privacy afforded the opportunity for introspection, and introspection provided the means for differentiating oneself from the crowd. The cultivation of the private life and the private point of view was one result of Renaissance individualism. It would not be long before the notions of private property and private gain became equally important.

The Demise of Print and the Rise of the Sound Culture

"We are today," writes McLuhan, "as far into the electric age as the Elizabethans had advanced into the typographical and mechanical age. And we are experiencing the same confusions and indecisions which they felt when living simultaneously in two contrasted forms of society."[10] Only we reverse their pattern. Theirs was a shift from medieval corporatism to modern individualism. We are going from individualism back to "corporate interdependence."[11] So the main source of confusion in our society is that some of us (the older ones) were brought up in a print environment, and the rest of us (the younger ones) were raised in a primarily electric environment: the generation gap is really a culture gap. This transition, so extensive that it rivals in magnitude the passage from medieval to modern times, marks the emergence of McLuhan's neo-tribal man.

As McLuhan and other commentators describe him, this new man finds his identity in the group—not apart from it. Among this new breed, communion with others is valued over self-reliance or character development, and collective participation is favored over individual initiative. Commitment to privacy and private property is not esteemed and, in general, communal and shared values predominate over private, personal ones. Property may be communally held or, if it is privately owned, it is easily available to others.

Although it is hard to pinpoint these trends precisely, the shift from print to electricity seems to favor a person who is egoless rather than introspective; who perceives globally rather than analytically; and who is oriented to the present rather than to the future.

1. *The decline of introspection and privacy.* Electricity, says McLuhan, has the effect of converting us all, in some degree, to a mentality that is both postprint and preprint. Included in this mentality is a lessening of the importance once attached to privacy and private parts. One need not be very observant to notice the increasing acceptance of nudity and near nudity in our society. Films without some form of nudity are now probably the exception rather than the rule—a marked change from the situation that prevailed only a dozen years ago. And one wonders if the modern reader would really react to the account of Louis XIII's childhood with the astonishment Philip Aries, writing in 1960, expected. Instead, one can imagine cries of

"far out" and "right on" emanating from certain postliterate quarters. Much of the current Zeitgeist can be summed up in the motto "Let it all hang out."

A concern with privacy seems to be a preoccupation of the visually oriented. Electricity, according to McLuhan, fosters a much more tactile approach to experience. It makes us into doubting Thomases who have to touch in order to believe. Intuitive feeling rather than insightful analysis becomes the order of the day. The high-voltage jabs of the electric media have already discolored the private eye and will eventually close it up. When this happens introspection and character formation will have been discredited. To some extent this is already the case. Even as sympathetic an observer as Paul Goodman commented on what he saw as a shallow inner development among the young:

> Except for a few like the young people of the resistance, I am not impressed by their moral courage or even honesty. For all their eccentricity they are singularly lacking in personality. They do not have enough world to have much character.[12]

Far from being insulted by such a characterization, many members of the youth culture are quite happy with it. They do not necessarily assign a pejorative value to a phrase like "singularly lacking in personality." Rather, it is the private pursuit of one's individual development that is now suspect. For a large number of young people the cardinal sin is to be on an "ego trip." It is not surprising, then, that when they look for wisdom they ignore Paul Goodman and turn to people like Baba Ram Dass, who said in a recent interview: "One of my strategies is not to know who I am."[13] Echoing this sentiment a young man recently advised me, "Getting to know yourself is imbecilic."

2. *Global perception.* Because print is fragmented and sequential it fosters a logical and analytical cast of mind. It now appears, however, that at some point in the last twenty years, print yielded its supremacy to television and the stereo; and

the visual-rational perspective gave way to a new mode of perceiving reality. Or better perhaps to say that a new reality —one not readily available to the logical-visual mind—became apparent to those capable of seeing the world in a new way. (This is overstating the case, of course. So far only the Mexican sorcerer/Indian Don Juan and his faithful companions have attained to an unclouded vision of this "separate reality," and for this we can only rely on the word of Carlos Castaneda.[14]) There seems to be a consensus among those who teach the young that a qualitative difference separates the new youth from those of only a few years ago. And this difference has to do with fundamental intellectual and perceptual habits. There is evidence that many of today's youth are deeply skeptical of logical and intellective approaches. They do not appear to read very much. At least they do not read what was once called "serious literature." Instead the bookstores overflow with the literature of astrology, Indian lore, magic, mysticism, and meditation. In general, it is the type of literature that does not lend itself to logical analysis but demands an intuitive grasp or simple faith. The young seem to have replaced faith in science with a new faith in intuition and the wisdom of the body—an understanding that "passeth knowledge." It would be easy to say in defense of the young that they have seen the deadening fragmentation rigid analysis and pure logic sometimes lead to, and they have as a result withdrawn their faith from traditional academic approaches to knowledge. Narrow scientific special- ization unleavened by a global perspective leads to napalmed villages and a ravaged ecology, and undoubtedly much of the current anti-intellectualism is a reaction to these Frankenstein creations of the logical mind. But once again the role of the electric media in this transformation of mind cannot be slighted. Is it really possible that all those countless hours watching television and vibrating to the drumbeat of the stereo has not had its effect on the perceptual apparatus?

How great or how subtle a shift in the sense ratio is required to turn an eye culture into an ear culture? In *In Bluebeard's*

Castle George Steiner provides a provocative sketch of the new dimensions sound injects into our life:

> This is being written in a study in a college of one of the great American universities. The walls are throbbing gently to the beat of music coming from one near and several more distant amplifiers. The walls quiver to the ear or to the touch roughly eighteen hours per day—sometimes twenty-four. The beat is literally unending. It matters little whether it is that of pop, folk, or rock. What counts is the all-pervasive pulsation, morning to night and into night, made indiscriminate by the cool burn of electronic timbre. A large segment of mankind, between the ages of thirteen and, say, twenty-five, now lives immersed in this constant throb. The hammering of rock or of pop creates an enveloping space. Activities such as reading, writing, private communication, learning, previously framed with silence, now take place in a field of strident vibrato. This means that the essentially linguistic nature of these pursuits is adulterated; they are vestigial modes of the old "logic."[15]

Walls provide privacy from searching eyes, but rarely from sound. And the sound culture penetrates not only physical walls but mental ones as well. Steiner continues:

> What is more important, but difficult to investigate, let alone quantify, is the question of the development of mental faculties, of self-awareness, when these take place in a perpetual sound-matrix. What are the sweet vociferous hammerings doing to the brain at key stages of development?[16]

We know, Steiner concludes, about the physical coarsening of the hearing apparatus when exposed to the unremitting rock echo, "But hardly anything is known of the psychological effects of saturation by volume and repetitive beat (often the same two or three tunes are played around the clock). What tissues of sensibility are being numbed or exacerbated?"[17]

If McLuhan is right, the shift from eye to ear banishes privacy and brings back the tribe. But along with this it deprives us of the analytic mode of thought and replaces it with something whose value, though possibly redeeming, is less certain. Experiencing various forces of communication simultaneously and through more than one sense (anyone who has sat near a stereo speaker knows that it is a tactile as well as audio experience), we begin to develop a field-view of reality. We become, as one writer has suggested, more like Zorba the Greek and less like his English companion: more intuitive, less rational; more spontaneous, less reserved; more generalist, less specialist; more inclined to live in the present than plan for the future. One may conjecture that the chief appeal of drug use in our culture is the release it provides from linear, fragmented thought patterns. To many, drugs must seem like the only antidote to the rigors of a rational-technological society; the closest they can come to a sense of tribal consciousness. For the majority of youth, however, music serves the same purpose. Over the divisive boundaries of separate egos it casts a net of cool electric sound. Steiner's way with words is as mesmeric as the beat of the stereo. When he writes, "The new sound-sphere is global. It ripples across languages, ideologies, frontiers, and races," we can almost believe that this "musical esperanto," as he calls it, is indeed the universal language that could tie the globe into a village.

3. *Orientation to the present.* The young, it sometimes seems, regard the past as totally irrelevant. What is more interesting is that their disregard of the past is matched by a lack of concern for the future. This is not a total unconcern, but compared to the intense future-orientation of past generations it marks a significant change in attitude. The idea of delayed gratification does not rank high among their priorities. But if we look among the young for a conscious revolt against the tyranny of the future we shall probably be disappointed. Instead of a philosophical repudiation of clock time we shall more likely find a perceptual and cognitive incapacity to deal with the future. It takes a linear, visual perspective to conceive of future sequences and consequences. Such a perspective is as difficult to cultivate in a postprint sound culture as it is in preprint sound cultures, many of which have no future tense in their language.

The electric media encourage and reflect this cultivation of the immediate present. Writing about the digital clock in the *Boston Globe,* David Wilson calls it "a 'now' gadget that tells nothing of the then on either side of the moment."[18] Digital calendars, the kind that can be found in banks, are equally disconcerting since they divorce us both from memories and anticipations. On a traditional calendar we can see that November 16 is only a week away from Thanksgiving and cherished reunions with family. On the digital calendar it is merely a number to be recorded on a deposit slip. These alterations in our time-measuring devices are very minor, but media work in subtle ways, and when one considers the numerous shifts from the mechanical to the electric, these digital devices reflect a general drift to a completely new time orientation.

Steiner calls this new departure "The denial of the future tense." It is manifested, he says, in "a deep embarrassment among the most gifted of the young about creating something that will endure, something that has the stamp of personal authorship."[19] The denial of the future tense is also revealed in a relative disregard for the older work ethic. The soaring rate of absenteeism among younger office and factory workers reflects a refusal to link one's job to the future or, for that matter, to worry about the future at all. Work is done, not to meet long-range commitments, but to meet immediate leisure needs: the next lid of grass, deck of tapes, or vacation to the sun. This orientation explains why the young are so often the target of adult hostility. Youngsters are a constant reminder to their future-oriented elders of opportunities and experiences that were never grasped when the time was ripe and have since flown out of reach.

McLuhan: Corroboration and Criticism

In these pages I have described some of the changes that seem to be entailed in a shift from a print to a sound culture. If the preceding speculations are correct—if the influences that created print-oriented, individualized man are on the wane—then the theory of identity based on observations of that older model ought to be called into question.

There remains, of course, the question of whether McLuhan is right or wrong about retribalization. His theory of history as media-determined is both his strength and weakness. There are certainly other ways of interpreting history; media do not explain everything, and McLuhan's chief fault is that he tries to make them do just that. But media do explain some crucial historical changes, and McLuhan's critics neglect that at their own peril. Despite the fact that he virtually ignores economics and politics, and despite the fact that some of his intellectual excesses make him an easy target for debunkers, McLuhan has made significant contributions to our understanding of history. Amidst the glitter of fancy phrasings there are gems of insight. Both Marx and Mumford have mined the theme of technological determinism, but McLuhan seems to have struck into the Mother Lode. With him we begin to understand how pervasive is the effect on us of our own inventions.

Objections can easily be raised against any single theory of history whether it be economic, cyclical, or "great man," and the same is true of McLuhan's media interpretation. Moreover, McLuhan's thesis cannot be proven in a statistical sense —it is too sweeping for that. Nevertheless, his approach has been successful in stimulating much-needed explorations into the state of our culture, and it does seem to resonate to many past and present realities. Under McLuhan's retribalization thesis, a number of recent and hitherto apparently diverse phenomena can be subsumed: tribelike communes, widespread drug use, more open sexuality, nongraded schools, a shift away from the sciences, a burgeoning interest in astrology, Eastern mysticism, and other nonlinear explanations of life, to name a few. These phenomena can be explained in other ways and by other theories, but none seems to have so captured the popular imagination. When a writer takes hold so quickly and so widely, it is an indication that he is probably hitting some nails on the head.

The fact that McLuhan is particularly popular with the young gives added weight to his analysis of youth. Sometimes acknowledged, sometimes not, McLuhan's terminology has crept into their self-description. Mark Gerzon, speaking for his generation, observes that "what McLuhan needs great insight to grasp, a young man recognizes readily because it is the only world he has ever experienced."[20]

Although the initial hoopla surrounding McLuhan's advent has faded, his influence has not. Nowadays, a familiarity with McLuhan's message and his esoteric vocabulary is simply assumed by the press as though electric retribalization were a first principle of social science. And McLuhanism is particularly congenial to people in the Human Potential Movement who want to move out of the cognitive domain and into the affective, out of the detached visual perspective and into contact with the other senses, out of individual isolation and into the group, out of past and future and into the shimmering present. Jane Howard, in recounting her year's odyssey through the encounter group circuit, indicated that her "Gutenbergian print-freak heritage" was somehow incompatible with the globalizing goals of the Human Potential Movement.[21]

Popularity aside, McLuhan's theory finds corroboration among some fairly substantial thinkers. Marx and Mumford have already been alluded to. Others have elaborated on themes quite similar to those advanced by McLuhan. For example, it is impossible to reread Teilhard de Chardin describing the "noösphere" and not be struck by the family resemblance to the global village.[22] And one can't avoid noticing that McLuhan's electric age bears striking similarities to anthropologist George Spindler's "transforming American culture."[23] McLuhan's print-oriented man is practically interchangeable with Riesman's inner-directed type.[24] Finally, any resemblance between Margaret Mead (postfigurative, configurative, prefigurative) and McLuhan (tribal, print-oriented, new tribal) is hardly coincidental.[25] They are all on to the same scent: a major transformation in the Western character. While they may differ on details and interpretations, the general drift of what they have to say is the same. McLuhan is not even the most radical of these observers; that honor goes to Chardin.

Is McLuhan correct? Future historians will be in a better position to answer that question and undoubtedly they will disagree among themselves. Right now, however, there is sufficient reason to take McLuhan quite seriously. His hypothesis is corroborated by other respected theories; it helps make sense out of recent cultural trends, and it has captured the popular imagination. Moreover, McLuhan has added significantly to our understanding of previously neglected historical dimensions and technological processes. He has stimulated further probes of our environment; and he has caused us to reexamine the meaning of identity. In brief, McLuhan appears to be correct in many ways about the drift of contemporary change.

Nevertheless, in certain crucial respects, his tribal analogy breaks down. And through the gaps in his theory there blows a chill wind which promises to bring neither individual salvation nor neo-tribal harmony.

5

Savages: Noble and Otherwise

*I*N light of McLuhan's scenario it is time to ask whether the anatomy of identity worked out by Erikson and other psychologists is any longer relevant for this society. Eriksonian identity, with its emphasis on the individual, assumes a print-oriented culture—a culture now on the wane, by McLuhan's account. But it is also necessary to ask if McLuhan's forecast is any more helpful.

Erikson first. Among some peoples there is no identity confusion, no identity crisis, no prolonged moratorium. Much of Erikson's vocabulary does not apply to the primitive tribesman. Instead of a moratorium there is a rite of passage; in place of confusion there is the certainty of a role and the solidarity of the tribe; instead of differentiation from the society there is incorporation into it.

For a long time this knowledge remained academic as far as the industrial West was concerned. It was the province of anthropologists and no concern of anyone else. From a practical standpoint it didn't seem to matter that what held true in Kansas City might not be applicable in Samoa. We were, after all, worlds apart. But all this changed in 1964, when the star of Marshall McLuhan rose above the horizon shining on a new

Bethlehem and pointing toward a new Jerusalem—or should I say a new Kansas City? For it now appears that electric-age Kansas City may be as far removed from the print-oriented Kansas City of twenty or thirty years ago as that society was distant from Samoa. The rough beast now slouching toward Kansas City to be born is neo-tribal man. Most psychological theorists were not prepared for his coming.

Irrelevance of Conventional Theories

One of the first, and one of the few, to recognize that something was amiss was the sociologist Edgar Friedenberg. In 1959, in a book prophetically titled *The Vanishing Adolescent*, Friedenberg described adolescence as he understood it and as it was then generally understood: the function of adolescence was to allow for individuation and self-definition. Self-definition means becoming a person in one's own right. It involves differentiating one's self from one's culture and finding a unique identity as an individual apart from the mass. "Inwardness," said Friedenberg, is what makes self-definition possible. Inwardness "is the capacity to attend to and respond to one's inner life and feelings, to the uniquely personal in experience, to personal relationships."[1] This inwardness was cultivated in private reflection and in private friendships marked by fidelity.

But adolescence so conceived was a vanishing phenomenon. The teenagers Friedenberg observed could no longer be characterized by traits like inwardness or uniqueness. At first Friedenberg assigned this change to the bland bureaucracy of institutions like the high school. Later, in 1965, one year after McLuhan's *Understanding Media* was published, he attributed the waning of adolescence to the far more pervasive but subtle workings of media:

> What I have been calling integrity is really the integrity of a print-oriented, individualized people; and the very self-awareness that I have conceived as the source of their nobility is also, it seems, the instrument of estrangement which saps their vitality.[2]

This suggests that it may be as unhealthy to remain print-oriented in a retribalized world as it is to retain a "fixed" identity in a future-shocked society.

Unlike Friedenberg, however, most authorities on adolescence and identity formation were slow to notice these changes in the atmospheric condition. Their formulations continued to be based on the print-oriented model. Their analysis of youth still hung on a framework of future orientation, self-examination, and even character formation.[3] Here is a sample from *Personality Development and Adjustment in Adolescence* by Alexander A. Schneiders:

> The adolescent personality is by its nature unstable, and thus tends toward disharmony; and the only effective antidote to these tendencies is the imposition of self-discipline through which the adolescent finally achieves character. Character is what a person makes of himself; and it is character above all which every adolescent should realize as the crowning achievement of his attempts to master himself and his environment on the difficult road to maturity and adulthood.[4]

Variations on this theme are still a standard prescription for remedying the adolescent crisis. But it seems that neo-tribal youth can no longer swallow this kind of medicine. Outside of a handful of Eagle Scouts, concern with character building does not flourish among electric age youth: building one's character smacks of deliberate ego-tripping.

When we come to Erikson we find the same concern with a character type that is distinguished by a self-made and even literate quality. For illustrative purposes he uses men like Freud, James, and Shaw. Hardly tribal types, they are, rather, men of letters with above average endowments of individualism and interiority. Erikson, recognizing that his models may pertain more to the past than the present is quick to qualify his use of them:

> But once we accept a historical perspective, we face the probability that the quotations [dealing with Freud and James] which I have offered as a massive motto are really

tied to a kind of identity formation highly dependent on cultural conditions of a sedentary middle class . . . their homes and their studies, their academic and clinical associations were, even when revolutionary in scientific matters, highly stable in their morals and ideals.[5]

"Their homes and their studies . . ." When we summon up a mental portrait of these individuals it is likely that we will picture them in their private studies, surrounded by books—the epitome of print-oriented virtues.

But in jumping ahead to the fifties and sixties, Erikson does not leave this print-oriented model behind. Rather he describes a particular type of boy whose cultivation is somehow linked with the maintenance of democracy in our society. This typical boy possesses some of the less worthy attributes of the print-oriented character shading over into other-directed "good guy." The family from which he comes is "Anglo-Saxon, mildly Protestant, of the white collar class."[6] The boy is emotionally restrictive "as if he were saving himself for something."[7] His fantasy ideal is a self-made individualist but he is well aware that he must temper this idealism in order to get along in an organization man society. He is not a "true individualist" but has an "individualistic core."[8] Erikson wants to know how one trains this boy for democracy. That is, how does one ensure that the old-fashioned qualities of autonomy, intelligence, and disciplined choice will survive in him? Erikson does not seem very satisfied with this young man but he will have to do in lieu of Freud, James, and Shaw.

Erikson discusses three main avenues which identity formation may take: "synthetic identity," "collective identity," and "democratic identity," but he appears to believe that only the last of these is worthy of a society that offers a wide variety of identity choices. Synthetic identity is really a "fake" identity. It is a prefabricated identity complete with ideals and ideology, and often a uniform; the Hitler youth, the Party member, the single-minded religious devotee are examples. There is no real identity here, only a slavish conformity to a code.

Collective identity is typical of primitive societies where

identity choices are limited by the size and technology of the culture. Because of the survival demands of such cultures there is little time for prolonged moratoriums of self-examination; consequently, the element of choice is minimized: the son of the village netmaker grows up to become the village netmaker. There is, moreover, no need to integrate a number of conflicting roles since all members share the same traditions and beliefs. It is a limited identity but it provides meaning and security along with a sense of communal and individual integrity.

Any healthy society supplies some sense of collective identity from which individual identities may partake. But identity in its fullest sense, democratic identity, has a quality of active choice which individualizes the collective tradition. As opposed to the mindless identity of the Hitler youth, democratic identity implies reflective decisions. It is a self-made identity that requires indulgence by society but promises a more autonomous individual. It is not the inherited identity of the tribes but a democratic achievement: a definition of self worked out from within, not an explanation of self imposed from without.[9]

The trouble is that Erikson's concept of democratic identity assumes a social and historical environment that may now be in eclipse. Take the phrase "self-definition." "Self-definition" is such a precise term that it is difficult to improve on it. The phrase explains itself. But the very clarity of the word prompts us to speculate on its meaning. What type of individual is it who is so intent on defining himself? Is it too much to see in this exact phrase the preoccupation of a historical type which may now be passé? I don't want to overstate this line of argument, but the print connotations of a phrase such as "self-definition" are too intriguing to be bypassed. It is a phrase that conjures up a picture of a certain type of intellectuality at work: a man alone in his study, poring over his dictionary of inward terms; an individual who already sees himself apart from his species as *sui generis*—a man in need of his own special definition.

How useful is Erikson's framework today? When we consider the media revolution heralded by McLuhan and when we reflect on the historical-cultural shifts suggested by people as diverse as Chardin and Mead, we are compelled to raise serious questions about this conventional analysis of youth. What is at issue is the very language used to conceptualize adolescence: "identity," "identity crisis," "personal identity," "self-definition," "fidelity." Can we any longer conceive of identity in these terms? Do we know what we are talking about? To be sure, these terms are still on everyone's lips, but what do they now mean? What does it mean, for instance, when a *Newsweek* staff writer can blandly assert that "young people found happiness and self-definition in the gigantic Woodstock gathering of the clans"?[10] Whatever this writer understands by self-definition, it is obviously poles apart from the meaning Erikson or Friedenberg assigns to the term. For Friedenberg self-definition is the result of inward reflection and selective friendships tempered with fidelity; not participation in mass gatherings. It is hard to avoid the impression, however, that this type of self-definition is not only difficult to achieve in the electric age, but possibly undesirable. The drift toward tribalism suggests that we abandon the quest for personal identity, that we stop looking for identity in the interstices of our own ego. Such lusting after self does not become the new primitive. We should instead go public.

That seems to be the direction suggested by McLuhan and the neo-McLuhanites. But there exists the strong possibility that in following this advice we will simply be selling our identities for a mess of neologisms.

McLuhan's False Analogy

If Erikson's framework is of limited applicability to the new condition, what about McLuhan's? McLuhan doesn't mourn the loss of personal identity because he thinks it will be compensated for by electric community; group identity will replace individual identity and we will be none the worse. All his reasoning, however, rests on a very mushy metaphor: the equation between tribal and neo-tribal. The fact is that McLuhan has made a bad analogy. Let me explain where it fails.

The global village cannot provide a sense of group identity because it is not really a village at all. And this is, in part, because electric media have the exact opposite effect from the one McLuhan envisions. McLuhan claims that the electric media, by recreating the oral bond of the tribe, make us all members of the same family, and thereby mend the fractures caused by print (print supposedly trains us to worry more about the poor in a Dickens novel than the poor in the street). McLuhan is right about the tribe. The oral bond does draw people together; but tribesmen do more than dance around fires to the beat of drums. They talk with one another, they get involved, they cooperate. Where there is communication there is interaction and the possibility of community. The trouble is that this analogy doesn't apply to electric media. Who can communicate with a television, a stereo, or a radio? Where is the involvement? How can a community emerge out of such one-way communication? If anything, the modern sound culture produces passivity and noninvolvement. The most isolated student among a group of eighth graders I once taught was a boy who went around with a transistor radio constantly plugged into his ear. His radio was all the company he seemed to need or want.

Another common accessory and symbol of the audio culture is the stereo headphone set, but it is hardly a symbol of involvement, since it effectively cuts the listener off from communication with others. Instead of creating the deep interdependence of the tribe, the TV and stereo create dependence; instead of fostering relationships in depth, electric media foster a "turn me on, or I'll switch you off" attitude. The trend toward neo-tribalism gives us the drawbacks of primitivism without the primitive compensations. Individual identity and responsibility are undermined, but no sense of collective identity or responsibility is substituted.

When one looks closely at the youth who are most involved

in the sound culture—the ones who should be building the global village—they seem to be mainly committed not to community but to "getting my head together." Developing a community requires a sense of commitment to others, as well as a willingness to communicate and work out problems together. But these youth are too self-involved to be able to structure communities, even if only on the small scale of a household. Yet their introspection is not of the type that leads to self-definition. Quite often, those who are deeply involved in the sound culture are also deeply involved in the drug culture, and although they may have the outward appearance of tribal types, they are inwardly as withdrawn from real contact and commitment as the uncommitted youth Kenneth Keniston studied. They tend to indulge in the same mystical fantasy of fusion but they do little about real fusion. Accompanied by drugs or loud music and without the bother of prayer or contemplation, they can float free into the realms explored by Jakob Boehme or Theresa of Avila. While carefully remaining unencumbered by self and others, they can in their imagination be at peace with all. They have, to paraphrase the poet, "slipped the surly bonds of self," but they have not achieved anything like oneness. What this fantasy of universal identification does do is to permit them to skip the intermediate stage of relating to actual others—the stage at which real tribal people exist. The cacophony that surrounds them, writes Erikson, ". . . can also camouflage a reciprocal isolation of desperate depth."[11]

These children of Morpheus are by no means representative of all youth. The youth culture is not a monolith any more than communism is or the Catholic Church. Still, there are few signs of an electrically induced spirit of involvement among young people or their elders. On the contrary, prolonged exposure to electric media seems to encourage a state bordering on inertia. Those who are reliant on the flick of the switch can easily develop a habit of passivity and an expectation of unsolicited entertainment.

Prepackaged Principles

It may be objected that there are plenty of signs of youthful commitment and involvement. In recent years we have seen a number of books dedicated to the proposition that youthful activism is changing the world. Often, however, these counter-culture commentaries turn out to be panegyrics rather than critiques, and they leave unanswered the question, "Which youth are creating the change?" As an antidote to the extreme optimism of youth culture apologists like Charles Reich, one ought to read a book like Clifford Adelman's *Generations.*[12] It is the print-visual orientation, he says, that stimulates involvement. (Ivan Illich makes the same point in observing how villagers who learn to read are compelled into political action.)[13] According to Adelman, prolonged exposure to television and other electric media only serves to cauterize brains and induce a numbing passivity. Furthermore, those who eulogize the commitment and activism of youth are failing to discriminate among generations. Between the ages of seventeen and thirty-two, said Adelman, writing in 1972, there were three more or less distinct subgenerations: 17–21, 21–25, and 26–32. It is from the latter group, he says, that most of the activism, organization, and change comes. The others simply lack the requisite conceptual abilities and "will-energy" needed to generate any change or movement. And where did the "older" youth get their energy and brains? From their print-visual exposure, replies Adelman: before TV, still in its infancy, had time to do its "dirty" work on their unformed minds.

Adelman's is an extreme position, but it does cut through some of the illusions surrounding the adolescent culture. There is, for instance, the all too easily accepted commonplace that young people today have deep ethical concerns and commitments. What passes for nobility is sometimes, however, not an individually and spontaneously worked through morality but a prepackaged ethic manufactured and distributed, as psychologist Lawrence Kohlberg puts it, by "a cultural industry called the 'counterculture.' "[14] The high-principled concern over political responsibility, poverty, pollution, racism, and civil liberties that is now the common inheritance of the young was worked out on a personal basis by the 26–32 (now 29–35) subgeneration. For them it was an achieved ethical identity, the result of personal experience combined with careful reflection and reading; but the moral stance of many younger people seems to be an ascribed posture that is put on along with jeans and sandals. Because their ethic often happens to coincide with many liberal and progressive values is no cause to rejoice. Not having been worked through on an individual basis, it always stands in danger of being sloughed off in favor of its opposite. Theirs is a moral stance, not a moral identity.

If they often happen to be on the side of the angels, the credit is not always due to clearly thought-out values. "The ethical attainments of one generation," writes Keniston, "often degenerate into the moral homilies of the next." Apparently something like this has happened—in a very short space of time—to American youth, although the moral homilies have descended not from parents but from the previous generation of youth. It is a case of conventional morality being replaced by conventional morality. This is Kohlberg's judgment:

> Although the impetus for the counterculture may have been once either principled or the expression of young people in identity crisis, the manufacture of the counterculture transforms it into yet another conventional system, although one lacking the solidarity of the traditional conventional society.[15]

Retribalization: Losses and Gains

The problem of ethical behavior brings us back to McLuhan's bad analogy, and exposes a rather dangerous fallacy that flows out of that analogy. As said before, McLuhan can remain sanguine about the various losses entailed in the shift to neo-tribalism because he believes his analogy to the tribal state is complete. The loss of individual identity will be more than compensated by group identity; the lessening of personal responsibility will be offset by the strengthening of collective morality. Typical of McLuhan's thinking is the following passage:

> The new feeling that people have about guilt is not something that can be privately assigned to some individual, but is, rather, something shared by everybody, in some mysterious way. . . . This feeling is an aspect of the new mass culture we are moving into—a world of total involvement in which everybody is so profoundly involved with everybody else and in which nobody can really imagine what private guilt can be anymore.[16]

The alarming suggestion here is that tribal people get along without a sense of individual responsibility, so why can't we? It is alarming because we do not have the compensating mechanisms by which tribal societies maintain order.

It is true enough that tribal societies lack a sense of individual guilt or personal responsibility. Ruth Benedict has observed that among the Zuni Indians there is no sense of either sin or guilt, and the psychiatrist J. C. Carothers has made similar observations based on his studies of several African tribes.[17] Moreover, Kohlberg's study of villagers in rural and isolated parts of Mexico and Turkey reveals that high-level moral reasoning (the ability to discern universal ethical principles) is generally absent among primitive people.[18]

This lack of principled morality combined with the absence of individual guilt might be expected to result in lawless behavior, but this is not generally the case. The primitive society has conventions and traditions that discourage and control antisocial behavior. And the tribal individual conforms to these rules because his identity merges with the tribe's: individual and group form one organism. This solidarity more than compensates for the lack of ethics, and it is this that McLuhan finds so attractive about the tribal state.

Village or Vacuum?

When, however, you have the primitive level of moral reasoning and no sense of community, traditions, or social ties, you are in moral (and social) trouble: you are heading toward the type of chaos depicted in the film *A Clockwork Orange*. There is nothing noble about the savage without his village. And if there is one clear trend in criminal behavior today, it is toward an increase in savagery. This, as one prominent sociologist puts it, is the Age of the Psychopath.[19] Psychopaths are notorious for their lack of either individual or social conscience, and they are the ones primarily responsible for crimes of violence, crimes which have increased eleven times faster than population size in recent years. Between 1960 and 1970 the incidence of murder increased 76 percent, forcible rape 121 percent, robbery 224 percent, and aggravated assault 117 percent. And recently released government statistics indicate that in many large cities the rate of crime is up to five times higher than that reported by the police. A large part of this total can be attributed to youth under eighteen. Adolescents—those who should have been mellowed most by media—commit about half of all serious crimes in the United States.[20]

Where is the sense of community that will offset this absence of conscience? Where is the global village? The answer, it is plain, is that there is no village, nor can there be, given the debilitating effect that occurs when the citizenry relies mainly on the support of impersonal electronic and chemical sources. What makes the village even more implausible is the growth of the Human Potential philosophy. It is no mere coincidence that we are witnessing a marriage of the "villagers" and the self-actualizers: irresponsibility makes strange bedfellows. It is doubtful that the electric age man really desires community, that he wishes to impose upon himself the obligations that the TV and stereo never did, or that the self-actualizer really wants to sacrifice any of his options for the sake of the whole, or that he wants to be anything but a law unto himself.

The word "irresponsibility" should not be thrown about in an irresponsible manner, so let me state the matter more clearly. Identity is linked not only with intimacy but also with responsibility, so that the new trends in identity will be accompanied by radical changes in our sense of personal obligation. Those with a sense of fluid identity will develop a sense of fluid responsibility; those with no sense of individual identity will have no sense of individual responsibility. We can see the first tendency at work in those who tell us that our self is in process, and therefore we needn't hold ourselves responsible for every little promise we made when we were somebody else. As an instance of the second tendency we have McLuhan telling us that "guilt is not something that can be privately assigned." I am not suggesting that your average mugger goes around with a copy of *Understanding Media* tucked under his arm, or that he spends his leisure hours attending encounter groups. But I am suggesting that, in the absence of community, the philosophy of fluidity in combination with neo-tribalism does nourish a general irresponsibility. Even if we ourselves keep the law and customs, we are increasingly unwilling to impose standards on others. "That's where they're coming from," or "That's where they're at," we say, as though it were the ultimate justification for any and all behavior. What we mean, of course, is "everybody to his own process." This attitude stems not from any concern for our fellows but from a habit of self-absorption bordering on self-indulgence—a habit which is shared equally by both tribal villagers and human potentialists.

At first glance it would seem that the McLuhanites, with their inclination to dissolve personhood, and the self-regarders, with an inclination to celebrate it, are poles apart. But just as the extreme left and the extreme right of the political spectrum finally merge to display the same totalistic outlook, so it is with self-abnegation and self-realization. At the core of it all is an overweening concern with self. This was clarified for me by reading a passage from Martin Pawley's *The Private Future*:

> The idea that nude theater and public sex mark the end of
> privacy is diametrically wrong: they represent its celebra-
> tion.[21]

Now such activities are generally endorsed both by global villagers and self-actualizers as evidence of a new frankness in interpersonal relations: communicating person-to-person instead of relating to clothes, roles, or status; an expression of oneness; even a return to the original innocence that supposedly prevailed before the sexes and the psyches were separated. On the contrary, Pawley suggests, the new openness is only an expression of self-gratification and self-obsession; and corresponding to this self-indulgence is a simple lack of concern not only for what others think, but for others, period.

In such a world there are no Thou's, only I's and Me's. Either, "I am a world sufficient to myself," or, "the world is me." Even among those who counsel the dissolution of ego boundaries we can see a subtle self-aggrandizement at work. From Allen Ginsberg to the latest Guru to McLuhan himself, this incongruous need asserts itself: the need for recognition, the dependence on publicity, the inability to practice what they preach and simply "drop out." One is reminded of Henderson the Rain King and his incessant inner refrain, "I want, I want, I want."

The electric global village, whether populated by fluid selves or tribal selves, is not a village at all, it is a world of self-absorption. As such it offers little hope for community and no compensation for the loss of individual ethics.

Morals and Ethics in the Global Village

Ethically speaking, our society is not shaping up along tribal lines but along pretribal ones. Private guilt, as McLuhan indicates, is on the wane, but there is no evidence of a new spirit of collective guilt to take its place. Collective guilt—the kind of guilt that a whole family suffers when one member does wrong—can still be found in this society, but it is *only* in the family that it is found. Elsewhere, the spirit of the times is better summed up by the motto Americans first adopted when their country was nothing more than a loose confederation of states: "Don't tread on me!"

The kind of morality McLuhan espouses simply is not possible in the electric-network world he envisions. To clarify this point let me elaborate on a distinction which Keniston makes between morals and ethics. Morals, he says, are the specific rules of conduct set out by the community and subscribed to by the individual as a part of the community. This understanding of "morals" is equivalent to the stage of moral development that Kohlberg calls "conventional." It works best in face-to-face situations, and it is, therefore, characteristic of families, small communities, and primitive societies. His adherence to conventional morality explains how the Mafia member can be completely loyal when dealing with his own "family," yet completely unscrupulous when dealing with the larger society.

Ethics, says Keniston, are a different matter. An ethical sense is really an extension of the sense of identity: "When an ethical man violates his own ethic, he feels not guilt but a sense of human failure, a kind of existential shame that he has not been who he thought himself to be . . . his ethical sense is a part (often the heart) of his central and best self."[22] The emergence of the ethical sense requires an ability to discern universal principles, applicable regardless of community mores. Ethics grant the stranger the same moral respect that is due one's family. In this sense, "ethics" is equivalent to the highest stage of moral development Kohlberg outlines—the postconventional stage, which is, by and large, absent from tribal societies.

The more technologically advanced a society becomes, and the less face-to-face contact it provides, the more it must depend on ethics rather than morals. Moral systems, observes Keniston, "were primarily intended to govern interpersonal relations, they are inadequate to the noninterpersonal dimensions of the twentieth century."[23] Once again the McLuhan analogy breaks down. The global village we are approaching is not an interpersonal one, but an impersonal one held together by TV, radio, and communications satellites, and endangered by faceless vendors of crime, pollution, and war. This highly electrified and highly impersonal global village, then, would require of its citizens precisely what McLuhan's tribal analogy implies we can do without: the highly developed ethical sense and the individualized identity out of which it grows. Tribal morals do not work in a global village.

Moral Imagination and the "Raskolnikoff Syndrome"

If anything, the electric media may work against the development of principled ethics. The reasons for this are complex but can best be understood via a brief excursion into the relationship between moral development and cognitive development. Cognitive development, according to the renowned Swiss psychologist Jean Piaget, proceeds according to stages, the highest of which is marked by the emergence of abstract thought (Piaget calls this the stage of formal operations). Kohlberg, the leading authority on moral development, says that it too takes place in stages. Moreover, says Kohlberg, the highest stage of moral development cannot emerge until the individual has reached the highest cognitive stage indicated by Piaget. Needless to say, abstract thought is not a universal phenomenon, and neither is principled morality. For example, a study by John Gay and Michael Cole reveals that the abstract thinking which comes "naturally" to adults in this culture is rarely to be found among certain tribes in Liberia.[24] And Kohlberg's own cross-cultural studies indicate that where high level cognition is absent, so also is high level moral development.[25]

What has this to do with electric media? Simply this: Print —the whole print-oriented milieu—seems to act as a spur to the development of formal operational thought and the careful abstractions and discriminations that go with it. The TV massage, on the other hand, is not very demanding and may even promote cognitive passivity. If the electric media do supplant print, we may well see an electronic erosion of abstract thought, and with it an erosion of ethical development.[26]

As Kohlberg's studies imply, ethicality requires a good bit of intellectual imagination. It takes a moral imagination to discern in the slave, the barbarian, the outlander, and other such "nonpeople," the same human qualities we cherish in ourselves; or—to put the matter in contemporary terms—imagination is required to understand that the ethical rules apply to "freaks," radicals, and dissenters, as well as to police, politicians, and other representatives of straight society. But the TV medium, since it leaves nothing to fancy, does not exercise the intellectual or moral imagination, as books, and even radio, once did.

Television is not the only culprit, perhaps not even the main culprit; still, we do seem to be witnessing a decline of the moral imagination. Thanks to Kohlberg's extensive and continuing research, it is possible to establish some solid evidence of this. Toward the end of adolescence it is not uncommon for young people to engage in a debunking of conventional morality (adult version). Today, in fact, it is quite common. Kohlberg observes that at this point many youngsters push on to a higher level of moral development, although many more simply shift to the conventional morality offered by the counterculture. Another sizable segment of the youth population, however, regresses to a preconventional moral stage—a phenomenon which Kohlberg terms the "Raskolnikoff Syndrome." This syndrome varies from those adolescents who revert to the childish rationale of "Why shouldn't I have fun?" to those who proclaim Nietzsche-like that they are "beyond good and evil." When Kohlberg first observed this moral backsliding it appeared to be only a normal developmental process in the transition to principled morality, for eventually his subjects took up again at the moral stage at which they had left off.[27] The whole affair could be explained in terms of what the psychoanalyst Ernst Kris called "regression in the service of the ego."

By 1971, however, Kohlberg was beginning to have his doubts. Moral nihilism and moral relativism seemed to be far more widespread than previously among the college and high school students he studied. And, "extreme relativism no longer appeared to be a temporary ego-developmental maneuver of a small group of subjects in crisis, but rather to represent a more stable, less crisislike pattern of low commitment."[28] In other words, it seems that for an increasing number of youngsters, the Raskolnikoff Syndrome is here to stay.

As establishment morals become more and more discredited in the eyes of youth, more and more of them will be faced with the choice of moral advancement or moral regression. It is, unfortunately, always easier to reject a system than to create alternatives to it, and without the exercise of the moral imagination it becomes doubly hard to envision a higher ethical substitute for conventional morality. Young people could, of course, shift their allegiance to the conventional morality of the counterculture, but that society lacks the bond of togetherness that makes conventional morality work in the first place. That leaves us with a bleak prospect. When the moral imagination fails, when conventional morality is discarded, and when there is no community to replace it, the first thing that comes to hand is moral anarchy—which is both a premoral and pretribal state.

The Present Dilemma

We are faced then with a dilemma. A neo-tribal society generates neither the individualized ethics a print-culture offers, nor the moral solidarity membership in a community affords. It thereby incurs many of the liabilities of the tribal state without its compensations.

The new electric age does produce some tribal characteristics, such as lessened personal responsibility, difficulty with abstract thinking, and indifference toward defining the self. It does not produce many tribal benefits. And this is primarily because electric media promote passivity, not involvement. They deprive us of the energy to commit ourselves to others either individually or in community; and they discourage both concrete perception and abstract thought. It is a commonplace observation of parents that TV watching is a passive activity, and they usually thank God for it. The screen provides hours of relief from romping youngsters and from insistent complaints that "There's nothing to do." Television has become the opiate of the tow-headed masses. How then can McLuhan say that television and the other electric media invite involvement-in-depth? Thirty million parents can't be wrong.

McLuhan's error lies, I believe, in making a bad analogy between one kind of ear culture and another. There is a large difference between an oral culture in which you listen to others and they listen to you and the resulting communication draws you closer together, and an audio culture in which the TV and the stereo do all the talking and you sit mesmerized like a dumb animal. The former really does promote involvement and community; the latter creates passivity and dependence. The electric media massage may foster certain habits characteristic of tribal man but it does not build villages—and that makes all the difference.

When speaking of the demise of print, however, McLuhan is more believable. He never said that we were entering into a printless world or beating a retreat back to illiteracy, but merely that print was losing its preeminent place among media and that this alone would create radical transformations. The print culture does seem to be declining. It is difficult to offer hard proof for this, only impressions. Other than Clifford Adelman's informal survey of reading habits (which does confirm McLuhan's theory), I am not aware of any hard research on the matter of quantity or quality of books read.[29] One is left then with individual impressions. But there are enough of these to indicate a real change. Where once there were shelves filled with books, there are now shelves filled with records and cassettes. Where once there were printed pages to power flights of speculation, there are now printed circuits to power tape players and TVs. The print culture is no longer king.

Under the new order the idea of personal identity has become a bit suspect. It doesn't seem particularly workable, nor does it seem quite befitting a global villager. The concept even has the faint odor of the bourgeois about it. Still, what else is there? The new media are creating not an electronic village but an electronic jungle. A continued trend in this direction is not pleasant to contemplate for if the print culture is on the wane and the electric culture cannot provide the village McLuhan promised, then we end up with a society situated between two shores and adrift on a windless sea. The electric media sap us of the conceptual- and will-energies needed to crystallize a well-defined individual identity, and they substitute no community by which we might find a corporate identity. We can reach neither the near shore of print-oriented integrity nor the far bank of neo-savage nobility. It would be pleasant to think that we could combine the best elements of both these worlds, but the culture we have now seems to be built mainly on the flotsam and wreckage that the tide carries out to us from those two shores.

6

Nonidentity

*I*N McLuhan's idea of a global village there are intimations of another, more radical attempt to go beyond identity. The speculations of Norman O. Brown represent one more articulation of a widespread discontent with the difficult task of structuring an identity, and reflect a deep skepticism about the wisdom of the whole enterprise.

What Brown, who is a humanities professor at Santa Cruz, serves up is a reinterpretation of Freud with none of the gritty inconveniences of either superego or ego; that is, he offers pure id unhampered by conscience or identity. Like McLuhan, Brown presents an alternative to fragmented print-oriented individualism; but instead of a return to the tribe he suggests a return to infancy—before identity or anything faintly resembling it can set in. It is a curiously attractive idea, but one, I think, which must ultimately be opposed. First let us look at Brown's argument, which is most forcefully presented in *Love's Body*.

McLuhan, Brown and Genital-Oriented Man

Love's Body might well have been prefaced with the same warning that Harry Haller, the Steppenwolf, encounters upon entering the magic theater:

TONIGHT AT THE MAGIC THEATER
FOR MADMEN ONLY
PRICE OF ADMITTANCE YOUR MIND[1]

It would be a fitting introduction to a book that flatly opposes the rational mind and requires its readers to adopt a stance of Dionysian madness. For Brown would have us lose our heads and become our bodies. In thus contrasting the whole (the body) with the part (the head), Brown is not unlike McLuhan, who contrasts the harmony of the senses with the extension of a single sense, sight. Brown's purpose is to reassert the primacy of the whole over the part.

One part in particular needs to be put in its place (here Brown is being metaphorical rather than literal) and that is the penis. Like the head, the phallus tends to dominate the rest of the body; the slang term "head" is in fact used to designate the glans of the erect penis. It is characteristic of Brown's topsy-turvy vision, that in a chapter entitled "Head" he speaks mostly about the phallus. Beyond this equation of head and penis, Brown makes a convincing case from myth and psychoanalysis that the phallus is representative of the whole person. The rest of the body is as "chorus to tragic hero,"[2] getting its pleasure vicariously in events to which it is only a passive spectator. The pleasure for the rest of the person is the pleasure of the voyeur. The voyeur, of course, turns out to be McLuhan's visually oriented man. (The connection between the visual-orientation and genital organization was perhaps first stated in the Book of Genesis: "then the eyes of both were opened and they realized that they were naked.")

If the penis is representative of the person, then all sorts of personality problems can be traced to it. One critic commenting on a recent performance of *Cyrano de Bergerac* takes Cyrano's elongated nose to be symbolic of a lack of size in another part of the body "where size is usually admired." Thus Cyrano's troublesome pugnacity can be interpreted as an attempt to defend and assert his underdeveloped personality. Brown opposes this tyranny of the genital as being a perversion of the true order of things. It is a state of trance imposed by the hypnotic power of a single part. The hypnotist imposes his will by fixing his subject's vision with his eyes; the seducer does it with his penis. Frank Harris, author of the autobiographical *My Secret Life*, believed that his penis had a hypnotic effect on women, but it is obvious to his reader that it had a more mesmeric effect on Harris himself. It, not he, was in charge. Harris' life was always under the sway of Harris' genitality.

To make his point, Brown utilizes a text from Blake which is also a favorite of McLuhan's:

> *Now I a fourfold vision see,*
> *And a fourfold vision is given to me;*
> *'Tis fourfold in my supreme delight*
> *And threefold in soft Beulah's night*
> *And two fold always. May God us keep*
> *From single vision and Newton's sleep!*[3]

"Newton's sleep" is the anaesthetizing of the rest of the body, the rest of the senses, which occurs when one part of the body (the genitals) or one sense (the visual) or one faculty (the rational) predominates. For McLuhan, "Newton's sleep" is the print-oriented age; for Brown it is the age of genital organization. It is the tyranny of the part over the whole, the tyranny of the genital over the body, the tyranny of the visual sense over the balanced sense ratio. McLuhan sees the Western world as print-oriented; Brown sees it as penis-oriented. "Single vision" is not, of course, enough for Brown. True vision comes with what he calls "polymorphous perversity." Polymorphous perversity is the sexual condition of the infant in which pleasure is not just focused on the genitals but dispersed through the entire body.

Let me offer a case in point. A friend recently recounted to me his experiences in a mixed sauna. The others in the group were taking turns giving and receiving massages. One person would recline on a bench while the other six or seven would play the role of masseuse and masseur. Not wishing to be considered asocial, my friend lent a willing hand to this communal enterprise, but out of modesty (the remnant no doubt of a print-oriented upbringing) confined himself to kneading ankles and calves, for whenever his hand or his eye moved up the subject's legs, another part of his anatomy would also begin to move up. This was particularly disconcerting since no one else in the group—all veterans—appeared similarly aroused. When his turn came to be massaged he begged off, fearing that he might display bad manners by violating some unwritten code of saunadom.

Whether the participants in this ritual were flaccid out of repression or out of jaded habituation or from a sense of delight in the whole body, I do not know. If it is the last, then it will serve as an illustration of polymorphous perversity as opposed to genital organization. And if, as appears to be the case, it is a scene which is increasingly familiar on the American landscape, it stands as proof of Brown's prophetic ability. Polymorphous perversity is a refusal to let the erogenous zones be culturally determined. It is the diffusion of sexual feeling throughout the whole body, a return to the pregenital condition of infancy where, before the imposition of fine discriminations, all the senses combined in global interplay. This is the part of Brown's mythology that has provoked the most widespread comment, but thus far he is not very different from Freud, who hypothesized in *Beyond the Pleasure Principle* that the purpose of eros, the sexual instinct, was ultimately to restore an earlier state of things "before life was sexually differentiated." The difference is only that Brown is more literal and more in earnest about this pregenital state of affairs.

Identity and Its Discontents

But Brown is out for bigger game than mere genitals. What he is really stalking is that which genitals only represent. He is, as it turns out, bent on abolishing the structure that Erikson carefully elaborated and that most of us spend our lives erecting. The fall of man, as Brown sees it, is not only the fall into the division of the two sexes but also the fall into the division of selves. It is identity, personality, the self, which he ultimately opposes. Underneath the startling juxtapositions, the fanciful metaphors, and the elaborate word play, Brown is quite serious about this. We must be willing to discard personality, he tells us, for "God is no respecter of persons." Like the Greek word from which it comes, personality is only a "persona"—a mask. The self is a "theatrical creation," a mere stage prop. Unconsciously we would all like to be one, to be free of these masks that separate us from each other. This world, says Brown, is an illusory theater in which we are all engaged in playacting. The real world is not unlike Hesse's Magic Theater: to enter it we must leave behind our questionable personalities, as Pablo, the theater manager, points out to Harry Haller:

> "You have no doubt guessed long since that the conquest of time and the escape from reality, or however else it may be that you choose to describe your longing, means simply the wish to be relieved of your so-called personality. That is the prison where you lie."[4]

What is wrong with the self that we should be rid of it? And what does Brown offer in return? Brown gives a clue to the first question when he writes:

> A person is never himself but always a mask; a person never owns his own person, but always represents another by whom he is possessed. And the other that one is, is always ancestors; one's soul is not one's own but daddy's. This is the meaning of the Oedipus complex.[5]

The trouble with the self is that it is derived from others. It is constructed in an attempt to live up to the expectations of elders. "The others . . ." to use the words of R. D. Laing, who echoes many of Brown's laments, ". . . have become installed in our hearts and we call them ourselves."[6] In short, the self belongs to daddy. And what does daddy stand for? The conventional Freudian response is to say that daddy stands in the way of the boy's desire for his mother. But to Brown's way of thinking, daddy stands for much more than this.

Conscience

Brown provides another clue to his thinking in asserting that "conventional Anglo-Saxon political theory, dismissing Nazism as an irrelevant aberration, a lunatic episode, in the history of the West, is all patriarchal."[7] Remembering Hitler's constant invocation of "The Fatherland," it is at first difficult to see how Brown could discern in Nazism the antithesis of patriarchy. But let us pause to consider what it was that characterized those people upon whom Hitler's enmity fell most heavily. "Conscience is a Jewish invention," Hitler once scoffed. In a way it was a true statement. The God of the Jews is the God of Abraham, Isaac, and Jacob: the God of the patriarchs. Judaism is the religion of patriarchy par excellence. And the patriarchs handed down to their children what fathers always hand down and more: conscience, morality, ethical demands, the Ten Commandments, the Law. There is a perceptive essay on this in George Steiner's book *In Bluebeard's Castle.* He reminds us just how alien and unwelcome was the interjection of monotheism into the ancient world. The God of the Jews is the God who forbids the making of images, whose own name is unspeakable, whose essence is unimaginable—and all this flew in the face of man's persistent tendency to familiarize his gods, to whittle them down to human terms and into graven objects. More than this, the single Deity posed a threat to man's pursuit of happiness, his liberty to follow his own impulses. Polytheism provided not only free reign to man's imagination but freedom of action as well. While the gods quarreled and reveled among themselves, man was free to go about his own earthly business. But the absolute and ever-watchful God of the Patriarchs put an end to this moratorium, banished Pan and pantheism, and imposed instead his Law.

Thousands of years later the spirit of Pan took its revenge. Steiner writes:

By killing the Jews, Western culture would eradicate those who had "invented" God, who had, however restively, been the declarers of His unbearable absence. The holocaust is a reflex, the more complete for being long-inhibited, of natural sensory consciousness, of instinctual polytheistic and animist needs. It speaks for a world both older than Sinai and newer than Nietzsche.[8]

Steiner tells us how in "Moses and Monotheism," written in the early years of Nazism, Freud attempted to lay the blame for the "invention" of God at the feet of an Egyptian prince. Perhaps not fully knowing it, Steiner suggests, "he [Freud] was trying to wrench the lightning rod out of the hands of the Jewish people"[9] before it was too late. But Freud himself had already introduced, via his concept of superego, the psychological equivalent of conscience. The ethical demands of the superego are patriarchal demands, the introjection of father's moral code. It is an interesting coincidence that makes Freud a Jew and, beyond that, a bearded patriarch—the father figure of modern psychology.

Performance Cancelled

What daddy stands for then, in both Freud and Brown, but more so in the latter, is conscience. More precisely, daddy embodies what Brown calls "the performance principle." Obeying the performance principle means living up to expectations, acting in a prescribed way, even denying one's impulses. Erich Fromm[10] tells us that mother's love is unconditional, even undeserved, while father's love is provisional; it is given on condition that children perform up to expectation. Under the pressure of these patriarchal expectations the child forms an ego, a superego, and eventually an identity. The trouble with an identity, according to Brown, is that it puts an artificial barrier around one's being and cuts it off from the world it was once merged with when it floated in the waterbed of the womb. Identity, self, ego, superego—whatever you wish to call it—it all spells repression and restriction. The idea that one has to live up to expectations, to mold a character, or to set oneself apart as a unique specimen is, for Brown, the source of all error.

New Resolution of the Oedipus Complex

In the face of the all-powerful father, Freud considered that there was only one wise course for the Oedipal child to follow: join him, identify with him, incorporate his personality into your own in the form of superego. But Brown would have the Oedipus conflict resolved in a way that Freud would not: by defeating the father and casting off the confines of the superego. This involves throwing off personality too, but that after all is only the imposition of daddy's self on you. There is no need to search through ancient myths in order to find the literary analog for this. We have it, albeit in diluted form, in Barrie's *Peter Pan*. Leslie Fiedler tells us that "even the most ordinary Broadway producer knows these days the poor papa in his doghouse and the evil Captain Hook ought to be played by the same actor."[11] In Peter Pan every Oedipal wish comes true: the father figure is slain (fed to a vagina with teeth, as Fiedler puts it), polymorphism reigns in Peter's androgynous body, and the irresponsible world of Pan is triumphant. Getting rid of daddy is really a wish to get rid of our own superego, our conscience, those gnawing ethical demands. The religion of Pan would abolish monotheism, patriarchy, and the Commandments. "Our only refuge," writes Brown, "is loss of shame, polymorphous perversity, pansexualism."[12] To be able to cast off patriarchy is to be able to return to the world of Pan, which is the world of the id. In Brown's version of the Oedipal drama, the father that has to be slain is the performance principle. This is not unlike McLuhan's wish for a tribal state where the only performance is collective performance and the only guilt is collective guilt. Brown approvingly quotes Freud: "It is a matter of indifference who actually committed the crime; psychology is only concerned to know who welcomed it when it was done. And for that reason all of the brothers [of the family Karamazov; or of the human family] are equally guilty."[13] The same idea occurs in the writing of R. D. Laing: "We are all murderers and prostitutes."[14] Brown merely carries the idea a little further by suggesting that the burden of bearing this universal guilt individually is what makes some people into actual murderers and prostitutes. His solution is the casting off of individual conscience.

Mother's Love

The opposite of patriarchy is not matriarchy, says Brown, but fraternity—a group of brothers who band together against the father's tyranny. The fraternity is an alliance with the mother against the father, but the sons must leave their real mothers and be born again through initiation to a new mother, this time the fraternity itself. Christ points to his disciples and says, "Behold my mother and my brothers." In primitive tribes the adolescent is initiated into the secret society by "male mothers." A young man who is initiated by an older homosexual into the mores of the gay world will call that man "my mother." Mothers don't demand as much as fathers, and they protect sons from fathers' demands with the excuse "he is just a boy." But the principle of patriarchy will not let boys be boys. The Nazis who reveled in the trappings of boyhood—uniforms, fraternities, secret societies—rebelled against patriarchal demands in the name of their fatherland, which was really their motherland. Brown rather facilely seems to assume that if Germany had not been so patriarchal there would have been no Nazi reaction.

Conscience, which was first invented by the Jews, was reinvented by the Protestants. After the war theologians like Reinhold Niebuhr and Karl Barth were once again to reassert the transcendence and absoluteness of God. They attempted to reestablish the God of the Old Testament that Nietzsche had wished dead. In doing so they proved that Protestantism is really a continuation of Hebraism, that is, of a patriarchal system. Brown is harshly critical of the legalism of the Jews and

Protestants but he spares the Catholic Church, even praises it in the person of Pope John XXIII. There are two obvious reasons for this preferential treatment. First, Catholicism retains elements of polytheism in its veneration of the saints, leaving more room for playing one deity off against another although in a much more restricted form than was available to pagans. Second, the Catholic Church tempers the performance principle with a large dose of unconditional mother love. It even refers to itself as "Holy Mother the Church." . This emphasis on maternity acts to mitigate the harshness of the patriarchal judgment. Holy Mother the Church or Mary the Mother of God can always be counted on to intercede on behalf of her children, perhaps with the excuse that they are after all "only children." There is a touching final scene in John Ford's screen adaptation of *The Informer* where the desperate Gypo Nolan and the mother of the murdered man he has betrayed are alone in a church, the altar of which is dominated by a large crucifix. In remorse Gypo turns to the old woman, pleads for forgiveness, and receives it. At this point he lifts his arms and face to the crucifix and shouts in a joyful voice: "Frankie, yer mother has forgiven me." Although the symbolism is obvious and the ending anticipated, the effect of the scene is always devastating. The mother provides the forgiveness which the fraternity—in this case the I.R.A.—will not; the Father in heaven turns back his anger; the performance principle is set aside. Mother's unconditional love prevails over father's demanding love. Salvation is by faith and not by works.

Salvation by Works

Strangely enough, it was on this last point that Martin Luther broke from the Catholic Church. He insisted that a man is saved by faith alone, not by works, certainly not by the purchase of indulgences; no, not even by keeping the law and the Commandments. I say "strangely" because Protestantism would soon after Luther take a turn which would lead it right back to a belief in salvation by works. I am speaking of that frame of mind which developed out of Protestantism and came to dominate industrial societies in the West. The Protestant ethic judged a man not by his faith but by his performance. It considered idleness to be the most capital of sins, condemned the poor for lack of enterprise, and in its most degenerate form equated cutthroat business practices with the will of God. How could Luther's best hopes come to such an end?—the very opposite of what he intended that day he nailed his ninety-five theses to the door of Wittenberg Cathedral. Perhaps this is what happens when there are no mothers around to soften the performance principle. For no sooner had Protestantism abolished the cult of Christ's mother than it found itself faced with the patriarchal prescriptions of a John Calvin. With Calvin, salvation by faith died and the law and the Commandments were reestablished with more efficiency than ever. Of Calvin's *Institutes,* the economic historian R. H. Tawney could write:

> Legalistic, mechanical, without imagination or compassion, the work of a jurist and organizer of genius, Calvin's system was more Roman than Christian, and more Jewish than either.[15]

In Calvin's *Institutes* the capitalistic spirit found the rationale it needed to prosper. The confidence that God's law could be fulfilled by the accumulation of worldly wealth only required a theology of justification by works. What Fromm would call the principle of motherly love was replaced in Protestantism by an extreme patriarchy which demanded that its sons and daughters work up to expectations. These children of patriarchy would now be all the more ready to defer to the demands of their superego and, since they now believed that salvation was a consequence of individual merit, they would fall victim to what Brown considers a crucial error: the mistaken notion that their separate identities were worth cultivating.

The Mystical Body

There is another characteristic of the Catholic Church that accounts for the soft spot which Brown has for it in his heart. Once upon a time—before Protestantism and print set in—the Western world did live in a harmonious state approaching the happy condition of oneness. In the Middle Ages the Church and society formed a cohesive organism held together by a vision of ultimate concord. This was the idea of the Mystical Body of Christ, a mysterious union of the faithful which seems more pantheistic than deistic. The doctrine developed in this way: Some six or seven years after Pentecost, on the road to Damascus, a young Jewish pharisee, a persecutor of Christians, was astonished by a flash of light and a voice saying to him: "Saul! Saul! Why do you persecute me?" "Who are you, Lord?" Saul asked, and was answered, "I am Jesus whom you are persecuting . . ."[16] The story is well known. Saul became Paul and Paul, against all odds, became a proselytizer of Gentiles. With the exception of Peter—and in his case also it required a vision—it did not occur to the earliest Christians that the word should go out to non-Jews. It was Paul's understanding of those words that caused him to exclaim the universal character of Christianity, for in Christ's Body "there is neither Jew nor Greek, there is neither bond nor free, there is neither male or female, for ye are all one in Christ Jesus."[17] Augustine, in commenting on Paul's vision, wrote: "Christ did not say 'Why do you persecute my saints—or my servants?' but 'Why do you persecute me, that is, my members?' "[18] As Paul and Augustine understood it, Christians form the Body of Christ; to persecute one of them is to persecute Christ. As it was used by Paul the expression appears to be more than a metaphor. Paul never says "the body of Christians," but always "the Body of Christ." In Paul's letters the doctrine of the Mystical Body becomes the basis for Christian charity. One cannot be indifferent to the other members of the body: "The eye can not say to the hand, 'I don't need you.' No, we really can't do without the parts of the body that we think are weaker—If one member suffers, all the others suffer with it. If one is honored, all the others are happy with it."[19]

Likewise the Mystical Body doctrine became the basis for chastity. In his letters to the Romans and the Corinthians, Paul makes it clear that Christians are no longer bound by the performance principle. Christians are above the Law of Moses. If a Christian should refrain from licentiousness, it is not because the law forbids it, but because by engaging in it he would be joining the body of Christ to a prostitute.

So the Church came to look upon itself as the body of Christ. Salvation lay not in individual effort but in being joined to the body; and being members of the same body each one of the faithful took care to build up that body, to live in close-knit harmony with the other members, and to take care lest any part of the body go undernourished. The reality of Christian life always fell short of the ideal, but the ideal helps to explain the corporate and communal nature of Christian society up until the end of the Middle Ages.

Dismemberment of the Body

But already in the Middle Ages certain forces were at work that were to cause that social fabric to unravel. One factor was Arianism, a "heresy" which spread through the Western Church in the fifth and sixth centuries. In reaction to the Arian denial of Christ's divinity, the Church began to play down his humanity. Instead of Christ joined together with a redeemed body of Christians, it became more orthodox to think of him as sitting in heaven alongside the Father. It then became necessary for the people to look for other mediators by whom the Father might be approached and petitioned. The position of the clergy and the saints as mediators was enhanced and Christian worship, which had begun as a family supper, became a private affair between the priest and God. Christian life became more private and introspective, less communal and interdependent.

Nevertheless, for a long time afterward, Christendom managed to retain its corporate and unitary nature. Then came Protestantism, Calvinism, salvation by works—in short, the performance principle. The performance of the individual parts gradually took precedence over the health of the whole body. And once the ruling belief in a mystical body was undermined the way was open for the Protestant ethic, for rugged individualism, for the belief that "it's every man for himself." In *Religion and the Rise of Capitalism,* R. H. Tawney writes:

> Individualism in religion led insensibly, if not quite logically, to an individualist morality, and individualist morality to a disparagement of the significance of the social fabric as compared with personal character.[20]

The question is, What led to individualism in religion? It was certainly not Luther's intention to subvert the fellowship of the Christian community. It was only that his emphasis on the direct communication of God's grace to man led to a circumvention of the social and religious organism and to a corresponding reliance on the inner revelation and the private life. Beyond this, Brown, like McLuhan, sees the insidious workings of print. In the Protestant reliance on the written word of scripture he sees the return of Judaic literalism and an inevitable relapse into patriarchy and law, conscience and superego. McLuhan says that print fragmentizes, analyzes, breaks down into component parts. Brown pushes the idea a little further: "The letter kills." The truth of scripture, Brown believes, lies in its metaphorical nature. The emphasis on the literal interpretation of scripture, on the book and on the letter of the law, takes the life out of the Body, gives over its members to their superegos, and leads to the cultivation of privacy, and worst of all, personality. Metaphorically speaking, print splintered the mystical body into a hundred divisions. With Protestantism and print comes the Protestant ethic: hard work, future orientation, denial of gratification, attachment to privacy and private property. It is an ethic that values ownership, possession, and secrecy, and wreaks havoc, Brown tells us, because it leads us to regard our own persons as property, leads to individualism, leads us to hide ourselves from one another.

Love's Body

What is Brown's solution to this rampant individualism? "The truth that will make us free," he writes, "is not in individual psychology, nor in the currently fashionable ego psychology, but in what the later Freud called 'mass psychology.' "[21] When Brown speaks disapprovingly of "ego psychology" (which is hardly the current fashion anymore) he is speaking of the school of thought to which Erikson belongs. Where Erikson stresses the importance of individual identity as a coherent and unique synthesis, Brown disparages it:

> There is no integration of the separate individual—integration of the individual is a strictly self-contradictory enterprise.[22]

The West, which has for centuries been bent on individualism, must turn back on its path. Back to what? To that body in which "there is neither Jew nor Greek . . . male or female" is Brown's reply. The true psychological salvation is the Mystical Body, secularized and sensualized for modern consumption and rechristened "Love's Body." Unconsciously, says Brown, we all yearn for incorporation into this body of mankind. Genital sex, because it is only partial incorporation of one body into another, is not enough. It is a poor substitute for the all-encompassing union of bodies which Brown has in mind. Better than genital sex is polymorphous perversity— sexuality diffused through the body, not just localized in the genitals. Sexuality diffused is genitality defused. That means an end to the performance principle, which in sex is the principle of the erection and the climax (Richard Kostelanetz compares polymorphous perversity to the "constant pleasures afforded by the electronic media, with their diffusion of attention and absence of climax").[23] What is important in this new sex is the skin contact, the touching, the warmth, the proximity of body to body. Polymorphous perversity means an end to all the exclusive one-to-one sexuality which now limits us, and the beginning of pansexualism—the first step toward a new mystical body. This new, egoless sexuality will help us go beyond the exclusivity and possessiveness, the emphasis on private parts and private property that plague the West. The whole stress on private parts is wrong, since we are all members of the same body. Genital sex is private sex, performance sex, partial sex; polymorphous perversity, on the other hand, is universal sharing.

The End of Identity

What all this means in practical terms is difficult to imagine. Does it mean that everyone's body should be at the disposal of every other body regardless of sex, age, or temperament— with no distinctions, no discretions, no lines drawn? It is hard to escape the conclusion that this is exactly what Brown has in mind. What it most certainly means is the end of anything like the search for identity. It is difficult to maintain an identity just as it is sometimes difficult to maintain an erection. Brown would have us give up both struggles. The outcome is no self. Only the entire Body counts. The Last Judgment, says Brown, does not consist in "the award of prizes to personalities for the performance of their parts."[24] The loss of personal identity is the price we must pay for incorporation into the body. For Brown it is a small price.

It all seems rather exotic and excessive, even a bit fantastic —this call to undifferentiated union. Yet the doctrine that identity must be abandoned is more popular than one might expect. Brown's whole vision is really a footnoted elaboration of the same fantasies that Keniston noted among his uncommitted students. These boys had resolved their Oedipus complex in the very way Brown suggests. They one and all had replaced their father as the object of their mother's affection. And they had discarded, by and large, the patriarchal performance principle in favor of mother's unconditional love. In sexual and romantic matters they displayed that passivity which one might expect from those who have gone beyond genital sex. Their fantasy ideal was to return to an Edenic state of oceanic oneness where there would be no differentiation or distinction—a state like that which had existed before they left their mother's body. Although in reality they led isolated lives, they consistently refused to delineate for themselves an individual identity. More recently we have seen a burgeoning interest in Eastern philosophy and its concept of the self which is so similar to Brown's. "Undoing the ego," Meher Baba called it.[25] And he is but one of many gurulike figures who have emerged in the past dozen or so years to exert an unprecedented Eastern influence on the attitude of Western youth, and not a few Western adults: Allen Ginsberg, Baba Ram Dass, Timothy Leary, Alan Watts, and R. D. Laing are a few names that come to mind. The message in each case is essentially the same: lose yourself.

Ever since Abraham Maslow touched head to Tao there has been a parallel trend in the Human Potential Movement—that is, a movement to the East, toward an identity so fluid that it really can't be called an identity. In *The Transformation*, George Leonard, who bridges whatever small gap may remain between the Human Potential idea and the Eastern/Brownian philosophy, suggests that it's just about time we in the West seek enlightenment by shedding our ego structures. As for privatized sex, that too has to go. In a chapter entitled "Beyond Incest," Leonard writes: "Recognizing that all bodies are part of the same field, ultimately one, we shall not hesitate to touch what is really ourselves."[26] The resemblance here to Norman O. Brown is really a family resemblance, for it is increasingly difficult to differentiate what is Human Potential from what is Brownian. It is no accident then that Theodore Roszak[27] sees in the touch-and-grow activities of the Human Potential centers, the practical application of polymorphous perversity.

There is a powerful attraction, a sort of seductive innocence, about Brown's vision that only a very hardened heart could ignore. The reasons for this appeal are many. Who has not tired of living up to expectations—so many expectations and so distant from what we feel to be our core self? And who has not wondered at the ironies of a performance principle that, when carried into the realms of sex, results in a lack of performance? The incidence of impotence is apparently rising (if that is the proper word) in this country, but not because individuals are embracing Brown's ideal of nongenital sex. Quite the contrary, they are determined to prove their genital prowess in a desperate attempt to keep up to the standard set by modern sex research. The lowered self-esteem and the anxious consultation with psychiatrists that accompany male impotence are a clear index that, in equating identity with the penis, Brown is not so farfetched after all. By reversing the accepted values of performance and striving, he offers an antidote not only to the current emphasis on sexual performance and techniques but also to the whole how-to-do-it orientation of our society.

But the allure of Brown goes deeper than this. Of all desires there is none so powerful as the desire for union, and of all fears there is none so fearsome as the fear of loneliness. Who has not experienced the sense of personal isolation, of being imprisoned in one's own ego, of being unable to break through to others? Who has not despaired of the emptiness of it all? And who has not wished to be born again into a more encompassing fellowship? When Brown, echoing the words of Christ, prays "that all may be one," he speaks for a yearning deep in every person.

The Trouble with Transcendence

Identity is not an end in itself; beyond it lies a more inclusive human identity. That is true enough. But Brown wants to skip the first stage altogether and fly straight to what the poet Schiller called "the universal kiss." There are several reasons to take issue with him, not the least of which is that his vision is ultimately unworkable. But first, the minor points. The performance principle has certainly been overdone. Life is nasty, brutish, and short enough without dressing it up in a hair shirt. Still, performance has its rewards. Keats said it long ago: "Do you not see how necessary a World of Pains and troubles is to school an Intelligence and make it a soul?"[28] Edgar Friedenberg said it in *The Vanishing Adolescent:* "Conflict is the instrument by which the individual learns the . . . difference between himself and his environment."[29] Victor and Mildred Goertzel, in their study of 400 of the most eminent people of the twentieth century, said it: "It may be possible to be both creative and comfortable, but we suspect it is not."[30] Finally, Herbert Marcuse, in a critique of Brown, said it: "There are divisions and boundaries that are real and will continue to exist even in the advent of freedom and fulfillment, because all pleasure and all happiness and all humanity originate and live in and with these divisions and boundaries."[31] Despite his own penchant for liberation, Marcuse is intransigent on the point of maintaining boundaries, clearly defined limits, demands and prescriptions, even a bit of repression. (There is an excellent treatment of this seeming anomaly in Marcuse in Lionel Trilling's book *Sincerity and Authenticity.*) He deplores the decline of the superego and the displacement of the father's role in the family, for, like Keats, he believes that identity is schooled in adversity.

The truth is that children seem to thrive in homes with defined limits and specific traditions.[32] And they seem to thrive on challenge. Time after time, in study after study, psychologists have demonstrated that self-esteem is built on competence, achievement, accomplishment—in short, the performance principle.[33] Challenge, when it is not overwhelming, does not debilitate people; it makes them grow. Conversely, it is well known that impotence—the inability to perform or to affect one's environment—is at the root of violence and despair. None of this is new: these principles guided the work of organizations like the Boy Scouts and YMCA long before the psychologists moved in with their measuring devices.

These have to stand as minor arguments, however, since they amount to saying that performance can't be that bad if it's good for identity. Since Brown thinks that identity itself isn't worth a tinker's damn, it doesn't do much good to argue from that direction. All one can do, then, is to point to the inconsistencies of his scheme and to suggest the consequences of following it. From various studies we know the consequences of a strong sense of identity: it makes individuals feel good about themselves; it can even make them happy, and it seems to give them the security they need to fall in love without fear of falling into a maelstrom. What little we are able to understand about the absence of identity or its loss is not at all encouraging. There is, for instance, the isolated unhappiness of the students whom Keniston described: their Brownian fantasy of fusion kept them from finding any real fusion. Whatever their inner longings, people who subscribe to this cosmic view tend to become more and more isolated from others. It's all quite logical: if one's self is coextensive with the universe then the problem of loving others is solved by loving one's self. Why bother with the others if you're a universe unto yourself? But the logic doesn't work very well; the uncommitted about whom Keniston wrote didn't seem to love even themselves.

The syndrome Keniston described was, however, only a mild case of ego transcendence. While it may raise doubts about the benefits of selflessness it does not confirm them. On a more serious level there is some tangible evidence that identity is not expendable—in our psychiatric wards, for example. Aside from babies, the only other recognizable part of the population who can't distinguish between their own bodies and the rest of the world are schizophrenics. In schizophrenia there is no sense of boundary, no sense of where "I" leave off and other people begin. It is remarkable in fact, how closely the clinical description of schizophrenia resembles Brown's description of the resurrected consciousness. Yet it is hard to imagine a ward of schizophrenics combining into anything approaching the body of love Brown speaks of. Crouched in a corner or engrossed with the workings of their ten fingers, they present instead a picture of ultimate isolation. Schizophrenics, like babies, aren't very loving; and unlike babies they aren't even very lovable. The ability to reach out to others and come together in a bond of unity depends on love of others, and to do that one needs an identity. Self-transcendence starts with the self, not with its negation. The keystone of Brown's high-arching theory is the stone that the builder himself has rejected. It is one thing for Brown—a middle-aged scholar who has presumably fashioned an identity and who can bring to his experiments in consciousness an intelligence schooled in the classics and the Bible—to reject identity. It is something else altogether when a nineteen-year-old, still in the thralls of identity confusion, is invited to skip the stage of individuation and to travel along with Brown and Nietzsche "beyond good and evil." The last word belongs to Erikson:

> If to those who seek an identity, Norman Brown advocates "Get lost" and Timothy Leary "Drop out," I would suggest that to get lost one must have found oneself and to drop out one must have been in.[34]

7

A Passage to Nowhere

*D*URING the spring I witnessed a baptism in a small church in a rural Berkshire village. It was not a separate ceremony as is so often the case, but was incorporated into the regular Sunday service. I had never seen a baptism done like that—in front of the whole congregation—and I was stirred by the power of the ritual. The minister, a huge man in a black robe, cradled the child in his arms and spoke in a very personal way first to the parents and then to the congregation, as though they also were the child's parents. The ceremony was for all of us, and I believe all of us felt its impact. It was conducted in such a way as to remind the parents that this small community realized the difficulties of bringing up a child and would be there to help when needed; the welfare of this child was not just the responsibility of two parents; the responsibility belonged to the whole village. I can't remember the exact words, but I do remember experiencing a genuine feeling of communion with all present, and somehow with all parents and all children everywhere. I also felt a renewed sense of appreciation to the friends and relatives who had lent a generous hand whenever I needed help (which was often) in raising my own children.

One does not need a formal occasion to undertake a responsibility or to celebrate a new awareness, but often such occasions will add a new dimension to the experience by intensifying our sense of belonging and by giving a universal character to our struggles and triumphs. Ritual has the power to solemnize, communalize, and universalize what might otherwise remain cries (whether of sorrow or joy) in the wilderness. Moreover the ritual confers a freedom to explore areas of emotionality that might otherwise be explored at one's peril. Andrew Weil in his recent book *The Natural Mind*[1] points out that those who benefit the most from the use of hallucinogens and who most consistently manage to avoid the pitfalls of chemical mind expanders are people like the Southwest Indians, who have learned to use these drugs within the context of a meaningful ritual. Likewise, the minister in my story has a fondness for formal meals, but within the setting of these ceremonial repasts there inevitably occurs a freedom of thought and expression which if not always irreverent is at least nearly always so. The formal dinner provides the backdrop and occasion for boisterous joking, sparkling repartee, and high flights of speculation.

But ritual and the structure which ritual can give to our lives have been largely lost. At some point we grew too sophisticated or at some point the rituals lost their vitality and became mere ornaments. As a concession to memory we may still keep their observance, but they are like old family retainers, kept on in vague remembrance of their past service. The original function of any ritual, however, is never merely ornamental but always highly pragmatic. If we can replace the ritual with another structure that performs the same function adequately, then its loss may be cause for nostalgia, but no more. But when we have nothing to take the place of a ritual that is now gone and that fulfilled a basic need, then we have suffered a serious privation.

The Moratorium vs.
the Rite of Passage

There is a particular type of ritual that has always been connected with the establishment of identity. The initiation rite or rite of passage is designed to confirm the adolescent in an adult identity, and more often than not, in a particular sex identity. The practical function of these rituals is to alleviate adolescent confusion while channeling adolescent energies and heading off adolescent rebellion. They assure among other things that the period of life we tag "storm and stress" will pass with a minimum of injury to the body politic. Rites of passage are generally associated with primitive societies, but in our own society, prior to the Industrial Revolution, there were institutions that served as extended initiations into adult life. Apprenticeship or simply working the farm served this purpose. In England there was the public school, which was only secondarily an educational institution. Its primary purpose was to provide a rite of passage to the ruling class. The hazings, the canings, the sports, and the traditions were meant to breed an adult with the character needed to rule an expanding empire or simply to live the life of a gentleman.

But technological societies seem to have grown too complex for any one ceremony or any one institution to provide a passage to adulthood. In the United States and in much of the industrial West, the moratorium replaced the rite of passage as the vehicle for achieving a meaningful integration of experience. Given enough time a young man or woman could work out an adult identity equal to the demands of a complex society. The system lacked the security and brevity of the primitive initiation. It dragged out the period of adolescence for years but promised a richer adulthood for it. Eventually, in the United States at least, the adolescent years took on a status of their own. Not just a transition from child to adult, but "the best years of our lives." Adolescents came to form a society unto themselves with their own customs, language, and dress.

It became an envied society. Young people showed less and less desire to leave it; adults betrayed a growing wish to return to it. Western societies had created a distinctive mode of identity formation which served a similar function to the rite of passage but was quite different from it.

Before considering what has happened to this moratorium, and whether it still fulfills its function, let us look at the advantages and disadvantages of a moratorium as compared to a tribal rite of passage. It's worth noting first off that the communal experience that primitives enjoy provides a strong sense of solidarity and belongingness—a group identity; for another thing there is little of the anxiety and confusion of our Western identity crisis. There simply is not enough psychological space or time for an identity crisis to occur. The young tribesman is not faced with a plethora of roles from which to choose. He does not spend years ruminating over questions like Who am I? Where do I fit in? What shall I do? Once he has met the test of initiation his identity is no longer in question. Rather it is affirmed by all.

One drawback of this process is that the sudden passage into adult society leaves little time for inwardness or self-definition. To the Western mind the identity of the tribesman seems to lack the complexity and subtlety that comes from an extended moratorium. By contrast, the Western brand of adolescence, when at its best, allowed one to find a unique identity apart from the crowd, to define oneself against a society that had a distinct identity of its own. The process was not without anxiety but the outcome was worth it. When successfully executed, this leisure-class brand of adolescence—for it assumes a society that has risen well above the struggle for survival—leads to a certain richness and complexity, to autonomy and individuality. The beauty of the moratorium was that it allowed for identity confusion. A certain amount of confusion would leave one open to change and help one to avoid a premature foreclosure of the self's possibilities. One needs a sense of sameness, but for the sake of growth and creativity one must be open to redefinitions of the self.

Societies and individuals can benefit immeasurably from this prolonged period of tentativeness, but some individuals pay a heavy price for their moratorium. Their adolescent lives are shrouded with a pervasive sense of anxiety, uncertainty, even dread. For them the identity crisis becomes a breeding ground for neurosis and psychosis. Hamlet is the symbol of the tragedy which can attend unrelieved self-analysis: the search for self can lead to admirable character traits but also to madness. The rite of passage—the primitive counterpart to the identity crisis—can also be fraught with anxiety, but the passage and the anxiety are of short duration, and on the other side are the waiting arms of the community. The absence of protracted identity confusion keeps the primitive relatively neurosis-free. However, where there is no moratorium there is no chance to develop those speculative and inventive skills upon which advanced societies are built.

The State of Our Culture

So take your choice: communal solidarity or creative crisis. Unfortunately, we seem to have arrived at some in-between stage where we get neither the advantages of the one nor the benefits of the other. We live in a transitional society that seems to allow for neither noble savages nor aristocratic adolescents. We get the anxiety without the autonomy, the confusion without the creativeness, the chaos without the character—in short, we get the crisis of identity without achieving identity. By the mid-sixties our Western brand of adolescence was producing a mass of alienated youth who had come to feel that as individuals they were neither master of their fate nor captain of their soul, but at the mercy of the winds and seas of a technocratic society. Individualism wasn't working for them and neither was the identity crisis. Many youth thought they had an answer. The antidote to identity confusion, they felt, was to emulate the primitives. And so the youth culture set its sights on simplicity, community, and the return to nature.

The beginnings were auspicious: flower children in the West and Woodstock in the East. The global village, it seemed, was at hand. But it was all too soon and too easy and too soon gone. Dissension, drugs, and distrust began to split the tribes apart. One commune after another failed, and with the passage of events, the Woodstock occurrence began to take on the quality of a mythic happening occurring in the dawn of time sometime before the Fall, but still within the memory of the tribal elders.

The many failures in communal living are an indication that individualism is still deeply ingrained in the American spirit. It is the spirit of Thoreau rather than the spirit of the Kibbutz that prompts many of the young to head for the communal woods, even when they adopt the organization of the latter. But a more underlying malady is the complete disorientation produced by cultural transition. The problem, as Peter Marin put it, is that:

> The dissolution of culture both releases and betrays us. It gives us the space to create new styles, new gods and connections but it denies us the strengths and talents to do it; for these are learned in relationships and community, and the dissolution of culture deprives us of them.[2]

The young then are doubly damned. They face their personal crisis of adolescence at the same time the entire culture is undergoing a crisis of identity. The old culture is in eclipse and the new culture is only half formed. The type of adolescence Friedenberg eulogized assumed a society with a strong identity of its own—something solid against which you could test yourself. We don't have this anymore; neither do we have a solid communal life within the counterculture. The young are caught in the "dissolution of culture" which Marin so eloquently describes, and they are not faring well. What gains they have made in other areas of their life tend to be offset by this double identity crisis. Living simultaneously in two contrasted cultures is not conducive to a secure identity, especially when there is nothing definitive about either one. The traditional culture with all its faults had some internal consistency. Occasionally it was capable of producing "men for all seasons" who, though they might stand in opposition to it, at least had some ground to stand on. But now the ground has become shaky and the consistency is gone. It's not a matter of a monolithic society being replaced by a pluralistic one, because all traditions have been leveled down to the lowest common denominator (usually money). Better perhaps to say that the ground upon which we stand has become mushy. In such a context the psychosocial moratorium leads not to autonomy and self-awareness but to alienation and confusion.

It's small wonder then that young people like to band together in groups large and small and no wonder that Woodstock became their symbol. Perhaps, as Paul Goodman contends, the young are grouping together at the price of character and personality, but perhaps there was never much of those traits to go around, and even less today, and at least the new youth are opting for solidarity, which is better than nothing—better, they feel, than the complete alienation that might otherwise be their lot. Unfortunately, the communal solidarity they seek is as elusive as the path back to inner-directed individualism. Possibly, when and if the transition to a neo-tribal society is complete, we won't have these problems. Possibly we will be as content as precolonial pygmies. That, for a number of reasons, does not seem a likely prospect. The transition will probably never be complete. Neither does it seem likely that the age of Holden Caulfield and Huck Finn is about to stage a revival.

There has been a tendency in recent years to make extravagant claims about the state of our culture. To listen to Charles Reich, Marshall McLuhan, and Theodore Roszak, one would think we had already crossed over to the Elysian Fields. This tendency toward hyperbole is forgivable in those who first propose the new paradigms. It is necessary to overstate the case if it is to get any sort of hearing. But ten years later, it is time to analyze the state of our culture with more precision. The truth is that the young are neither in a print-oriented society, nor a neo-tribal one, but suspended between two identities, one "civilized," the other "neo-primitive." They may have some of the earmarks of a tribal culture but certain crucial elements are missing: the bond of solidarity, the rite of passage, the sense of ascribed identity. As I indicated before, the tribal analogy is not a very good one. Yet the rational, individualized print culture is on the wane.

A better analogy for locating the position of our culture can be found in the Old Testament story of the exodus from Egypt. After crossing the Red Sea, the Israelites did not enter immediately into the land of milk and honey. They landed, instead, in the desert. If Biblical time can be taken literally in this instance, they were forty years wandering in a wasteland, forty years marred by hardship, dissension, and idolatry. By the time Canaan was reached most of the original emigrees were dead. I tend to think that for those involved in cultural change, now is the time of wandering in the desert. If a Red Sea of sorts has been crossed, Canaan is still far in the distance. But for an increasing number of Americans, most of them young, there may be no going back to Egypt. This is, of course, the argument of Charles Reich and Marshall McLuhan: there has been a change in consciousness, a change in the way the world is perceived. Reich can be criticized for naiveté, for oversimplification, for wearing rose-colored specs, but his contention about consciousness change should not be lightly dismissed.

I wouldn't argue with Reich on the point of consciousness change, only with the extent of it and with his implication that the young are home free when, in fact, they are in various states of confusion. The confusion runs deepest for those who have precipitously plunged themselves into the new culture without fully understanding where they are going or where they come from. They have cut themselves off from one society and have immersed themselves in another which is only half-formed and in which only the strong can as yet find sustenance. The stronger ones are usually those who have thought carefully and deeply about the steps they have taken into the counterculture. But prepared or not, the pioneers of the new culture are like canaries in a coal mine set free only to find which tunnels are safe, which poisonous—they are being sacrificed to those who will follow. The drug culture is replete with examples of those who came back from their trips to guide others—and those who never came back. The activist ranks are filled with those who never imagined the real terror of confrontation with the police until it happened to them. Perhaps most disillusioning of all for the culture pioneer is the discovery that, cultures aside, there is such a thing as the human condition, and it cannot be escaped by switching societies. These people have chosen to be or have been forced to be at the cutting edge of cultural change. It is not surprising that they often bleed for it.

For others the counterculture pose is merely a veneer covering the same violence, exploitation, and commercialism that plague the old culture. They maintain the vices with none of the amenities and comfortable compromises that make establishment life at least livable and without which life approaches savagery.

On another level are those—perhaps the majority of young people—who sit on the establishment shore with their feet dipped in the counterculture currents. They would like to plunge in but for one reason or another hold back.

To see in this motley crew the hope of the West requires either a high degree of optimism or a lack of acquaintance with non-Ivy League youth. They are not the millennium. Possibly within their confused culture they carry the seeds of love and unity which our society aches for, but to sit back and wait for Con III youth to bring about a new order of serenity is as much a disservice to them as it is to everyone else. We do not need any more panegyrics to Consciousness III, but we can't refuse to admit the reality of significant cultural changes. We must be aware that we are determined to some extent by the media around us, but we must not expect those media to automatically create a new level of tranquility. What we do need is a realization that we live in a state of ambiguity, and will continue to do so for some time. Ambiguity is not necessarily a disaster. It is a normal state of affairs for most human beings. Although for many it is a source of great anxiety, others seem to profit from it. Instead of resorting to repression, the healthy individual will try to find a synthesis of the polarities and contradictions in his life. For instance, when Erikson talks about resolving identity he does not suggest that one pole be rejected and the other embraced, but that a ratio be obtained in which both elements, identity and identity confusion, are retained.

The Need for Synthesis

At the present time there is an urgent need to find a synthesis between the dichotomies of tribal and Western. The rapid transition—possibly dissolution—of our Western culture generates more crisis than identity and makes of adolescence a vast gray area with no boundaries nor guidelines. One consequence is that the adolescent moratorium no longer works very well—doesn't fulfill the function it was meant to. I am not suggesting an abandonment of the Western tradition, since that would mean abandoning the flexibility needed to cope with a changing future. Neither am I suggesting that we get rid of the moratorium period. But there is an important lesson to be learned from the tribes which, properly applied to our culture, could lift the fog that hangs over the adolescent years. We have to learn or relearn the importance of ritual. In particular we need to seek a Western equivalent of the primitive rite of passage which could provide the solidarity of the tribe and still avoid the shortcomings of synthetic or ascribed identity. Our society has many minor rites of passage, none of which really works because none provides that integration into the community that the primitive passage does. As it stands now, no one really knows what the criterion for adulthood is in this country. Is it the driver's license? The high school diploma? The vote? The army? Marriage? Child rearing? The achievement of economic independence? Even after passing all these plateaus there are often nagging doubts about one's identity. Killing a lion with a spear (one form of primitive initiation) at least has the advantage of being clear-cut. When it's over, it's over. An initiation rite that leads somewhere is a better tool for identity formation than a prolonged and confused moratorium that leads nowhere.

Rituals of Rebirth

The fact that youngsters usually invent their own rites of passage attests to a proposition mentioned earlier: these rituals fulfill a pragmatic need. The fact that for boys these spontaneous rituals have to do with "proving you're a man" points to what one of those needs is. The anthropological studies of Whiting, Kluckhohn, and Anthony[3] suggest that male initiation rites at puberty are most likely to be found in societies in which boys are particularly dependent on their mothers and hostile toward their fathers. Seen in this light the puberty rite for boys is a way of finally cutting the apron strings, of asserting male identity while at the same time heading off filial rebellion. Among the Kwoma, a tribe living in the interior of New Guinea, initiation rites for boys consist of severe hazings and beatings, painful genital operations, exposure to the elements, and lengthy seclusion from all women. That this same society allows the infant boy to sleep cuddled by night in his mother's arms and seated all day in her lap for the first three years of his life; that during this period the mother refrains from intercourse with the father, who sleeps apart on a slab of bark; that the boy child's every wish is indulged—all this seems highly incongruous with the harsh initiation rites unless one is familiar with the Whiting thesis. In our society, when we speak of the decline of the father's authority, we speak about it in tones which imply that the father's authority over his children is a natural state of affairs. Quite the contrary is true in many primitive societies, where the father leaves both the nurturing and the disciplining up to the mother. He either has no right to exercise authority over his son or no wish to. All this lack of male authority ends with a vengeance at puberty. The pain of initiation is the pain of birth. It is only by being born again into a man's world that the youngster can break with the long years of mother dependency. The initiators are the male mothers. The initiation rite is a passage through the womb to a new birth. Among some tribes in New Guinea, initiation calls for the boy to crawl into the mouth of a newly slain crocodile (vagina dentatis again) and out the other side. As part of his initiation the Yurok Indian goes into the sweat house until his body is supple enough to squeeze through a small hole in the wall. He is born again to a new male identity.

Delinquency and Identity

What happens if there is no rebirth, no initiation, no affirmation of the boy's male identity? In our society—a society with no definitive rites of passage—those families that conform most closely to the Kwoma method of child rearing; i.e., exclusive mother-child relationships and lack of paternal authority, are the families that most consistently produce delinquents. That such family patterns cry out for a formal role ratification is manifested in the delinquent's proclivity for joining tribelike gangs and undergoing harsh initiation rites, all in the service of proving his manhood. Much of the trouble that these youth get into serves the same function as primitive rituals. To compensate for the dominant role of the mother in his childhood, the boy needs a dramatic event or series of them to establish male identity. There are a number of interesting parallels to the tribal state. As in the primitive initiation, the delinquent protest often takes the form of a compulsive rejection of anything feminine. Girls, if they are given any status at all in the gang, are kept in a subordinate position. As with primitives, there is a cultivation of scars obtained in fights or tattoos that are self-inflicted. And, as with the primitive, some ordeal must be undergone; often it is to participate in a dangerous and illegal act. Bravery and nonchalance in the face of danger are, as with the primitive, highly respected.

Delinquency is one way to prove your masculinity when society provides no other means. The gang also provides the sense of belongingness and security that society does not. To the delinquent it is his alma mater and his identity. The pragmatism of the tribes is to co-opt this spontaneous urge to prove masculinity. The initiation rite heads off open revolt against society while at the same time allowing the youth to assert his male identity. It is a conspiracy with the father figures rather than against them.

That this pragmatism can be adapted to American youth is evident in the recent success of the Outward Bound program in rehabilitating delinquents. Outward Bound provides an experience that is similar in some crucial ways to the rite of passage. The school was founded in Aberdovy, Wales, in 1941 for the training of Merchant Seamen during the battle of the Atlantic. Its purpose was to expose young men to a program of severe physical challenge involving tests of stamina and the threat of danger. While encouraging competition against oneself, the program fostered cooperation within the group. Obstacles were devised that could only be overcome by combined effort. The idea spread. At present there are over twenty Outward Bound schools throughout the world, including three in the United States located in Colorado, Maine, and Minnesota:

> The Colorado Outward Bound School is located on the western slopes of the Rocky Mountains at an altitude of 8,800 feet. The course involves mountain walking, high altitude camping, rock climbing, and rappelling. Each patrol climbs at least one of the 14,000 foot peaks in the area. As a climax, unsupervised groups of three or four boys cover 60 to 90 miles of unfamiliar terrain in three days.

> The Minnesota Outward Bound is located in the Superior National Forest near Ely, Minnesota, on the edge of the Superior-Quetico Wilderness. Participants are trained at the main camp for twelve days and then leave on a two-week, two hundred mile canoe expedition. Selected readings, films, and discussions related to the students' experiences are presented upon return from the expedition.

> Hurricane Island Outward Bound School is located ten

miles off the coast of Maine at the entrance of Penobscot Bay. More than half the program involves training in seamanship and navigation. The course climax is a five-day cruise in 30 foot whaleboats. Each group of 12 boys must live together in these small open boats without an instructor.[4]

In 1968 two Boston College Professors, Francis Kelly and Daniel Baer, studied a group of delinquents who were sent through these Outward Bound programs in lieu of reform school, and compared them with a matched group who went through the traditional rehabilitation route; i.e., reform school. They found that the return-to-crime rate was much lower for the first group than for the second, and concluded that a program of severe physical challenge could be an effective preventive as well as treatment for juvenile offenders. As Kelly sees it, the crucial difference lies in the fact that Outward Bound provides what society does not: a chance to prove one's masculine identity and have it ratified by others. For many youngsters delinquency is a matter of one or two years, a stage they pass through on the way to proving their identities, unless they are unlucky enough to get thrown into an institution where the chances are they will come out as hardened criminals. The lesson of the Outward Bound study is clear: if society would only confirm a boy in his masculinity instead of waiting to confirm him in his delinquency it would have less delinquency to contend with.[5]

Where's Poppa?

If we take matriarchy to mean the exercise of political power by women, then there have been few if any matriarchal societies in world history. If we use the word in another sense to indicate a society where the life of the family is dominated by the mother and where the father has abdicated his paternal authority, then there are many matriarchates. In this latter sense our own society is becoming increasingly matriarchal. And this poses a problem. If matriarchal societies require harsh rites of passage for the purpose of establishing male identification, and our own society though increasingly matriarchal has no definitive rites at all—let alone harsh ones—then we can anticipate more confusion over sexual identity and more delinquency.

It is not only our delinquents who are in need of a rite of ratification, but all our youth. The entire society has for some time now been shifting toward a pattern of exclusive mother-child relationships and relinquishment of the father's authority. We are still a long way from the indulgence of the Kwoma, but not so far removed as we were twenty or thirty years ago. The lack of discipline exercised by American fathers has been commented on at length by many sociologists. Less obvious is the way in which technology perpetuates the child's dependence on his mother or a mother substitute. We are a child-centered culture, not because we enjoy our children more than other peoples do theirs, but because we gear so many of our activities and inventions to their amusement and benefit. Where mother leaves off, the TV, the stereo, and the refrigerator take over. These electronic mothers nurse, pacify, and rock to sleep. Like mother's love, their ministrations do not have to be deserved. They provide unconditional succor, and like the indulgent mothers of the Kwoma tribe they encourage passivity. After childhood comes a further postponement of responsibilities. Mother moratorium provides the equivalent of an undemanding environment. By now the young man or woman is quite unwilling to leave the narcissistic environment which has been provided for him or her. Luckily he or she lives in a society where middle-class children are no longer expected to be fully self-supporting upon leaving high school or college. Next they enter an economic system that, because it is actually a superpatriarchy, has the effect of breeding more dependency. In a superpatriarchy (the term was coined by the German sociologist Karl Bednarik), only a few men are allowed the exercise of real power or initiative. For the ordinary male it encourages a passive pattern of consumerism. The economy and the political system as well, offer little scope for the exercise of traditional masculine assertiveness. The net result is that most important decisions are out of the common man's hands, and more likely than not he retires to the sphere of recreation, play, and instant gratification that he knew as a child.[6]

This is not meant to be an outcry on my part against an effete society or a call for the restoration of patriarchy. Compared to most primitive societies, the United States has until recently been unusually severe in its child raising practices. It is not gratification as such that is in question but some of the forms it has been taking, and the lack of any compensating mechanism at a later stage. It is better for children that the sins against them be committed in the name of indulgence rather than deprivation, but continued into late adolescence these matriarchal practices can prevent the full development of identity.

Sports as a Rite of Passage

We have seen how tribal societies attempt to counterbalance the lack of fatherly discipline by the imposition of male organized initiation rites. In the United States, an unconscious recognition of this need for ballast is manifested in the male's concern for organized sports. For the adolescent male the playing field or basketball court is still a more crucial arena for testing identity and masculinity than any other that society has devised. The sense of solidarity that team sports can engender is also without parallel. Grown men are just as serious about sports. Most adult males show greater concern for the struggles of a Sunday afternoon than for the power contests of local and national politics, although it is the latter that will most decisively influence their individual destinies. The spectacle of young men testing their physical powers in ritual combat taps a deep well of emotion. Perhaps it is regret for an identity that could be won once and for all in a decisive and clear-cut way. Most revealing of all is the way in which American fathers try to initiate their sons into organized sports of the roughest kind, and this at an age when their physical and emotional growth would be better served by those informal games youngsters create when left to their own devices. There are a variety of reasons why fathers may encourage their sons in such endeavors, and some of these motivations may be innocent of the psychological shadings we would like to find in them, but it is finally difficult to escape the impression that the father is, among other things, belatedly trying to make up for an earlier noninvolvement with his son. And if we also discern in these activities a semiformal attempt to wean the boy from mother dependency and turn him toward the "man's world" we shall probably be close to the mark. In thus encouraging his tender-aged son to join the world of organized sport, the American father is acting out of a primitive urge. It is probably a sound instinct, although it is marred by what Piaget calls "The American Problem"—the headlong acceleration of children into activities for which they are not ready. But, although we do need some form of passage for our adolescents, it is naive to suppose that identity can be achieved in a single football game or a series of them. Our society has grown far too complicated for that.

The Moral Equivalent of War

We are so far removed from our preindustrial roots that it is almost impossible to conceive of a rite of passage that would work in America. Two institutions that have partially served this purpose come to mind, although one is disbanded, and the other has serious drawbacks. The first is the Civilian Conservation Corps, which during the Depression served to channel the frustrations of unemployed young men into constructive works. The physical accomplishments of the C.C.C. were impressive, and its success in imbuing its members with a sense of purpose was no less admirable. The war, of course, brought a hasty end to the C.C.C. The other institution that promises to confer adulthood is the army, and very often it seems to make good on that promise. The number of men who claim that their maturity was forged in the army are myriad and probably exceed the numbers of those who considered it a waste of time. The boast of the Marines that they "make men" is not to be taken lightly. The Marines do sometimes seem to make men—at any rate better men than we might have got otherwise. Probably everyone knows of some hopeless case who was transformed by a four-year hitch in the service. The objection to the Marines is that they can as easily breed monsters as men, and even the "men" they develop often seem lacking in those qualities a full maturity would call for. I am not by any means suggesting the Armed Forces as an initiation institution—only drawing attention to the fact that such organizations are capable of transforming, whether for better or worse, the lives of the young.

William James once suggested that we needed to develop a "moral equivalent of war." He meant, I believe, not an institution that would cater to men's violent instincts while avoiding actual bloodshed, but a cause or commitment that would summon the same energies, passions, and loyalties as does war. These energies are at their peak in adolescence, and it is a pity that when the young are looking for dragons to slay we hand them computer cards to fill out. They would like to feel that they are useful to society and that their existence does make an immediate difference. They would like to be involved in a great enterprise, but we tell them that their importance lies in getting good grades and otherwise keeping out of the way. If we are to consider developing a moral equivalent for war or for the initiation rite, it must be an institution that is capable of marshaling the fidelity young people are waiting to commit. But to merit that fidelity it must take as much as it gives. There is much important work to be done in this country, some of it a matter of life and death, that our youth could help get done: there are deserts to be made green, rivers and lakes to be purified, cities to be made livable, children to be taught, racial barriers to be overcome, and political corruption to be fought. But as long as we conceive that there is only one important task for adolescence—to finish high school, then finish college—

these problems will get worse and the young will continue to feel useless.

Continuities and Discontinuities

Here we touch upon a crucial difference between our society and most others. Americans are not disposed to allow youthful participation in important enterprises. In America there are sharp discontinuities between the role of child and adult, and little opportunity for the child or adolescent to learn those adult roles. The child is expected to be submissive, the adult dominant; the child has no responsibilities, the adult must shoulder many; the child is expected to be innocent, the adult should be sexually experienced. Many societies do not allow these discrepancies to develop in the first place. For example, in traditional Chinese communities there is no attempt to separate children from the adult world. Children accompany fathers to business meetings and temple fairs; they are witness to family fights and family failures. Not much is hidden and not much distinction is made between child and adult. Chinese youth enter adulthood not as novices but as old hands wise in the ways of grown-ups. As a consequence there is little confusion about what one is supposed to do, and little inclination to rebel against the adult world, since one has always been an integral part of that world. It is not surprising, then, that the phenomenon of adolescent delinquency is largely unknown in the Chinese community. (The Chinese in Hawaii are a good example.) Where boys participate in the activities of men from the start, there is no need for them to prove their manhood later on in antisocial ways.[7]

Other societies recognize that where discontinuities exist between adult and child status, they have to be compensated for at some stage. Societies like the Kwoma which provide an easy childhood compensate with harsh initiation rites. The more the child is indulged in infancy, the more he will be challenged in adolescence. The ritual of initiation allows the adult member of the tribe to play the role of adversary, first testing the initiate, then embracing him as a comrade.

In America the discontinuities are allowed to stand: youth are left to grow to adulthood by their own devices, there is no sense of participation in meaningful activities, and there is no attempt to marshal adolescent energies by way of an initiation. Whatever adversary role we may have played in the past has been yielded up in the name of gratification. This is too bad, because an adversary culture—one which sets and defines limits and challenges—is better for the young than a spongy culture that soaks up youthful energies and enthusiasms and leaves no channel down which they might flow. If we are not prepared to provide rites of passage that would supply the opportunity for boys to cope with severe physical and mental challenge or in some way prove their courage and resourcefulness, then we should stop demanding the type of masculine identity that has to be proved. This would be a step in the direction advocated by Norman Brown—abandonment of the performance principle—but it would not really be such a drastic step. After all, the maintenance of our society and economy no longer depends on the physical strength and physical courage that the struggle with nature demands of preindustrial people. But this we seem unwilling to do. We continue to peddle a model of masculinity that is more suited to frontier survival than to the realities of twentieth-century life in America.

The only other solution to our adolescent malaise lies in the direction taken by communities like the Chinese in Hawaii (a direction long advocated by Paul Goodman and more recently by Ivan Illich in *Deschooling Society*). Such communities can be characterized as "participation societies": they gradually, almost imperceptibly, initiate the child into the adult world so that the passage is accomplished with a minimum of discontinuity. The drawback here is the absence of a moratorium and the flexibility which an exploratory period can provide. A further disadvantage is the relative absence of that kind of idealism that can result when, sometime in his teens, a protected child collides with an imperfect world. The adolescent who is abruptly awakened to the ills of his society is going to be more reform-minded than one who through long experience has been habituated to compromise with imperfection. The naive idealism of the former, while it may prove irritating to the world of affairs, becomes, when tutored, the source of renewal for that society. The protected child may be the one who later on provides the editing that society always stands in need of.

Lessons to Be Learned

As McLuhan and Brown and a number of others suggest, we have much to learn from primitive and communal societies; but instead of waiting for a Brave New World filled with polymorphous villagers, instead of losing ourselves in cosmic contemplation while doing nothing, we ought to specify exactly what other societies have to offer and what price we must pay for applying their experience to our own. We have to learn to break down the barriers between child and adult without suffocating youthful idealism; we ought to develop rituals of passage that confirm identity without closing it up. To this end it would be to our advantage to look to primitive cultures, to ethnic communities, to the Kibbutz, and to communist societies to see what we can learn about community and identity. But if, in our haste to transform ourselves, we were to put our own cultural heritage behind us, it would indeed be folly. If we want a unique and creative identity we had better not neglect the Western tradition. The type of autonomous and self-achieved identity which that tradition is capable of fostering is as vital and currently lacking as the sense of community. Unfortunately the counterculture sometimes seems to be quite willing to abandon that tradition in favor of Eastern thought and tribal mores. There often seem to be a dangerous lack of reason and a primitive use of language within the youth culture, as well as a disconcerting tendency to want to merge their undeveloped egos with some mystical cosmic consciousness unrelated to real relationships with real people. It would be a tragedy to go in that direction. It would mean reversing an historical process out of which has flowered some of mankind's greatest achievements.

The adolescent moratorium is one of the first signs of an advancing civilization. It indicates that a society has moved beyond the struggle for survival and is beginning to reflect upon itself. It signals the advent of a degree of diversity and variety that is unavailable elsewhere. For a long time this adolescent moratorium was the province of the wealthy and the privileged. The sons of the aristocrats were afforded the opportunity to study, to dream, to aspire, to travel, to explore, to try on roles without commitment—in short, to find their possibilities. Gradually these privileged years became the birthright of ever-increasing numbers of youth. The opportunity to test one's soul, to define and delineate the subtleties that make men more human and less brutish became available to more and more adolescents. The West is fortunate in being able to provide these years to so many. The opportunity that is provided is not just a chance to develop charm and subtlety and fine mental distinctions. We could probably do without those qualities although it would be more than a pity to lose them. But that tradition holds something more substantial: the opportunity to choose and create a unique identity. It would be tragic if, having reached the goal of providing this chance to so many, we now retreated from it.

Part four
Identity and Love

8

Some Love Proposals

*I*N Part Four I want to call attention to certain consequences that may result if the elements of continuity,
purposefulness, and self-definition are diluted by liquid identity.

One consequence that is already apparent is widespread
confusion over sex roles and sex identity. The blurring of
gender contains both a promise and a threat: a promise of a
wider, more human identity for both men and women; a threat
that fluid sex roles will dissolve personal responsibility in an
acid bath of noncommitment. Paradoxically, the path to a
more relaxed sex identity lies by way of a confident and persistent sense of self, not by way of fluidity. Just as a secure identity
allows us to take real risks in intimacy, it allows us also to take
liberties with our masculinity and femininity. Without that
base, however, sex role liberation gets mingled with slipperi-
ness and evasion of responsibility and becomes part of the
general slime that laps against the piers of committed relationships.

Another consequence of the transformations in identity is
the apparent death of romance. From time to time there are
reports of romantic souls being sighted in remote corners of

the countryside, but for the most part the breed has been killed off—victims of mobility, restlessness, instant intimacy, and temporary love systems. If the decline of romance were a prelude to the general agape which the transformationists promise will replace it, then we could chalk up its loss to progress. What the decline seems to herald, unfortunately, is the enfeeblement of intimacy, and a further collapse of commitment. Disappointed by romance, we leap, not to agape, but to the opposite extreme—Don Juanism. Don Juan, the completely uncommitted lover, becomes emblematic of the current intimacy.

The legendary Don Juan was disdainful of any limitations over his freedom. But it is often the case that those who experiment with the new intimacy do so, not out of any love of freedom, but because they have no idea who they are or what they want. Their identity is anchored not in choices but in "spontaneous" feelings. Love is conceived as one of these spontaneous feelings, and it is, therefore, considered subject to spontaneous change. A final consequence of the identity transformation, then, is a paralysis of mature love and the substitution of a spurious love—what Rollo May calls "love without will." Love without will can only be a transitory love; love that endures has to be made of sterner stuff than feelings alone.

In the following chapters the relationships and interrelationships connecting identity, sexuality, romance, and love will be explored. Hopefully, these pages can shed some light on what has become the murkiest corner of our lives.

9

Redefining Sex Roles

*T*HE new philosophies of identity imply radical changes in sex roles, in patterns of intimacy, and in matters of love. For instance, the current rethinking of sex roles is not only the result of political and social reforms initiated by the Women's Movement, it is also an expression of a new and more fluid understanding of the self. In short, the loosening of identity advocated by the Human Potential people leads inevitably to a loosening of sex roles. It is important, however, to make a distinction: the Human Potential Movement is not the Women's Movement. One obvious difference is that the Women's Movement is, in general, concerned with the liberation of women, while the Human Potential Movement expresses concern over a more general human liberation. Another major difference is that the Women's Movement considers the heightening of female consciousness to be a necessary step toward liberation from old patterns of exploitation; the Human Potential Movement, having no grievances to redress, is more inclined to believe we can skip this "detour," forget maleness and femaleness, and just get on with the task of being persons. Finally, while the Human Potential Movement is concerned with purely psychological states, the

Women's Movement is concerned as well with political and social change. The observations to follow are directed to the Human Potential philosophy, not to the Women's Movement.

Changing Sex Roles

A major focus of the recent debate over sex roles is to what extent they are biologically based and to what extent they are learned. And this is really a question of whether and to what extent they can be changed. Without getting into the research used to buttress one side of the debate or the other it is possible to make two observations. One: there is a shift away from biologic instincts and toward learning as one traces up the phyletic scale. Lower animals are almost completely controlled by instincts, while human beings are low on instincts and high on learning. In comparison to all other creatures, the human being is a cultural rather than a biological animal—and becomes more so with each passing decade. Two: whatever biological basis there may be for sex roles, there is enough research and enough common sense observation to indicate that sex roles can be far more flexible than they are now. Humankind has proved to be sufficiently adaptable in so many areas that it is difficult to find fault with the contention that sex roles can be widely restructured.

The question is, To what purposes are sex roles to be shifted? The Human Potential answer is that liberation from traditional patterns will open up new areas of awareness to men and women alike, will allow them to realize new capacities, and will make possible more relationships and more meaningful ones. It is an invitation to leave our polar habitats and move to the temperate zones where the sexes mix more easily and where life is warmer, more livable. Why should men and women live in emotional igloos when they could be basking in the warm sun of liberation?

There are some problems with this view, however. For example, there are plenty of bisexual and homosexual men who have no trouble in expressing the feminine side of their nature

(I am not talking about the effeminate stereotype); and there are plenty of bisexual and homosexual women who have no difficulty in expressing the masculine component in their lives, yet there is no evidence that bisexuals or homosexuals have a corner on the deep and meaningful relationship market—or on self-actualization. I am not suggesting that homosexual relationships are any worse than heterosexual ones, only that they don't appear to be any better—and logically they should be, for these are men and women who have liberated themselves rather completely from the old stereotypes. Obviously something more than sex-role liberation is needed to assure self-actualization and meaningful relationships (I anticipate that there may be objections to this example, but the objections can only come from those who believe that homosexuals and bisexuals form a separate or even deviant class of people who lack the capacity for normal human relationships—a view that is completely unsupported).

The Male Myth: Escape

I am not suggesting that we remain stuck in old roles but I would suggest that life becomes meaningful mainly through transpersonal commitment, and where that is absent no amount of self-actualization or sex-role liberation is going to make life more meaningful. Self-actualization, as Frankl maintains, comes only as a by-product of commitment. But the current emphasis on the liberation of human potential is not at all conducive to commitment; in fact it leads right back to the pattern of noninvolvement that it is supposed to liberate us from. As a case in point, take the masculine image as it is popularly portrayed by the advertising and entertainment media. What is really wrong with these images? Is it simply that the men portrayed aren't allowed to express their expressive side—or is it something more? The mythic model that is presently held up to the male for imitation is a collage of the tough, cool, leave-it-all-down-in-the-guts, John Wayne, James Bond, Schlitz gusto, Marlboro Country type of man; or it is the image

of the sophisticated playboy who resists emotional involvement as effectively as his permanent-press clothes resist wrin-
kles. In place of the full life, expressive and involved, the
media substitute what might be called the "cool philosophy":
an attitude that devalues emotional expression and personal
involvement. The film world has been generous in providing
for our edification a succession of "cool heroes," from un-
flinching tough guys like Bogart and Cagney to the more sophisticated cool of Sean Connery, Clint Eastwood, or even
Peter Fonda's portrayal of Wyatt, the easy rider. James Bond
represents the cool hero to perfection. He is tough, self-reli-
ant, emotionally inexpressive, capable of sexual intimacy and
emotional detachment at one and the same time. True, movies
are changing with the times: it is no longer a Bond market. But
even films aimed at younger, hipper audiences still stick with
the cool formula. Take *Easy Rider* as an example. The character of Fonda-Wyatt, although an improvement over Bond, is
not that much different from the standard cowboy hero—
strong but silent—who has been a mainstay of the American
film. Fonda is as laconic as Gary Cooper ever was, and not
since William S. Hart has an actor so effectively concealed
emotion.

Magazine and television advertisements, by conveying a
similar cool message, help to keep the masculinity myth alive:
thus we have the "ale men," the "Marlboro men," and the
rather detached and aloof young males who drive the latest
sports car or model the unwrinkable and unspottable rain-
wear. Much of this is laughable—yet still we hesitate to laugh,
for there is something appealing here: the image of the capable but noninvolved man, free of problems, free of doubts,
free of human entanglements and human frailties. Burdened
as we are with multiple involvements and problems of relating
to parents, friends, wives, children, and associates, it is small
wonder that the image of the adventurous and unattached life
should seem so appealing. The promise of escape offered by
adopting such a role is indeed hard to resist. The popular
Playboy magazine does its part in sustaining the image: its

pages portray the ideal male as one who possesses the proper accessories to the good life. Pretty girls are an important accessory, but one should not get emotionally attached to them any more than he would to his collection of sweaters or his new stereo kit. A glance through the advertising copy will indicate that the proper attitude for the playboy to cultivate is one of studied unconcern.

Now what is the element in all this that men must be liberated from? Is it, as has been supposed, the prohibition on tenderness and emotional expression? This is the argument that is usually presented for abolishing male stereotypes. Men can never be free, it is said, as long as they labor to conform to these restrictive images. On another level, however, these stereotypes are not at all restrictive: while they may require a certain emotional restraint, they promise unlimited freedom. The major motif that runs through the advertising copy directed at men is escape: escape from responsibilities or limitations. The heroes of film and advertising seem to lead lives unburdened with responsibilities or commitments. It is this aspect, not their emotional control, that makes them so appealing. Yet it is this aspect of the masculine myth—the escapism—that most men successfully manage to resist. The promise of escape is a very appealing one; and resisting it is no easy accomplishment. Nevertheless, most men do lead responsible, committed lives. Perhaps it is their boyish wish for complete freedom that men have to keep down-in-the-guts. But instead of being given credit for their sense of responsibility, they are now censured for their lack of emotionality. Paradoxically, those who are willing to liberate men from the idea that they must be tough and aggressive are often blind to the fact that males must also be liberated from the illusion that they can have boundless freedom.

The essential male myth is not strength or self-control, and certainly not patriarchy. The essential myth is escape and irresponsibility. It is a myth that prevailed long before the advent of film or videotape. And it cannot be accounted for simply in terms of conformity to a cultural model.

Leslie Fiedler, in his brilliant book of criticism, *Love and Death in the American Novel,*[1] gives some substantial insights into the problem. To understand the central myth of our culture, he says, we must look to our literature. And to find the most deeply underlying image of ourselves in literature there is no better place to look than to the original Pathfinder and Indian fighter, hero of the Leatherstocking Tales, Natty Bumpo. As Fiedler sees him, the Deerslayer of Fenimore Cooper's prototypical novel is the patriarch of a long line of literary heroes that includes Seymour Glass and Gene Forrester as well as Ishmael and Huckleberry Finn. Cooper's protagonist is the embodiment of a mythic ideal, for he represents a world to which the American male secretly aspires: a world of nature; a world without women; a world of male camaraderie—even male love. According to Fiedler's analysis, our literature is a literature of escape: the typical hero of American fiction is a man on the run; forever running away from women and responsibilities, and back to nature and childhood, innocence and irresponsibility.

American men, Fiedler implies, are by and large Peter Pans who would rather not grow up, would rather not assume the responsibilities of marriage, sex, fatherhood, and society. But *Peter Pan* is too British and too obviously a child's story to serve as any model. It is the native legend of Rip Van Winkle that is the real archetype. The figure of Rip sums up and embodies the literature of escape: the story of a man, as Fiedler puts it,

> . . . who slips off with a dog and gun into the hills; who ends up bowling and drinking with a ghostly collection of the boys; and who wakes up to find, when he has slept off his superhuman drunk, that he has also slept away the life of the shrew who bullied him, as well as that of George III, who oppressed his country.[2]

Indeed the theme of "gone hunting" or "gone fishing" is forever being played out in the American imagination (consider Hemingway, or the really big fishing trips of Melville's novels) and in American life. The best places to go hunting or fishing are, of course, places where there are no females—

womanless, wilderness places. How appropriate that the gutsy beer drinkers of the Schlitz commercial should be met on board ship where a woman is traditionally considered bad luck. How fitting that the Marlboro men find their home on the range where women rarely venture. It seems that there is something in the heart of the American male that forever beckons him to "come to Marlboro Country" and all that it represents. That something, Fiedler suggests, is an underlying fear of women.

Sex Roles and Commitment

Still, why should there be this underlying fear of women? In positing such a fear we are still scratching at the surface of the problem. For a more penetrating analysis we must look again at the problem of time orientation, only this time from a different perspective. In his book *Sexual Suicide,*[3] George Gilder makes a useful time distinction between masculine and feminine sexuality. Women, says Gilder, are tied to a long-range, future-oriented cycle of sexuality necessary for the bearing and nurturing of children. The male pattern of sexuality, however, is episodic, present-oriented, in search of immediate gratification, unconcerned about long-term involvements—even frightened by them. While I cannot agree with many of the conclusions that Gilder draws from this initial assumption, the assumption itself has some merit. Such a distinction in time orientation does seem to exist. For example, in situations such as homosexuality, where no children are involved, it is still the case that lesbians exhibit more of a facility for stable long-term relationships than do male homosexuals. The reputed promiscuity of the latter can be attributed to the short-range male pattern multiplied by two. Whether the distinction is biologically based—as Gilder thinks—or whether it is culturally conditioned is secondary to the fact that civilized societies require the long-term orientation from a large number of their citizens, both male and female. It is the job of women, Gilder asserts, to convert men to their long-range pattern of sexuality. Whether or not they wish to, and whether or not it is truly their job, women have come to represent deferred gratification and submission to long-term involvements. Why the underlying fear of women? Because they represent commitment. The "natural" masculine propensity is to keep free of entangling alliances. So males are always retreating: like Ishmael, they retreat to the sea; or like Rip Van Winkle, they retreat to the woods; or they escape to the companionship of a woman who won't tie them down.

However, this pattern is eventually unsatisfying, since most human beings are intent on finding meaning in their lives. And meaning comes, not from short-term self-indulgence, but from durable commitment to others. Throughout history the majority of civilized males have found meaning as providers and protectors for their families. As work has become increasingly senseless, family and children have become increasingly more important. For the majority of males who are unable to achieve artistic, intellectual, or political satisfaction, their commitment to children is their link to society and the future. It is their assurance that they play a part in the historical process. It is the reason that so many blue-collar workers carry pictures of their children with them, and why the desks of so many businessmen and office workers are graced with family portraits. For most males it is the only answer to the question, What the hell am I doing here? Except for those lucky enough to be engaged in highly creative or professional work, most men find their work incredibly meaningless. The main thing their job gives to them is the wherewithal to play the role of provider and thus find meaning. Most males look to their breadwinning role to confirm their masculinity. If a man is poor or jobless and can't make the economic grade, he's forced to seek about for other ways to validate his masculinity. Too often his only recourse is to adopt the more blatant forms of machismo: boasting, brawling, and aimless procreation. In the ghetto we can see what happens to men who have been deprived of their masculine props and denied the means to make and keep long-range commitments to family and children. It is in the ghetto and particularly among single, unemployed males that we find the highest rates of violent crime, mental illness, alcoholism, drug addiction and suicide. And wherever else males are unable to play a constructive part in family or community they make their presence felt in socially destructive or self-destructive ways.

The solution to all this male irresponsibility would seem to be an effort to encourage and cultivate in males an orientation to the future, to children, to society; and to give men a sense that their economic sacrifices and struggles are not without meaning while we strive to find ways to make work itself more meaningful. Men need to feel that their identity as males does not depend on episodic proofs of manhood but on an ongoing involvement in the care and cultivation of society.

Instead, at a time of rapid change when individuals desperately need to find continuity in their lives, we find an ethic of present-orientation and noninvolvement being preached to men and women alike. The faults of the irresponsible and uncommitted male are held up as virtues to be emulated by all. What is happening is that the fluid-identity advocates have moved into the sex-role arena and are trying to capture center spotlight. With no real understanding of the identity problems involved in changing sex roles, with scant appreciation of the need for continuity and purpose, they cater instead to a burgeoning desire for escape and experimentation.

Carl Rogers' contribution to sexual liberation is *Becoming Partners: Marriage and Its Alternatives.*[4] The important thing in marriage, as Rogers sees it, is "my growth" and "your growth" and freedom from role restrictions and constraints of any kind. But once again Rogers is pushing the idea of personhood at the expense of any ties or commitments to past or future, friends or relatives, home or career. To one couple whose experimental marriage has become a prolonged flirtation with disaster, Rogers can only offer his usual nondirective enthusiasm when they proclaim: "We're selling our home . . . all our properties," "we're leaving our friends, our jobs, professional positions, we're leaving the country we were married in."[5] The

Rogerian solution to every problem is to keep growing. It doesn't seem to matter in which direction people move or grow, as long as there's motion. If you get into a tight situation you can either "process it," or if it proves to be too great an impediment to your growth, why just move on. But at all costs keep your options fluid. Rogers would have marriage and other relationships conducted along the lines of a scientific experiment. "Any modern industry," he observes, "is judged in part by the size of its investment in R and D—research and development."[6] Now, he suggests, is our chance to follow their example, and convert the field of personal relationships into a "vast laboratory."[7] According to Rogers, this experimental attitude will make it possible for the "person of tomorrow" to "establish closeness quickly" and to "leave these close relationships behind without excessive conflict or mourning."[8] Presumably the pioneering scientist does not waste much time in mourning experiments that didn't work out.

What the new breed of best-selling marriage counselors offer is what everyone has fantasized about: the security and reliability of a spouse along with the excitement of experimentation. Writing in the Rogerian vein, Nena and George O'-Neill[9] encourage an "open marriage" in which the partners will be free of circumscribed sex roles, social conventions, and —if they are really with it—of parenthood. Like Rogers, they trundle out all the currently fashionable talk about "openness," "spontaneity," "flexibility," and becoming "more fully human." John and Mimi Lobell[10] go them one step further in positively endorsing what used to be called "messing around," but which has now become a high art form by which people actualize themselves. The Lobells can mess around with other couples in all manner of permutations and combinations because they keep themselves fluid and loose: "I can see our lives. We are like two liquid films floating on an endless field reflecting all the rainbow . . . continuously, slowly shifting . . . free to slip apart and float off . . ."[11]

What the Lobells are really celebrating is not a relationship but a fiercely guarded avoidance of commitment. One of Rogers' disciples, Barry Stevens (a woman), is even more explicit about this new brand of love:

> I do not *want* anyone to love me exclusively. That pinches me. It binds me, demands that my love flow in one direction, when my *love* is free. When it is not free, it is not love to me. "You are *mine*," gives me the shudders. I wish to be free myself, and to let others be free of me.[12]

This has a high-sounding ring to it, but where does it lead? To find the answer I refer again to F. M. Esfandiary's manifesto *Up-Wingers.* Even the Lobells do not come up to the high standards of fluidity that Esfandiary demands of up-wingers. Here are some samples of his futuristic credo:

> Attempts are under way to modernize marriage—trial marriage serial-marriage group marriage open marriage celibate marriage . . .

> These timid gropings do not go to the roots of our family problems. . . . Marriage itself must go. . . .

> We must settle for nothing less than the total elimination of the family.

> Singling is an attempt to assert independence and achieve fluidity. A way of maximizing opportunities to maintain psychological sexual professional economic political freedoms . . . [Esfandiary does not employ commas. Presumably they interfere with fluidity.]

Esfandiary will admit communes into his scheme, but he considers modern communes to be too durable (anyone who is familiar with the literature on modern communes knows that the exact opposite is true). He wants a more fluid type of commune—a "mobilia":

> The mobilia is simply a stopover—any place the individual who wishes to be unalone may stop at to be with peers and with children.

This mobilia is to "replace homes families communes." As the name implies, it is no place to settle down:

—No one should stay at a mobilia longer than a few days a few weeks or at most a few months. *Six months ought to be the maximum.* Move on. Don't fester.[13]

This sounds not like the future but like hoofbeats out of the past. "Who was that masked man?" In the mobilia few will be able to answer, most having arrived just the previous night. Instead of *Up-Wingers* the book should have been titled *High Plains Drifter.* Unfortunately an increasing number of people are buying a diluted version of this credo. What they fail to see is that this fluidity does not lead to the bright place that these optimists envision, but to a much dimmer landscape. It leads back to the nomadic restlessness of the frontier cowboy—a theme which the ad industry had been playing variations on long before Esfandiary ever set pen to paper. If we want a perfect picture of individuals who keep their options open and who are ever ready to move on when involvement rears its ugly head, we have only to look at the creations of Hollywood and Madison Avenue. The *Playboy* males, the James Bond types, and the easy riders may not be "fully human," but they certainly don't fester from immobility. Whatever else these types may represent, and whatever product is being peddled, the basic idea that is being sold is the image of the man who won't let himself get tied down. The ubiquitous presence of these images makes it exceedingly difficult for any man to enter into relationships marked by commitment. Yet, most men do fight against these perversions of the masculine image. They realize, whether consciously or unconsciously, that these images symbolize not strength, but noninvolvement and noncommitment—and most men want more meaning in their lives than that.

But by confusing liberation with escapism, the Human Potential School is following a path that leads right back to that present-oriented, live-for-the-moment, love-'em-and-leave-'em male image. What Madison Avenue has always promised the male is escape, and now the advocates of open relationships have renewed that promise. Only now it's an escape into feelings which they offer—feelings without fidelity. In doing so, the proponents of fluid identity undermine the average male's attempt to make provision for those who rely on him. In addition to encouraging the male to lapse into the episodic pursuit of immediate gratification, they likewise persuade many women to adopt the primitive short-term horizon of masculinity: from bed to bed, from experience to experience, always on the move, and always shunning lasting responsibilities. It is a mistake to suppose that as women become oriented to the male style, men will now adopt a female pattern of nurturing children and caring for family. They never have—not without the incentive of feeling that they play an indispensable part in the future of family and society. Where the mother or the state has taken over the job of provision and protection, the men simply leave. If they are now told that deep meaning can be found apart from society, family, children, or the future, that it can instead be found in a continuous round of sensual experimentation—it is not difficult to guess in what direction they will head. And women along with them. Already certain patterns are emerging which indicate the direction in which the fluid philosophy is taking us. Art Buchwald said it humorously when he wrote of the day when a poll would show that 67 percent of all adults over thirty years of age "would rather have a good time than have children."[14] Psychologist Urie Bronfenbrenner put the matter more seriously in remarking that "the growing number of divorces is now accompanied by a new phenomenon: the unwillingness of either parent to take custody of the child."[15] Even more serious is the dramatic increase in violent crimes by women which occurred during 1074—an indication that women are being converted to the less responsible male pattern rather than the opposite.[16]

Sex Identity and Sex Roles

It has been the common judgment of psychologists, psychiatrists, and sociologists for the last six decades that boys have a more difficult time in establishing sexual identity than do girls; that they are more anxious regarding sex identity than females; and that many more males than females fail completely in achieving same sex identification. There are, as one example of the last, many more male to female transexuals than female to male. Biology may be at the root of this. Or it may simply derive from the fact that a boy initially identifies with his mother (because he spends the most time with her) and then has to switch his identification to the father and the male role.

For both boys and girls, the earliest and most formative experiences are with their mother. The father, if he has not abandoned the home completely, usually spends a good part of his time away from it. When he is home, he still tends to leave most of the intimate child raising activities—bathing, feeding, putting-to-bed—to the mother. Moreover, in the typical family situation, the child follows the mother through her daily round of activities, but has little notion of what the father is doing. Small wonder, then, that the mother becomes the first object of identification for boys as well as for girls. In both cases the earliest stirrings of sexual identity are decidedly female. As an illustration, let me recount one mother's anecdote: her husband, an army doctor, had just returned from a long tour of duty in Vietnam. In an effort to establish a bit of male camaraderie with their four-year-old son, he invited the boy to watch him shave, whereupon his son, who already had a solid understanding of the shaving process, began applying shaving cream to his legs.

Sooner or later, the male child is expected to repent his error and convert over to male identification. This means that much of his early sexual identity has to be unlearned. But many boys are so thoroughly identified with their mothers that they would prefer not to switch or else they are unable to. For the majority of boys who do make the switch, the transfer may involve vehemently putting away the things of a girl in order to better consolidate their newfound masculinity. At this stage of life the worst epithet that one boy can hurl at another is, "Johnny likes girls!" Johnny will, of course, deny having anything to do with the creatures. Some males carry this hostility for females throughout their lives. They secure their masculine identity in a negative way by repudiating femininity.

Society's demand that boys make a sexual about-face accounts for much of the insecurity that males have about their sex identity, but there is a further reason. The male model the boy is expected to transfer to is not generally a warm, personal, individual model of identification, but a broad, culturally defined stereotype of "masculinity" which he first learns about, not so much from personal contact with significant older males, but secondhand from his mother, female teachers, primary school readers, and television. This is in contrast to his first sexual identification, which was very special and very individual. It is likely that, even after his reconditioning, many of his deepest, most "natural" responses will be female. But society is powerful. If a discrepancy arises between his natural inclinations and society's definition of maleness, he will likely suppress the former in favor of the latter; he will come to depend more on the cultural role and less on his spontaneous reflexes. The point is simply this: a sexual identity based on an intimate personal model (as it is for girls) is more secure than one based on a generalized abstraction (as it is for boys). In the second case we can expect to see—and we do see—many more attempts to compensate for a felt weakness in sexual identity by playing a sexual role to the hilt.

If males are less secure about their sexual identity, why is it that so many more females are interested in liberation? One way out of the confusion is to make a distinction between sexual identity and sex-role preference. Sexual identity runs deeper and is less conscious. It is an inner conviction about which sex one does in fact belong to—a basic contentment with one's maleness or femaleness. Sex-role preference refers to a more conscious desire to play the part which society assigns to one sex or the other. Starting from the premise that boys have to make a switch in identification, it seems logical to conclude that males will be less comfortable in their *sex* than females. Starting from the fact that this is a male-oriented society, it is likely that females will be less comfortable in their *role.* Although females may be more secure about their femininity, they are more likely to be envious of the privileges and prerogatives that go with the male role. They will tend to be more content with their sex but discontent with the limited scope of action afforded to it. Because preference is a more conscious process, it is not unusual for women to voice the wish that they had been born men. This is a wish, not for male identity, but for the male role. Men, however, since they already belong to the "man's world," will rarely show a preference for the more limited role of the women. Yet their underlying sense of identity may in many cases be more feminine than masculine.[17]

If in fact men are less secure in their identity (though more happy in their role) than women, it helps to explain and relate two curious phenomena. One is that men have always grabbed the superior roles in relation to women; the other is that men are generally less flexible when it comes to role experimentation. Men seem to have to shore up their shakier sense of identity with the props that roles provide; the strongest, most dominant roles provide the strongest props, and men actively seek these out and hold on tenaciously once they have achieved them. All the traditional male institutions—the initiation rites, the clubs, the sport teams—betray a male's need for some special province he can call his own: a place where, joined with other males and surrounded by ceremony, he can ritually affirm his ever shaky identity as a man. To do without these props one needs a secure sense of sexual identity; to experiment with sex roles or to express facets of the opposite sex in one's personality requires an even stronger sense of self. One reason that males experience difficulty in accepting their feminine side is that they lack a clear sense of masculine identity in the first place. Women, however, freely adopt many aspects of the male role because, being secure in their femininity, they can afford to express a wider range of their personality.

It would seem then that the route to more flexible sex roles lies by way of a secure identity. Persons with a strong sense of personal identity rely less on ascribed cultural definitions of masculinity and femininity; they have the security to make their own definitions. Conversely, the more an individual relies on the formal role trappings of masculinity or femininity, the less secure is his or her sexual identity.

Sex Roles and the Sense of Purpose

Still, sex roles are so closely linked with identity that liberation from one threatens liberation from the other. The question is, What roles are dispensable and what roles are not? How fluid can sexuality get without washing away identity? Perhaps it would be better to rephrase that last question to, How far can we liberate individuals from sex roles without taking away their sense of purpose? One's identity can to some extent be abstracted from one's sex—though never completely—but one's sense of identity is inextricably bound up with one's sense of purpose, and sex roles have traditionally provided a sense of purpose to both men and women. That sex roles can be shifted—even reversed—is evident from the cross-cultural studies done by psychologist David Gutmann.[18] In most societies, says Gutmann, sex roles are normally reversed, but not until late middle age—after the children are grown up. After that is ushered in what Gutmann calls the "normal unisex of later life": "Grandpa becomes sweet, affable, but rather vague, Grandma becomes tough-minded and intrusive." The reason that the switch does not occur earlier is that grown up children seem to elicit from parents "a sense of chronic emergency" to which the male reacts by suppressing his expressive side in favor of the instrumental role, and vice versa for females. When the child-raising years are over, a natural process sets in by which each sex tends to live out the life it had suppressed. The passive yearnings of the male which at a younger age might have weakened his resolve to provide for his children can now be indulged; the competitive and aggressive impulses of the female which at one time might have been directed toward her children can now be given freer rein. But until that time, Gutmann suggests, parents must be content to live out some of their potentialities vicariously through their spouse. Sex roles, he concludes, are ultimately derived from "the parental imperative."

While supporting the view that sex roles can indeed be changed, Gutmann raises the question, Should they be changed? Or more exactly, When should they be changed? His answer is, "not until children are grown up." The possibility that children require a certain polarity from their parents is supported by a study conducted by psychologist Urie Bronfenbrenner. His conclusion is that "the most dependent and least dependable adolescents describe family arrangements that are neither patriarchal nor matriarchal but equalitarian." Those families in which sex roles are not differentiated tend "to produce young people who do not take initiative, look to others for direction and decision, and cannot be counted on to fulfill obligations."[19] Sex roles, then, may serve the interests of growing children; and, in truth, children are more adamant about maintaining sex-role distinctions than are adults. In return for exacting this polarity from adults, writes Gutmann, children give back "an unquestioned sense of life's meaning."[20]

For males the role of protector and provider can supply for the first time a secure sense of masculine identity. This role may be looked upon as merely a prop, but it represents a considerable advancement over the attitude of males in primitive societies. What distinguishes civilized from primitive societies is the orientation of males to children, which is also an orientation to the future, because children represent the future. In place of secret ceremonies, civilized males substitute a different proof of their manhood: the ability to provide for their children and their children's future. Civilized man is a historical creature, and for most civilized males it is through their children that they enter into the stream of history. Their faith in the future is expressed in their wish to bring up specific children and to have those children carry their name and something of their identity into the future. In short, civilized man adopts a future-orientation and affirms his unsteady male identity by his commitment to his offspring. This commitment provides both a sense of continuity and an ever-present confirmation of identity that short-term sexuality cannot.[21]

Thus, in a civilized society the job or career takes on many of the mysterious aspects that secret rituals hold for the primitive. It allows a man to play the role of civilized provider, and its loss can be a crushing blow to male identity. Psychologists, who usually have secure careers and plenty of money, often fail to realize what a job and money can mean to one's sense of identity. One's identity cannot be so easily abstracted from these "extraneous" factors. I believe Erikson was well aware of this when he emphasized that a sense of industry must come before a sense of identity. People must feel that they are useful, that they can do something, and that they can do something for someone. It may be a sad fact but it is nevertheless true that money is often the major factor in allowing one person to do something useful for another. Mark Twain's remark, "the lack of money is the root of all evil," has more truth than humor when applied to a society like ours. When people are denied the means to make and keep long-range commitments to family or friends, their sense of identity suffers. It is not just that they have been deprived of an artificial role: they are also robbed of a sense of duration and continuity.

On Being Fully Human

The idea of childhood as a special and protected time of life came late in history, but the invention of the child seems to mark an evolutionary step upward. Advances in civilization have always been preceded by special allowances for the education and protection of the young. There is for instance a definite correlation between the length of the adolescent moratorium and progress. And while it may be true that human beings are less instinctive than other animals, it is also true, for that same reason, that human infants require a longer period of dependency than any other creature. Consequently a distinctively human society requires long-term commitments from its adult members. Now, this pattern of commitment to children and the future, which civilized men and women have built up over the centuries, is being subverted by a philosophy of fluidity disguised as sex-role liberation. The Human Potential Movement claims to be liberating people to be more fully human—but what exactly does it mean to be "fully human"? One thing that distinguishes humans from other creatures is the long period of childhood dependence which allows for our greater fluidity and adaptability. Another trait that certainly distinguishes humans from most other animals is the willingness of male parents in the human race to take on a long-range responsibility for their offspring. This is a cultural, distinctively human accomplishment—not a natural process. When the Human Potential advocates talk about making people more fully human they are really talking about making people more "natural"—but they seem to forget that humans are cultural animals: it is in their nature to transcend nature and its instinctual limitations.

While men and women do need to be liberated from emotional paralysis, they hardly need to be liberated from their sense of responsibility. This is especially true for males. As Phyllis Chesler writes in *Women and Madness:* "Telling men to withdraw from deep or monogamous commitments is not very revolutionary: few men are committed to the ethic of love or sexual monogamy."[22] Too many men are already anxious to interpret the liberation phenomenon as a green light to put their hit-and-run fantasies into action. One of the goals of the women's movement is to make women independent of men. This is understandable. And, as the feminists say, it will also liberate men. Men may take this opportunity to cultivate their "feminine" side—to enhance the nurturant and intuitive aspects of their life—but it is just as likely that they will take it as an opportunity to plunge deeper into the short-horizon male pattern or else to slip off in pursuit of the old male myth of irresponsibility. Hopefully, men can liberate themselves emotionally, without abandoning their role in the socialization process. But this hope is best served when males have a solid sense of masculine identity; and this in turn rests on their conviction that they can make a distinctively important contribution to society. The dissolution of sex divisions may lead to more tender, human males, but before men can become more human they must first be sure that they are men. Before they dare express those more tender elements of their personality, men need a distinctive masculine identity and that depends on their having a sense of purpose. Both men and women do need to free themselves from restrictive roles, but above all they need to find meaning in life. And meaning does not come from spontaneity or openness or tender feelings but from something more durable.

New Purposes

I hope that none of this is construed as an argument for the status quo. We may have to find new and better purposes in life than those defined by tradition. We need to reevaluate the kind of commitments we make and reconsider to whom we will make them. In the past most men and women have found meaning in raising a family, but this may no longer be a feasible pattern for most. The important thing is that one has a sense of being involved in history and in the future. Raising children usually provides such a sense of purpose and is, perhaps, the most convenient model of meaningful commitment to society; but it is by no means the only one. Moreover, there are ways of contributing to the welfare of children without reproducing them: any action that betters society also serves children. A concern for the quality of society is a concern for the future children will grow up in. For many people in these transitional times, raising children can simply be a hellish mistake. While providing a sense of meaning, children can also provide a sense of desperation. They can be quite literally maddening, especially now that there are no longer servants in the house and no extended family to ease the burden on the mother. We have, moreover, a serious population problem that requires us to limit the number of children born into the world. It is irresponsible to push parenthood in a world of limited space and resources. Finally there is a "vicious circle" problem involved in assigning profound meaning to parental commitment. Why should parents make sacrificial commitments to children just so those children can grow up and sacrifice their lives to their children, and so on? Doesn't anyone ever get to enjoy?

There has to be more to life and love than pure commitment. Obviously there has to be a balance in each person's life between commitment and self-actualization, responsibility and gratification. My objection is to the idea that deep meaning can be found solely in the latter. It is interesting to note that the self-actualizing people Abraham Maslow studied were invariably deeply committed individuals. And these original self-actualizers tended to limit the number of their intimate friends to a few. It was their feeling that a close relationship demanded a great deal of time and commitment and could not therefore be had with a large number of people.[23] It seems to me that we could all profit by their example by being more judicious and realistic in the commitments we undertake. Premature or unrealistic commitments can be as damaging to identity as no commitment at all. It does take a long time to consolidate a sense of self, and a too early commitment can put an end to one's growing season as effectively as an early frost puts an end to summer. Moreover, what was at one time a realistic commitment may now be a precarious one: parenthood, for example, was once a manageable proposition, but without the support of either the community or the extended family, and possibly without the support of a spouse, it comes to seem like a trap instead of a commitment.

Perhaps in the present dispensation the responsibilities of parenthood need to be illuminated only in the harshest light as a caution to the overconfident and the overly sentimental. But there ought to be some middle ground between this kind of realism and the kind of escapism by which one generation cuts itself off from the next. In this regard we seem to be afflicted with an all-or-nothing mentality: either parenthood as a perfected state, and therefore the only state worth being in, or parenthood as a pitiable state, and therefore a state not even to be approximated. If it is unwise to encourage parenthood, is it therefore wise to discourage any commitment to younger generations? We could, for instance, do something to resurrect the role of aunt or uncle and return it to its former respected status. As a corollary to our campaigns for zero population growth and child-free marriages we could extol the virtues of aunthood or unclehood. Since birth control campaigns are never completely heeded, there will always be a need for supportive relatives. Aunts and uncles who aren't burdened with their own children can make a significant difference in the lives of their nieces and nephews without overextending their capacity for commitment. And certainly we have arrived at a stage in our culture which calls for fewer parents and more aunts, uncles, and friends of the family.

What I am arguing for is what Erikson calls "generativity": "the concern for establishing and guiding the next generation." Without generativity, identity is not complete; and without it the life cycles of separate individuals cease to be mutually supportive. The fact is, that the life cycles of many people, young and old, intertwine, and where a sense of generativity is lacking, the whole social fabric soon unravels. But, as Erikson takes care to establish, generativity need not be confined to taking care of one's own children; it need not specifically involve children at all: "Generativity . . . potentially extends to whatever a man creates and produces (or helps to produce)."[24] And in the future, suggests Erikson, generativity must be exercised "in a more informed manner." It must be conceived in terms of a "universal responsibility of each individual for the potentialities of all generations."[25]

Finally, I have deliberately avoided ascribing life's meaning to heterosexual commitments. There is a sense of generativity involved in all friendships and love relationships in which, as Erikson puts it, friends "become sons of each other"[26] (or daughters of each other). It seems to me that this understanding of generativity applies also to friendships and love relationships of a homosexual nature. There is no reason that one cannot find deep meaning in commitment to another of the same sex, nor is there any reason that sexual preference should prevent an individual from finding ties to society and society's future. The significance of a commitment lies in its freely chosen nature; the liberty to choose whomever one will is essential to identity. The real significance of the coming revolution in sex roles lies not merely in the opportunity it will provide for greater self-actualization, but also in the possibility it holds for forming freer, deeper, and more realistic commitments.

10

The End of Romance

*I*N the fifties and early sixties pop singers sang of romance, true love, and undying loyalty. "Only you," crooned the Platters, would make their dream come true. And if this was not consolation enough, we always had Elvis Presley's pledge to love us tender and love us true; or the assurance of Johnny Mathis that his love would last until the "twelfth of never."

Not that the tender ballad can't still be heard—but the pop songs of the late sixties and early seventies indicate a marked change: they are much more sexual and much less romantic; much more concerned with the pleasures of the present than with the dreams of the future. "Light My Fire" (The Doors) is a far cry from "Love Me Tender," and even further removed from the sentimental ballads of the forties and early fifties—as are such current favorites as "I'm Horny, I'm Stoned" (The Doors) and "Let's Spend the Night Together" (The Rolling Stones). At one time the voices from the Victrola counseled us to be true to each other. Now we are advised to "Love the One You're With" (Stephen Stills), if the one we love doesn't happen to be around.

The explanation for this abrupt change in our musical

mores is that within the space of a decade, the romantic love ideal has been taken from its pedestal. An increasing number of contemporary youth are unswayed by the myth of romance which ruled an earlier generation. One reason is that romantic love is based on a fantasy of commitment ("I'll love you forever") and exclusiveness ("You're mine alone"), and this type of fantasy doesn't hold up very well against the prevailing emphasis on fluidity and on nonpossessive, nonexclusive relationships. Another reason is that romantic love depends upon a consciousness that is more print-oriented than neo-tribal.

This demythologizing of romance has as yet gained little notice from historians and sociologists, but if the social and psychological consequences of the romantic love ideal are as profound as Denis de Rougemont maintained in his classic *Love in the Western World,*[1] then its demise may prove to be one of the paramount transformations in modern history.

The Romantic Myth

The romantic love ideal—the idea that for every girl there is a boy; that one day they will meet and fall in love and live happily thereafter—is one of the powerful underlying myths which shape our lives. And the theme of its frustration by external forces has preoccupied the Western literary tradition since the time of the troubadors. From Tristan and Iseult, through Romeo and Juliet down to Zhivago and Lara the formula hardly varies: a forbidden person, an impossible love, forced separations, temporary reunions, and eventual tragic death. Because of its inherent frustration, de Rougemont considered the romantic love myth to be the chief curse of Western man. To be in love passionately, he maintained, is to be in love with suffering—for that is what passion means: to love that person who is inaccessible or who exists mainly in fantasy is to suffer.[2]

Star-crossed lovers still take their own lives no doubt, but for most of us nonliterary types who have an aversion to tragic death the myth has been watered down to less than epic proportions. Still, it takes its toll in disappointment or disillusion or in a lifetime of deferment, waiting for "the right person" to come along. In compensation we have evolved a number of cultural supports for those disappointed in love. The jilted lover is extended almost the same sympathy as the bereaved widow, and we have ten hundred songs to celebrate the sweet misery of heartbreak. The pains and pangs of romance have become as dear to us as the ecstasy. Watered down or not, the myth of romance is a powerful one—but there are signs that it is losing its hold.

Consider the popularity of films like *Ryan's Daughter* and *Love Story*. Both films are replete with obstacles to love's fulfillment and, at the last, death makes a sudden end to romance. The obstacles in *Love Story* are a bit strained: Jennie Cavalleri comes from lower-class, ethnic Cranston, Rhode Island; Oliver Barrett III comes from upper-class, Waspish Boston Brahmin stock. But they easily leap over these obstructions only to have their dreams crushed by Jennie's untimely death. In *Ryan's Daughter* the obstacles are more real: she is Irish, he is a British officer, and the setting is occupied Ireland. She, moreover, is married. They temporarily overcome these barriers by meeting clandestinely in the heather, but in the end the villagers find out their secret and take revenge on her. He blows himself up with a hand grenade. The convenient solution of tragic death obviates the need to invent further obstacles to keep romance alive. One can go away from these films with an image of intense romance preserved forever by death —as one could not, for instance, if Jennie had lived and the film had followed her through married life. Or picture, if you will, Romeo and Juliet celebrating their fortieth wedding anniversary among children and grandchildren. Not much romance there. But their early and unfortunate deaths place a seal of eternity on their passion. Obviously, stories like *Ryan's Daughter* and *Love Story* are quite in keeping with the romantic tradition of the West. One could cite these films as evidence that the myth is still very much alive but to do so would be to miss the main point about both—the fact that they are blatantly nostalgic. The audience may shed tears but the tears are for days gone by. We live in such a psychologically sophisticated period—such a decidedly unromantic time—that it is hard for any viewer to believe that such a romance can happen to him. The current penchant for nostalgia does not signal a revival of the romantic love ideal. It marks its obituary.

Demythologizing Romance

This demythologizing of romance is primarily the result of certain transformations within the youth culture that have altered long-standing attitudes and conditions. That the process should be activated by youth is only natural, since those chiefly affected (or victimized) by the romantic love myth have been adolescents. In the not-so-long-ago, adolescents were known to pine away for months at a time over girls (or boys) they had never talked to, and probably never would for fear of breaking the spell—all the time elaborating a fantasy of eventual marriage and lifelong bliss. Such behavior presupposed a quasi-puritanical society willing to put obstacles in the way of young love, for passionate love is not conceivable in a world where everything is permitted. A decade ago these obstacles were real enough. There were still strong prohibitions against sex before marriage; and there were class barriers and ethnic barriers and religious barriers and age barriers. These obstacles, however, are increasingly difficult to find in a society that tends to put few restrictions on the object of one's love—and passion is likely to encounter fewer and fewer prohibitions as our society becomes more and more liberalized. It is, however, a tribute to our literary inventiveness that Western writers still manage to devise new obstacles to keep the flame of passion burning bright. The class barrier between Jennifer Cavalleri and Oliver Barrett III is as nothing compared to the obstructions which forbid the love of Humbert Humbert for Lolita or the love of Ulrich for his sister in Robert Musil's novel *The Man Without Qualities*.[3]

The world still does not take kindly to romantic affairs between middle-aged men and teenage nymphets, or to incest. Given a few such exceptions, however, there now exists a general state of permissiveness which is not a good climate for the romantic flower to take root. But beyond the fact that we lack obstacles as a spur to romance there are other factors that contribute to the decline of the myth. Romantic behavior presupposes a certain way of looking at the world—a consciousness, if you will, that is increasingly rare among adolescents growing up in McLuhan's electric age. This consciousness involved:

1. an orientation to the future
2. an assumption of scarcity
3. a sharp polarity between the sexes
4. an individualistic rather than communal outlook

1. *Future orientation.* In order to prosper, the romantic love myth requires a society that is incurably future-oriented, one that is willing to defer satisfactions almost indefinitely. The future-oriented man defers present pleasure for the sake of reaping greater rewards in the future. Like the characters in *Waiting for Godot,* he is forever waiting for his life to begin, forever postponing the present. His attitude toward time infects his attitude toward love. "To love in the sense of passion-love," wrote de Rougemont, "is the contrary of to live. It is . . . an inability to enjoy the present."[4] It seems that those who are willing to wait for Godot will also wait for Prince Charming or "the girl of my dreams." They turn down what is possible *now* for what *might* be possible. They live not in the present but in their fantasies of the future. Out of this future-oriented attitude grew the philosophy of "I'm saving myself" and the phenomenon of the old maid. But now, thanks to future shock, electricity, and the Human Potential Movement, there prevails a general orientation to the present, and, despite whatever benefits that may bring, it is not conducive to romance.

2. *Scarcity assumption.* The extreme future-oriented frame of mind is built in part upon what Philip Slater calls "the scarcity premise":[5] the belief that there is simply not enough of the

goods of life to go around. If everything, including love and sex, is scarce, then a high premium is placed on the ability to defer gratification. Moreover, what is scarce tends to be idealized and romanticized. Dante's Beatrice, loved from afar (the obstacles here were her tender age and her social class), attained near-divinity in his imagination.

But, according to Slater, the scarcity assumption is no longer subscribed to by the young; and sociologists from Spindler down to William Foote Whyte, Keniston, and Roszak have chronicled the steady erosion of the future-oriented outlook and the cultivation of the present by the young. Among counterculture youth there is less inclination to defer gratification to some future romanticized time; less disposition to fantasize about some elusive Beatrice or to dream of an evanescent Jeannie with light brown hair and perfect body. Neither do they appear to have much interest in the pursuit, the chase, the long courtship. The girl who plays hard to get, gets no one. Instead of, "You're the only one for me," the current attitude is "Love the one you're with," or, to repeat an older proverb, "there're plenty of fish in the sea." Since the current emphasis is on keeping one's options open, on tentativeness, and fluidity, there exists a general unwillingness even among the reckless young to make the kind of reckless vows that romance calls for.

3. *Separation of the sexes.* In all the great love stories the flame of romance is fanned higher in the absence of the beloved. Tristan and Iseult are separated by the sea and their love waxes rather than wanes. Zhivago and Lara are separated by a thousand miles of tundra and their love grows stronger. It's easier to fantasize about someone who is not present. It is likewise easier to romanticize about a person of the opposite sex when sex roles provide distance. There is a sense of mystery created by the "otherness" of the other sex. The less we know about the other, the higher our imagination soars. The British officer with whom Ryan's daughter falls in love is a mysterious figure and thereby all the more romantic. He says little. What past does his silence conceal? He walks with a

slight limp. A war wound? A fine scar traces the corner of his eye. A duel? He suffers from occasional tremors. What anguished memories?

Familiarity, on the contrary, while it may not breed contempt, does not foster romance. Among the members of the same Kibbutz, romance is rare. The Kibbutzim generally go outside their commune in search of romance and marriage partners. Since they have all been raised together, in one big family as it were, they apparently find little room to romanticize about one another.[6] The threat that familiarity poses to romance is well recognized. A whole literature, in fact, has grown up in women's magazines that purports to tell housewives how to put romance back into their tired marriages. The secret is to add some novelty by, say, having sex in a different room each night. The unromantic dangers of familiarity have also provided fertile ground for authors and playwrights. In *The Fantastiks* two widowed fathers live side by side. They are great friends and their fondest wish is to see their children married to each other. To encourage this romance they build a high stone wall between their yards and feign hostility toward each other. The ruse works. The neighboring son and daughter grow up, fall in love, and nightly clamber over the wall. And against the pretended opposition of both fathers the boy asks for the girl's hand in marriage. But once the ruse is discovered and the element of mystery dissolves, the lovers fall quickly out of love.

In the United States, sex segregation was once practiced to a much greater extent than it is now. Males grew up with only hazy notions about the "weaker" sex, and females fantasized about the "strong, silent" male who would someday enter their life like a prince out of a fairy book. But now we seem to be headed the way of the Kibbutz. There appears to be more a convergence of sex roles than a separation. Young people see less of a need to specialize themselves into highly defined and rigid sex roles. Implicit in the dress and behavior of a growing number of young people is the assumption that masculinity and femininity form not a polarity but a continuum. As the sexes come to live closer together, to know each other better, and as the psychic distance between them closes, the possibilities for romantic love, which thrives on separation and distance and unrealistic perceptions, decrease. Romantic love assumes a polarity between the sexes, not a continuum. When the element of mystery and otherness is removed, the tendency to fantasize and romanticize about the opposite sex is discouraged. The differences between the sexes seem less important to modern youth; so does romantic love.

It is not only youthful unisexuals who are creating this change in the romantic climate. The Women's Movement is also dedicated to breaking down the roles that divide the sexes. Those who associate themselves with the movement are, in general, adamant in their refusal to accept a "mysterious woman" status. Although these trends may lead to liberation and greater self-fulfillment, they also lead inexorably to a diminution of romantic love.

4. *Individualistic outlook.* A final factor involved in the demythologizing of love is an increasing interest in community. The romantic outlook seems to flourish in future-oriented, individualized societies, but is practically unknown in many communal and tribal societies; and when it does appear it is often considered a form of illness. There are some signs of a drift toward a more communal pattern in America, illustrated most clearly in the widespread experimentation with rural and urban communes. And for every well-known and well-organized commune, there are ten thousand smaller household communes: semicommunal clusters of males and females living together in groups of four, six, eight, or ten—not a global village by any means, but certainly a new phenomenon in the American experience. In addition there are a number of other communal trends: the proliferation of community action groups, consumer groups, food cooperatives—even the switch back to the communal form of confession among Catholics. McLuhan, of course, would explain these trends in terms of the communalizing power of electricity. Whether the current togetherness is electrically caused and whether it is really com-

munal in nature or simply an aggregation of bodies in proximity are moot questions. Either way romance suffers. One rarely becomes romantic about those with whom one lives or works on a daily familiar basis. It is not surprising, then, that for many of the young the ideal of love is not the love of one individual for another, but rather the "universal love" that animated the Woodstock festival. Individualized, romantic love is often seen as just one more manifestation of the ego trip that isolates.

We have been conditioned to accept as normal a love that expresses itself in relationships based partly on jealousy and the exclusion of others. Romantic love does not want to share the beloved; it wants to hold an exclusive place in the beloved's heart. In its preoccupation with "the two of us," it stands at the opposite pole from universal or communal love. But jealousy and possessiveness no longer seem the natural and necessary accompaniment of love. Romanticized, individualized love appears as selfish and childish to a growing number of people. To them the attitude that one intimate relationship precludes any other, smacks of exclusivity and an inability to love on a wider scale.

The first question that comes to mind in considering the demythologizing of romance is, Where does it lead? At first the decline of romance seemed evidence of a new maturity about love. I was of this opinion a few years ago. At that time it was possible to interpret the demythologizing phenomenon in the best possible light: to see in it the beginnings of a secularized revival of a tradition that preceded the romantic myth—the tradition of Christian love or agape with its roots in the Talmudic tradition of love for the stranger and love for one's neighbor. A demythologizing of our notions about romance seemed the first step toward the realization of that older and more hopeful tradition: love that spreads and unites, rather than love that confines and restricts. During the halcyon Woodstock days it was easy to believe that the romantic mythology would be replaced by a more encompassing neighbor love. Now it is much more difficult to believe that this is the direction we are taking. It appears that the nonexclusive, non-jealous love now gaining currency may simply signify an incapacity for intimacy or commitment. What is replacing the romantic love myth is not agape but simply another myth.

Two Myths of Romance

Actually, there are two myths of romance: the myth of Tristan and the myth of Don Juan. What I have been calling romantic love is really the Tristan version of romance. And that intensely individualistic myth is being replaced not by a community of love but by a crude version of the Don Juan myth.[7] I say "crude" because the modern rendition has none of the grand style or drama that Don Juan displayed, nor any of the adventure, even danger, of midnight rendezvous and risky assignations. Nevertheless, the current pattern retains the essential elements of Don Juanism.

According to legend, Don Juan possessed a thousand and three women in Spain alone and one thousand and sixty-two elsewhere. To perform such a restless feat must have required almost constant motion. And indeed this is how Don Juan is depicted both in literature and in opera: a man in perpetual motion. An air of restlessness pervades Mozart's opera *Don Giovanni*. Don Juan is the hit-and-run lover, the man in constant pursuit. He no sooner makes one conquest than he is off to another. Don Juan is pure movement: a "power" rather than a "person or individual," wrote Kierkegaard in *Either/Or*. His life is "a sum of distinct moments . . . a total of instants"; "he has no time."[8] To de Rougemont, Don Juan is "a stone skipping along the surface of water." He "can not have a biography. . . . He is the genius of the moment. His conquests are without history. . . . Without past, without memory (he needs the Catalogue!), without future, and without nostalgia, he turns up, takes his pleasure, and takes off."[9] Don Juan is the present-oriented man par excellence. He lives for the moment —nothing else. If he were to stop, to pause, to reflect, his energy would dissipate. Like a gyroscope he must keep spinning to keep his balance. Without motion he is nothing.

In his perpetual quest for novelty and change, Don Juan stands as a prototype for the highly mobile individual about whom Toffler writes in *Future Shock*. Don Juanism is in fact the romantic corollary of accelerating change. A future-shocked society is one in which our attachments to others become tenuous because we must always be prepared to move on. Incessant moving deprives us of the wish to make commitments and, eventually, the ability to do so. In the face of ever-changing life-styles we are reluctant to settle: either to settle down or to settle for someone. The nomadic hit-and-run pattern seems to better suit our fast-moving times. Ceaseless change, moreover, quickly erases the past and renders the future unknowable. Increasingly we live for the moment-to-moment pleasures. Living in a state of constant flux, we are, like Don Juan, without a past or a future, without continuity and therefore without identity. A sense of identity depends on continuity, and Don Juan, because he has no continuity, has no identity either. This is the meaning of his reply to a woman who seeks to know his identity: "Ah, Heaven! Man, who art thou?" she asks, and he answers, "Who am I? A man without a name."[10] Don Juan refuses to define himself by choices, and thus he remains "a man without a name"—a man without an identity. His is the type of eroticism suitable for those who lack identities: individuals who restlessly search everywhere for themselves. Never, in fact, has there been a time more congenial to this type of lover. True, no one today speaks of Don Juan. In rationalizing the nomadic pursuit of eroticism we speak instead of "freedom." But that also is a line from *Don Giovanni:* "Viva la libertà!" proclaims Don Juan. "Hurrah for freedom!"[11]

What is the attraction Don Juan holds for women and for the men (even Kierkegaard was fascinated by him) who would like to emulate him? Don Juan represents the man without commitments; the man for whom all possibilities, sensual and sexual, remain open; the man who lives for the moment and for himself alone. In him there is no constancy, only the immediate present. Like Richard Rich he is full of deceit, and like Rich he could not answer for himself "even so far as tonight,"[12] for he has no self to be held answerable. To Kierkegaard he was a "power rather than a person." And being a power he cannot be held responsible. The energy that propels him is a "natural" force like a tornado or a bolt of lightning striking where it will. He is no more accountable than a gust of wind.

Don Juan is, of course, only a symbol for a certain attitude toward love. Real men and women are too complex to be fitted into any one category: the curious mixture of hedonism and altruism, commitment and irresponsibility we can find in any average man or woman simply defies classification. Still, the figure of Don Juan is an appropriate symbol for the direction in which many relationships now tend.

In speaking of Don Juan as "a power rather than a person," Kierkegaard touches on an important connection between identity and sexuality. Don Juan is a power, or what we today might call a self-in-process; his identity is subject to change without notice and so is the object of his pursuit; he is all fluidity—one can only count on his absence of accountability. Such a figure naturally invites comparison with the more fluid human type that the Human Potential Movement wishes to encourage. While I would not equate Don Juanism with human potentialism, I would suggest that it is a logical extension of the philosophy of self which the Human Potential Movement promulgates. It is not a very great jump from the exploratory, experimental approach to identity, to the experimental, noncommittal approach toward persons, and from thence to Don Juanism.

But most of the devotees of the process philosophy are not yet of this persuasion. They sail more slowly over the sea of possibilities. Their lingering belief in "closeness" and "relationships" constrains them to temper their pursuit of experience with short-term fidelities. They adopt a more moderate pace in their wanderings from encounter to encounter and bedroom to bedroom, lest their espousal of loving one another become completely empty talk. They are what de Rougemont calls "Don Juans in slow time."[13] Another factor which slows them down is the American habit of organization. In their craving for consensus, Americans tend to institutionalize the Don Juan syndrome. It is the Kiwanis Club approach to eroticism. By joining a swingers club or singles club one can play Don Juan without courting danger. Leave it to Americans to organize adultery. Nevertheless, the essential motif is to keep moving—as evidenced, for example, by those swingers clubs which discourage members from dallying twice with the same couple.

What fuels the incessant motion of the new breed of "lovers" is a wish to experience all possibilities before it is too late. Whenever a philosophy of experience is elaborated it is accompanied by a sense of urgency; a sense that one must move quickly before time seals up the options. This element of restlessness is obvious, for instance, in the arguments the Cavalier Poets posed to the young ladies they wished to seduce. Robert Herrick's most famous poem is addressed "to the Virgins, to make much of time" because it's "still a-flying";[14] and Andrew Marvell is anxious to get his "Coy Mistress" quickly into bed because he can "always hear time's wingéd chariot hurrying near."[15] Though the modern cavaliers suffer by comparison to those of the seventeenth century, there is the same anxiety to get on with it. But such restlessness almost always signifies that inability to choose that Erikson calls identity confusion. This is the fear that in defining our identity by choices we also limit it. We have been schooled to believe that all our potentialities should be exercised and that all relationship possibilities should be explored, but we are so afraid of making the wrong choices—choices that will get in the way of further exploration —that we don't make any at all, or else we make sure that our commitments are refundable. To do otherwise is to go against the grain of the prevailing wisdom. Safer to keep moving.

We cannot overlook the likelihood that for others there is a more sinister side to this restlessness; more than a simple fear of losing out on attractive possibilities. For some it is a deeper, more stubborn refusal to commit: an absolute hardness of heart. It is the latter certainly that characterizes Don Juan, and it is worth asking whether the current celebration of the fluid personality is not at bottom a tribute to the same callousness. Apologists for fluid man purport to find in him the same heroic qualities that the poet Tennyson found in that prototypical wanderer, Ulysses:

> *I can not rest from travel; I will drink*
> *Life to the lees: . . .*

Here Ulysses is pictured as an early actualizer:

> *How dull it is to pause, to make an end,*
> *To rust unburnished, not to shine in use!*[16]

But there is another poem about Ulysses and the nomadic type he represents. And it may be a more accurate description of the type of individual who is now surfacing from the swift-flowing streams of self-fulfillment:

> *. . . being in love with no one; hard and*
> *isolated, in love with change alone,*
> *With a bird's yearning to move seasonally*
> *and the sharp, mean eyes of a bird.*[17]

Ulysses, at any rate, was forced by the gods to wander. Moreover, he always yearned to return to Ithaca, to his wife and son. No such sense of final commitment motivates today's experience seekers or those who counsel them from the pages of books and articles devoted to the unquestioning pursuit of self-actualization; their only commitment is to change itself. "Novelty," wrote Casanova, speaking for those of all eras who follow Don Juan's persuasion, "Novelty is the tyrant of our soul."

If Don Juan wants to experience all possibilities, Tristan refuses the possible; and if Don Juan can't wait, Tristan can wait forever. At first glance the Tristan myth and the Don Juan myth seem poles apart, but in fact one leads to the other.

Again, I rely heavily on de Rougemont's analysis of the myths.

Here in highly abridged form is the ancient legend of Tristan and Iseult. Tristan, an orphan, is raised to manhood by King Mark of Cornwall. He is sent by King Mark to Ireland to fetch Iseult for his (King Mark's) bride. On the return trip they both mistakenly drink a love potion intended for Iseult and King Mark, and Tristan and Iseult thereby fall passionately in love. Iseult does marry King Mark, but by a series of ruses she continues to meet with Tristan although their meetings are few and far between, Tristan being alternately banished and recalled. Finally they both escape to a forest where Tristan takes to laying a drawn sword between himself and Iseult. After the effect of the love potion wears off, Tristan returns Iseult to King Mark, asks forgiveness, and gets it. The two lovers continue, however, to rendezvous in the woods. Then they are separated once again and Tristan for no particular reason marries another lady. At the end, wounded by a poisoned spear, Tristan sends for Iseult but gives up his life before she comes. She arrives and, overcome by grief, dies by his side.

The key element in this intricate tale, as de Rougemont makes clear, is obstruction. From beginning to end, all sorts of obstacles are raised between the love of Tristan and Iseult, and for this their love becomes the more passionate. As if Iseult's marriage to King Mark and Tristan's fealty to him were not enough of a hindrance, the two actively seek more barriers to their love. Where society puts obstacles in his way Tristan boldly leaps over them, and where it does not he invents them. As an example of the first instance, Tristan vaults from his bed to Iseult's to avoid leaving footprints in the flour which has been scattered between by the less trusting members of King Mark's court. As an example of Tristan's inventiveness when no one else will provide obstacles, there is the naked sword between the two clothed lovers. Beyond this there is Tristan's marriage, which seems to serve only the purpose of presenting him one more obstruction to overcome.

At one point in his analysis of the myth, de Rougemont

poses a question that borders on the irreverent, given the inspirational effect the story has always had: "Does Tristan care for Iseult, and she for him?"[18] His answer is no. They are not in love with each other but with love itself. What makes Tristan swoon is not Iseult but his own passionately cultivated feelings. What makes Tristan fascinating to Iseult is his inaccessibility. The distance between them allows full play to their fantasy. And since they love the fantasies better than they love each other, they make sure that obstacles keep coming between them. Tristan is not in love with Iseult; he is in love with the image of Iseult which he carries in his mind. He must see enough of her to keep that image alive but not enough to tarnish it with reality.

Beyond his love of love, Tristan is in love with death. For what he wants can never be found in this life of limited possibilities and corruptible flesh. Since he wants the impossible, wants the constant ecstasy of pain or joy that only a dream can bring, he refuses what is possible. He wants the eternity of ecstasy that death alone provides and he will do what he can to hasten that eternity. (Throughout the story he is constantly courting death.) What Tristan finally "longs for with all his being is the annihilation of his being."[19] He is indeed mad with love.

It is almost a holy madness. De Rougemont sees Tristan as a relative of the Christian mystics who longed to be consumed in a flaming unity with God. Tristan, however, is not concerned with God but with his own fantasies. De Rougemont brings us closer to the nature of that fantasy when he remarks on the "twin narcissism of Tristan and Iseult."[20] Those of Tristan's persuasion seem to conceive of death as a return to some kind of narcissistic state where the distinction between selves is blurred and the world becomes, once again as it was in the womb, an extension of the self. Here we are back to Norman O. Brown and the fusion fantasies of Keniston's uncommitted youth. The latter, interestingly enough, though they gave lip service to sensual experimentation, were like Tristan, inclined to solitary ruminations on the misery of life, and like him they were all waiting for something better to come along.

The significance of the Tristan myth lies in the fact that it became the prototype for all other love stories in the West. If it were not woven into the fabric of Western life there would be no need to talk about it. But it is. From *Romeo and Juliet* to *Love Story* the Western mind has been following a siren song of romance: an impossible dream, generating impossible expectations, generating incredible misery. In one sense it is even more frustrating for us than it was for Tristan. He somehow understood that the ecstasy he sought would only be found in death. But now the myth has been diluted to the point where the element of death is often left out altogether. We are no longer apprised of the true price that the unrelenting search for romance exacts. We are instead led to believe that we can find some kind of heaven on earth.

From Victim to Victimizer

If many now turn away from this myth of romance to the myth of Don Juan, it is not difficult to see why. Our dreams of Iseult have been disappointed too often, and so "Don Juan appears, as though to avenge Tristan's inhuman suffering."[21] There is still enough of the Tristan legend to keep expectations high. And there are still many who feel the sting of romantic love unrealized. Now as Don Juan they will make up for the "good times" Tristan never saw.

But at heart both legends are the same. Both refuse to deal with the span of time. Intense romantic love (Tristan's kind) is oriented to a future beyond time and founders on the reality of daily continuity and familiarity. Don Juanism rejects continuity because it lives only for the present. Both refuse to deal realistically with choice: Don Juan jumps from possibility to possibility, while Tristan seeks the impossible. Both are alike in their inability to commit themselves to a possible future. And in both there is no question of the love of one person for another—the type of love by which a self might be defined:

Tristan loves only his own feeling of love; Don Juan is in love with change alone.

And for both, the pursuit of love is an outlaw affair. Tristan breaks all the rules of knighthood and fealty. Don Juan plays havoc with customs and law. In many respects the distance between these two mythic figures is not really so great. In our time it has, in a symbolic sense, taken only a decade or so to make the transition from starry-eyed victims of passion to mean-eyed victimizers.

11

Unscientific Postscript
on Romance

WHAT would be the difference if romance were to fade away? Romantic love as I have described it so far may seem very adolescent. So it is. It may seem rather unrealistic. It is. And so, aren't we better off without such adolescent fantasies? The chance to debunk a myth is a very tempting one, especially when it has led to as much misery as this one has. But the romantic love myth should not, I think, be approached in an iconoclastic manner, as though by freeing ourselves from it we were casting off the chains of yet another oppressor. Although in some respects we are well rid of the myth (as we are well rid of most fantasy), we shouldn't be too hasty to bury it. There always remains an element of mystery about myths that can never be completely demythologized. It is mysterious, for instance, that perfectly rational people—even those who are well acquainted with the myth—still come under its sway and fall romantically in love. And such people are somehow— at least to me—more appealing than those complete realists who, as Wordsworth put it, "murder to dissect." Realism too often misses the point and ceases to be realistic. Richard Schickel gives a good illustration of misguided realism in reviewing a film attempt at demythologizing sex. The film was the screen adaptation of D. H. Lawrence's *The Fox,* and Schickel had some comments to make about the sexual explicitness that was present in the film though not in Lawrence's novel. Such explicit realism ought usually to be avoided, writes Schickel, "not out of prudery but out of the knowledge that the true drama of the sexual encounter often occurs not in the act of love itself but in the life that surrounds it, conditioning and creating its quality."[1] The same comment may apply to any attempt to overexplain the romantic myth. Having laid bare the workings of the myth, do we now really understand it? Schickel goes on to say that "naked truth, literal and figurative, is often the biggest lie of all, disguising the creator's inability to recognize where the heart of the enigmatic drama lies and implying, too, that he knows all about a subject that is, finally, unknowable."[2] This search for the "naked truth" is rampant today in the behavioral sciences and it manifests itself in an unfortunate tendency to view all behavioral phenomena as ultimately reducible to the terms of science. Thus a great deal of behavior gets explained away as "nothing but a defense mechanism" or "nothing but a conditioned response." I think it would be doubly unfortunate if we tried to explain away romantic love in the same manner as "nothing but an illusion created by distance."

It is in an altogether different spirit that I would like to probe further into the nature of romantic love. If a romantic myth has developed and lasted for centuries in the West, despite the heartbreak it almost invariably brings, there may be good reason for it. One key to the purpose of the myth is the fact that it first takes hold in adolescence and is generally unknown in societies with no adolescent moratorium. (In many tribal societies when romance does occur, which is rare, it is considered a lamentable sickness.) Romantic love may be adolescent, and we could probably do without it just as we could probably do without adolescence itself. But adolescence is not a stage that can be skipped with impunity; it is the necessary transition to the type of rich and varied adulthood we value in the West. Romantic love, I believe, provides a similar transitional function; it leads on to a fuller and more realistic type of love: that love which the ancients called Eros.

Up to this point I have been speaking somewhat loosely about different kinds of love, and, for the sake of establishing the existence of a general decline in romance, I have been avoiding certain distinctions that I now want to make. Let me distinguish five types of love: sexual love, Don Juanism, romantic love, Eros, and agape. Romantic love and Eros are usually equated (de Rougemont does this) and often both are equated with sexual passion. A good initial distinction, then, is the one made by C. S. Lewis[3] to distinguish sexual desire from Eros (under which heading I will temporarily include romantic love). Lewis observed that sex makes a man want a woman whereas Eros makes a man want one particular woman. The psychiatrist Harry Stack Sullivan made a similar point in describing pure sexual desire as "undifferentiated lust": in other words, just about anyone will do. Don Juanism is sexual desire compounded with a desire for novelty—and indeed the novelty is as important as the sex. In this case, just about anyone will do as long as it is a different person each time. Eros is the force that intertwines two lives in love and gives them one common destiny. It is a drive, but also an attraction toward union. It involves sexuality, but unlike sexual desire it does not seek merely its own pleasure; rather it seeks to give pleasure to another. Its ultimate purpose is to create one new life out of two old ones. Finally Eros sweeps us up into promises and commitments with very little thought as to how they will be kept. But Eros cannot by itself keep the promises it makes— for that it has to be rescued by a more mature love. This mature love that the Greeks called *agape* is a care and concern for the other as other. It seeks not so much union of souls as communion. Where the other loves are all to some extent need-loves, agape is what C. S. Lewis calls "appreciative love";[4] that is, it loves another not for this or that aspect that fulfills a need in us but it loves them in themselves, in their wholeness. In mature love, moreover, there is a large component of will. Mature love is more under the control of will than is Eros and less under the control of emotions, and for this reason it has the staying power to keep the commitments that Eros in its rashness makes. Most loves are a mixture of these various types of love; most loves combine need-love with appreciative love, sexual love with altruistic love, and emotional love with love under the control of will. Agape for instance does not preclude sex but it does not *have* to do with sex at all. Without an infusion of agape, however, the other loves tend to burn up under their own heat.

Where does romantic love fit in this scheme? It is a preparation for Eros: it gears us toward individuals and commitments, but it is still a self-centered love, more in love with the feeling of love than with the beloved. Romantic love doesn't really know what to do with the beloved once the obstacles are out of the way. It fantasizes fusion—in the sense of an interpretation of souls—because it doesn't know how to cope with the other as other. It is, like Don Juanism, more in love with a state of being (the pursuit) than with a person. Eros is closer to appreciative love; it involves a more realistic perception of the other's qualities although it still has difficulty in imagining the other as separate with a life of her own. And Eros is always sexual, though romantic love may not as yet be so. The basic difference perhaps is that where romantic love cultivates the absence of the beloved, Eros cultivates her presence.

The point I would like to make is that, providing one does not permanently go off on the Don Juan detour, there is a progression from romantic love to Eros to mature and committed love. Everything in a sense starts with romantic love. In its willingness to overcome any obstacle and make any sacrifice it is a preparation for the real sacrifices that love requires. It is, moreover, the beginning of a love that looks to the future and therefore can make commitments that last. And it is, finally, a prelude to a love that transcends the self. All the promises of romantic love will, of course, lie fallow unless they are eventually redeemed by a more realistic understanding of love, but it does not seem that this initial stage can be altogether skipped without losing something basic. Perhaps there is something to be said for not getting too realistic too quickly. The whole process of adolescence as it has developed in the West is, after all, a deferment of realism. And it is for that reason a time to develop passions: passionate devotion to causes and passions of the intellect as well as passions of the heart. Passions are not very realistic but they make life a good deal more interesting than it would otherwise be; they also are a goad to the search for identity—and perhaps passionate romantic love is chief among these goads. Falling in love for the first time may be the essential mystery that starts the adolescent asking those questions that eventually lead to identity. A good deal of romantic love is unrequited, and such sweet misery is bound to generate some very basic questions in the adolescent heart: Why was he chosen to suffer like this? And who is he that he has been singled out to feel what (he is sure) no one else has ever felt? And who is he?

Before a child develops fine motor coordination, he first has to develop gross motor skills. Romantic love seems to play a similar role as a preparation for more mature forms of love. Just how important a role it plays is hard to say. But we may soon find out, for romance is certainly on the decline. The demise of romantic love may merely prove to be the end of a foolish myth—or it may portend something more serious: the death of Eros. And the death of Eros could be the death of agape.

12

Love: Identity and Constancy

*T*HE ability to love is today being undercut by three forces. From one direction it is assailed by the rising tide of rapid technical and social change. From another direction it is subjected to the eroding action of the self-in-process psychology. And from still another direction it is exposed to the numbing vibrations of the new tribalism. Together these forces deprive us of the capacity to make commitments and therefore the ability to love.

Whether one resonates to the McLuhan wavelength or to the Human Potential frequency, the result is the same: an end to romance, but also—and more seriously—a diminished capacity for sustained love. The romantic love of adolescence, when it does not succumb to the pounding of electric drums, all too often gives way not to real intimacy but to galloping Don Juanism. Those who are raised in the sound culture lack the imagination to romanticize and the will-energy to commit themselves to others. Those who follow the siren song of pop psychology and pop sexology believe that such commitment will limit their potential. Both camps lack the future perspective upon which mature love relies: the one, because it came of age in a post-print, present-oriented electric field; the other, because it embraces an ethic of spontaneous gratification. And both, because both are surrounded by a society of flux. Together these forces pull at the foundations of identity and love. Romantic love has been all but obliterated. And the next victim appears to be the mature and lasting love upon which most people anchor their ultimate hopes.

Love: Commitment and Feelings

Almost every recent serious attempt to define that love is but a postscript to Kierkegaard's analysis.[1] And Kierkegaard's treatment of love is, in turn, an explication of a single sentence in the New Testament: "Thou shalt love thy neighbor as thyself" (Matthew 22:39). It is, as Kierkegaard took pains to show, a startling statement. How can something like love be commanded? Even the most foolish parent realizes that although he can command a child to do something, he cannot command the child to love what he is doing. Sentiment simply cannot be decreed. You can perhaps require me to be polite to someone, to treat him civilly and with respect, but you cannot require me to like him. The statement "I can't help how I feel" is psychologically quite valid. Our feelings are of such a spontaneous nature that we rightly believe we cannot be held fully responsible for them. Kierkegaard reasoned that if love is something that can be commanded, it cannot be a feeling or sentiment but must be something entirely different.

If you cannot help how you feel, you can, however, help what you do. While we do not hold people legally responsible for their feelings, we do hold them responsible for their acts. If something can be commanded, it must be an act that we are capable of performing; something we can choose to do or not to do. Love, Kierkegaard concluded, is not a feeling but a choice. It is an act of will. More precisely, he said, it is a duty to which we freely commit ourselves.

This pairing of love and duty is odious to the modern sensibility, schooled in the tradition of spontaneity. The romantic notion of love as something into which one falls unaware is far more attractive than the concept of love as a chosen duty. Kierkegaard, more of a romantic than most, was well aware of this objection and sought to show that it is only when love is perceived as a duty that it is free from the double blight that always plagues romantic love, that is, uncertainty and anxiety. A love that is based merely on feelings is always threatened, because feelings are always subject to change. We cannot, after all, help how we feel. The love that is based on a chosen commitment, however, is secure against the vagaries of sentiment. "Only when it is a duty to love," wrote Kierkegaard, "only then is love everlastingly secure against every change."[2]

It is the love based only on feelings—what Kierkegaard called "the immediate love"—that is constantly concerned with putting love to the test ("Do you really love me?"), precisely because that kind of love is always in doubt. That the immediate love is no love at all is evident by how readily it can be changed into its opposite—hate—when it feels that the beloved has not met the test. Romantic love is of this kind. It is based on a feeling of love. It is in fact more delighted with the feelings than with the beloved. The romantic has a type in mind: someone like Iseult or Juliet. She comes along and he falls in love. At first she fits his mental image to perfection and he is in heaven. But presently the ecstasy fades. With time and familiarity the veneer of emotionality begins to wear thin, and since he is sure that there is nothing wrong with his feelings, he assumes that there is something wrong with his choice. She is not his type after all. But let him discard her and he feels certain the right girl will soon take her place: the type of girl who will keep his feelings at a high pitch. And so on. He is already on his way toward becoming a "Don Juan in slow time." As for Don Juanism, it makes no pretense of being anything but a transitory kind of love. It too is based on feelings: either a zesty mixture of pleasure, excitement, and adventure, or an anxious compulsion to confirm one's potency.

The New Look in Love

Love today supposedly has a new look. But it still appears to be a love based on feelings. Today's love experts make no excuse about this—it is, in fact, their proudest boast. Some examples of this type of thinking may be found in *Love Today: A New Explanation,* which is a compilation of the newest opinions on the oldest topic. One contributor, Joe K. Adams, defines love this way: "By love I mean a sentiment; i.e., a feeling for another person."[3] The utter simplicity of this statement is matched by the complete inconsistency of another definition appearing in the same anthology. Alexander Lowen sounds almost Kierkegaardian when he writes, "Love—is a feeling of total commitment." It's just a "feeling," however, not a real commitment because it "imposes no obligations." After all, Lowen observes, "Love is a feeling and, as such, is not subject to one's volition."[4] This of course is the exact opposite of the way Kierkegaard defined the matter.

A number of observers remark that our society is heading in the direction of temporary encounters, short-term intimacies, sequential and simultaneous affairs, sequential marriages, group marriages, and communal love. These new types of love are meant to replace "old-fashioned" romantic love. They are supposed to be more meaningful because they are endorsed by psychologists. They are supposedly more in line with natural human propensities than the outmoded pattern of lifelong love. This may be the direction in which love is headed, but the question is, Will it then be love? Even though today's emotional evangelists are no longer fooled by romantic love (they're too hip for that), even though they are more "realistic" about love, it still seems as though the love they are talking about is based strictly on feelings. True, they no longer endorse the starry-eyed, head-in-the-clouds feelings of a Tristan. But the feelings they do promote—"warmth," "sensitivity," "peak experiences"—are equally transitory.

In *The Transformation*, George Leonard writes that "unconditional joy may . . . turn out to be the real pornography of these transition years."[5] I am inclined to think that not joy but committed love will be the new obscenity. Like liberal theologians who are embarrassed to speak about God, the new relationship counselors are embarrassed to talk about love. When they do, they are quick to add that it "imposes no obligations." They would prefer to talk about "sensuality," "freedom," and "openness." Anything but love. Since they hesitate to attach a word with the lasting connotations of "love" to the growth encounters they advocate, and since they refuse to burden their followers with the language of commitment, they aren't left with much to say about the kind of love that might endure.

In fact the type of intimacy that is currently in fashion works best in the absence of commitment. This is evident, for example, in encounter group situations where complete strangers suddenly take to touching and hugging one another as though the Last Judgment were at hand. Given the supercharged atmosphere and the short duration of these groups, such behavior is understandable. It's easy to summon up warm feelings for people to whom one has only the most tenuous commitments, provided the group gives encouragement. And it does (as soon as everyone has confessed his sins). It also provides an experimental atmosphere which assures its participants that they don't really have to carry through on their pledges of affection. It has to be that way, of course, but it is unfortunate when the participants are deluded into thinking that such experiences are a prelude to real loving in the real world.

Another medium that furnishes a portal to the hassle-free world of warm feelings is the "personals" section of the classified ads. It is interesting to note how these lonely hearts pick up on the vocabulary of the Human Potential Movement, and how they often link it to noncommitment. Here are some typical excerpts:

> "Looking for WF 20's pretty, educated, to share occasional meetings of sex and warmth."

"Male grad, 22, seeks warm, gentle, honest, fun-loving female to show me city. My interests are varied, active, expanding—no limitations or expectations, closeness is all I seek."

"WM 25—seeks understanding older WF 30–35 for companionship and sexual encounters. No heavy relationship, just open and happy one."

"I am F 35, attractive, intelligent, caring. My credo: I do my thing, and you do your thing. I am not in this world to live up to your expectations, and you are not in this world to live up to mine. You are you and I am I. And if by chance we find each other, it's beautiful. If not, it can't be helped! [Fritz Perls.] I would like to meet a man who lives the above. He should be over 30, aware, dynamic and looking for a close relationship."

Once again behind all this avoidance of entanglements is the assumption that love is only a feeling. Since feelings are fluid and changeable it is no good trying to account for them. Love, yes; commitment, no. That is the current wisdom.

The Limitations of Love

Opposed to this view is Kierkegaard's belief that love is a freely chosen duty—a proposition that was never very well received and is even less popular today. As said before, the present tendency is to rebel at the limitations of choice. There is a refusal to choose, or else a conviction that one ought to be able to take back one's choice and all the lost possibilities that went with it. This, however, is more than a refusal of choice; it is also a refusal of love. And beyond this it is a refusal of identity. As we have seen, our identity does lie in choices and in whom or to what we choose to commit ourselves. There is no way to avoid this uncomfortable fact, nor the fact that choices are limiting. If a man involves himself with one woman, he may be lessening his chance for involvement with someone else—perhaps someone more interesting. But true actualization requires such decisions. Although choices are limiting, they are the medium by which we define ourselves. This is why Don

Juan, who cannot settle, is best described as a power rather than a person. He has no identity because he will not choose. Once again de Rougemont puts the matter quite succinctly: "Don Juan might be the man who cannot love, because loving is first of all choosing, and to choose one must *be* and Don Juan has no being."[6]

"To choose one must be." That is, one must have an identity. And that presumably is why Erikson places identity before intimacy in the development toward maturity. An individual without a firm sense of identity will be frightened by the thought of intimacy or commitment. He must find himself before he can afford to lose himself in love. Without that sense of identity he will always be asking himself: "What am I doing with *this* person when I don't even know who *I* am?" And always he will be moving on with "a desperate wish . . . to start all over again."[7]

Intimacy requires a relaxation of the definition of self. But to do that one must first have a grip on one's self. Otherwise the proposition becomes too risky. The fantasy of fusion with another becomes a bad dream when there is no prior self-delineation. In that case, as Erikson puts it, "fusion with another becomes identity loss."[8] A young person with an uncertain sense of self will often react in one of three ways when he arrives at the stage of intimacy. He will either avoid intimacies altogether. Or he will embark on a ceaseless round of sexual and romantic experimentation in the manner of Don Juan. Or he will seek to submerge his self under the auspices of some older, more powerful person—a guru, a religious master, an experienced lover—who seems to have everything under control. In the latter case there is at least a possibility that the "leader's" seemingly sure sense of self might rub off on the disciple.

It is an oversimplification of the case, however, to place identity before intimacy, as though a complete sense of identity can be obtained in the absence of intimacy. Identity is constructed in part on the fidelities and commitments that intimacy evokes. Identity is never complete until it is shared. This is what Martin Buber means when he writes: "Through the *thou* a man becomes I."[9] Buber, as is plain from his translator's preface, was heavily influenced by Kierkegaard. The same emphasis on love as choice and duty permeates *I and thou*. Buber speaks of the *I-thou* relationship in terms of taking a stand: "Love is the responsibility of an I for a *thou.*"[10] And like Kierkegaard he does not see love as limited to feelings: "Feelings accompany the metaphysical and metapsychical fact of love, but they do not constitute it."[11] In the writings of Buber, Kierkegaard, and Erikson we find this persistent theme: love is a matter not of feeling, but of choosing. And choosing is a matter of identity. By our choices we create ourselves, and that is why we ought to try to be faithful to them.

Loving Everyone

Even if we can bring ourselves to accept love as a duty, that problematic statement from the Bible still remains problematic. The commandment with which Kierkegaard was so concerned goes on to tell us that the object of our love is to be our "neighbor." This is generally interpreted to mean "everyone." And that, it would seem, is asking too much. We are not, after all, saints and we can plainly see that many of our "neighbors" are either scoundrels, fools, or madmen, or a combination of the three. The commandment was certainly a stumbling block for Freud. Like Kierkegaard, he clearly recognized the significance of this "Love thy neighbor"—but with an entirely different reaction: "Why should we do it? What good will it do us?" But, above all, "How shall we achieve it? How can it be possible?"[12] Freud's argument is all the more difficult to refute when he continues in a very Kierkegaardian manner that "it [my love] imposes duties on me for whose fulfillment I must be ready to make sacrifices." Under these conditions, says Freud, it is hard to love any stranger: "Indeed," he writes, "I should be wrong to do so, for my love is valued by all my own people as a sign of my preferring them, and it is an injustice to them if I put a stranger on a par with them."[13]

Freud goes on to say that, if anything, this universal stranger probably has more claim to his hatred than his love, considering what we know about the aggressive nature of man. But his most telling argument is the simple economic one that if love is spread out, it is spread thin. How many duties can one shoulder simultaneously? How many commitments can one carry? "Love thy neighbor" is "unpsychological," Freud wrote. "Such an enormous inflation of love can only lower its value."[14]

Now the currently popular reply to anything we find disagreeable in Freud is to say that he was a product of his times. It is said (I have said it myself) that Freud's theoretical constructs were colored by the scientific and economic assumptions of his culture. And that in true capitalist fashion Freud assumed a scarcity economy in the psyche: There was just so much libido to go around and one had to be careful where one invested it. Since libido could only be in one place at one time there was no such thing as a diversified psychic portfolio. So for Freud, self-love and love of others were incompatible and brotherly love close to impossible.

But it is not enough to claim that Freud's vision was limited by his times. Common sense tells us that there are just too many people coming in and out of our lives on a daily basis to love them all in any but the most diluted fashion. If we conceive of love in Kierkegaard's and Freud's sense of a chosen duty that carries responsibilities—as opposed to a warm glowy feeling of "love" for all mankind that can come or go depending on our mood—then it is not possible to love so many. Long before I had ever heard of Freud, back in my youth, in confessional days, I was bothered by the same commandment and I once confessed to a priest that I couldn't keep it. Instead of urging me to "pray for God's grace" and to "try harder" as I expected he would—for that was the way priests talked in those days—he replied in a gruff tone, "You can't love everyone," and dismissed me with a hasty absolution. That put me in a good humor. It was a relief not to have to love everybody. And I determined to go to that priest for confession from then on, in the hope that he would help me dispense with the rest of my scruples.

Still, the commandment says "Love thy neighbor," which seems to imply "everyone." And although we live in nonreligious times, there is no reason not to give this Biblical injunction the same consideration we allot to a passage from, say, Eric Berne or B. F. Skinner. Once again Kierkegaard's analysis is most astute. It focuses on the parable of the man who fell among thieves and the good Samaritan who came to his aid:

> After having related the parable of the good Samaritan, Christ says to the Pharisees, "Which of these three do you think was neighbor to him who fell among thieves?" And the Pharisees answer "rightly," "the one who showed mercy to him." That is by recognizing your duty to him you readily discover who your neighbor is—He to whom I have an obligation is my neighbor, and when I fulfill my obligation I show that I am his neighbor.[15]

Your neighbor is, according to Kierkegaard's interpretation, the one to whom you have a responsibility. More often than not this means family and friends, but it could mean anyone who through circumstances demands a responsibility of us. You can't love everyone but you can choose to love the ones you have a duty to. Buber has written that the *thou* "implicates the whole world."[16] In loving the *thou*—your neighbor—you love all others in potential. In this sense it is enough to love one person to fulfill the command "Love thy neighbor." To think that every relationship with every person should be an *I—thou* relation is foolish. *I—it* relationships characterize the majority of our dealings with other people and rightly so, for as Harvey Cox[17] points out in *The Secular City,* we simply could not otherwise accomplish our daily routines. If we wish to carry on an *I—thou* relationship with the clerk at the check-out counter of the supermarket, we will only succeed in winning the ire of a dozen other customers and the possible dismissal of "thou" from his job. What we must be aware of is that any individual has the potential for becoming a *thou* and that any stranger may through circumstances become our "neighbor." So neither Buber nor the Bible enjoins us to love everyone; instead they remind us that everyone is a potential neighbor.

The Death of Love

It is another matter altogether when certain modish thinkers inform us that we are indistinguishable from our neighbor. In an article on "the Future of Sex," Marshall McLuhan and George Leonard predict that, "Sex as we now think of it may soon be dead."[18] What will replace it, they say, is the polymorphous perverse nonspecialist, nonprivate, tribal sex that is so dear to Norman O. Brown. Even prostitution and homosexuality will have to go, since they are too specialized for this nonlinear age. In support of these contentions they pull out the usual McLuhan adages about the electric age and mix it in with some Human Potential philosophy—which is more in Leonard's line.

It can also be argued, however, that love as we now know it will soon be dead—and for the same reasons that will kill sex. McLuhan and Leonard are quite explicit about the demise of romantic love: a specialist "invention of the late Middle Ages," a triumph of highly individualistic enterprise."[19] And they tell us that, "A couple of teen-agers like Romeo and Juliet would now have some of their most dramatic moments deciding on the kind of education they want for their children, plus a second career for Romeo in middle age."[20] Not very romantic, but perhaps preferable to death at an early age. Romance may not, however, be much missed since the ability to romanticize seems to require certain abstractive powers and McLuhan's neo-tribal youth appear to be phasing themselves out of the stage of formal operations. This, by the way, may be another reason that romance is uncommon in many primitive tribes, where conceptual thought is also rare.

Even if we have to get along without romantic love (which

was always a mixed blessing), how well can we get along without committed love (which though also a mixed blessing has always been a more necessary one)? The same neo-tribal currents that threaten to wash away sex and romance also threaten responsible love. What makes love responsible is the fact that it goes out from one individual to another: "The responsibility of an *I* for a *thou,*"[21] as Buber puts it. Contrary to the commune philosophy, people are much more responsible when they don't have a group to disappear in. Following the much-publicized murder of Kitty Genovese in front of forty or so witnesses, two psychologists, John Darley and Bibb Latané undertook to study the dynamics of responsibility.[22] They found that individuals are far more likely to take responsibility for another when they are alone than when they are in a group. In a group, responsibility is so diffused that everyone feels a lessened obligation and everyone is less likely to take responsible action. In one of a variety of experiments two individuals are placed in adjacent rooms separated by a thin partition. One man, an accomplice of the researcher, imitates the sounds that a heart attack victim might make: wheezing, gasping for breath, and eventually a resounding thud. The object of the research is to determine how quickly and under what conditions one individual would take action to help another. It was found that when the number of individuals in the adjoining room was increased, the tendency for any one of them to take action in aid of the "victim" was considerably delayed or completely absent. In light of such studies one wonders what would have been the fate of the man who fell among thieves if, instead of one Samaritan, a whole caravan of them had passed by. The point here is that although responsibility can flourish in a communal setting, it must first be a personal matter—a matter of *I* and *thou.*

In the McLuhan-Brown version of the future there will be no more *I*'s and *thou*'s. One wonders what will then become of responsibility. The answer is not hard to find. Both McLuhan and Brown have broadly hinted that the concept of individual guilt and individual responsibility is passé. In fact, the concept of the individual per se is out of date. It is to be replaced by a "mystical body" or a "global village" or a combination of both. In any event it means that individual identity is to be submerged in the mass.

As I see it, this spells the death of love. If you lose the self then you have no basis for love, since mature love, which is communion, requires two separate identities. Without a sense of identity, people will not commit themselves to other people. And if love is not such an individual commitment, then what is it: a feeling? a vibration? electricity? The neo-tribalism of the present day does not replace individualized Western identity with communal identity but with an inability to define any kind of identity. The sound culture tends to produce an individual who is too far into his own head to really communalize, let alone commit; and it can leave him deficient in the particularizing skills the intellect requires to delineate an identity. Both self-definition and commitment also require that characteristic Adelman has dubbed "will-energy."[23] And in that also the neo-tribal young are sadly deficient. Finally, when we consider how difficult it is to cultivate a future perspective in a post-print culture we are forced to picture a society in which long-term committed love will be largely absent.

The Paradox of Fluidity

The McLuhan-Leonard article propounds an interesting thesis. What is more interesting to note is that in the collaboration of McLuhan and Leonard, the Human Potential Movement and the electric age philosophy have joined up. We can expect more of these alliances in the future because these two schools of thought are highly compatible. Both argue for a breakdown of specialist roles and their replacement by a more fluid self —one more adaptable to the high-speed world of electric circuitry. Both emphasize the advantages of living for the present as primitives supposedly do; and both, finally, advocate the expression of spontaneous "natural" or "primitive" instincts.

It is possible to enumerate other similarities between the two, but I think it more important to comment on another facet of this merger.

Separately or together these twin philosophies of transformation are caught in an enormous paradox. The biological corollary of fluidity is the phenomenon of neoteny. Neoteny refers to the retention of some embryonic or immature characteristics in adulthood. But this immaturity also connotes flexibility and plasticity. The neotenous creature is, so to speak, an unfinished product. It is not bound to the stereotyped patterns of behavior that characterize those animals which grow quickly to maturity. The phenomenon of neoteny accounts in part for the supreme adaptability of the human species, but it also accounts for the long dependency of human offspring. Commenting on this phenomenon the biologist J. Bronowski urges that the specifically human thing about us is our mutability. But this is not quite the same as the process philosophy. Rather, Bronowski says that human advancement depends on long-term strategies; and that the ability to devise such strategies rests with minds that are allowed to put off decisions, to play, to have, as it were, a "long childhood" of the intellect. This "play period" of the mind is the biological equivalent of the adolescent moratorium. It is as essential to the evolution of mankind as the moratorium is to the development of identity. All of this, says Bronowski, depends on a long, protected childhood. The more plastic human nature becomes, the more slowly men and women must mature, the more dependent human children will become:

> In man, before the brain is an instrument for action, it has to be an instrument of preparation. For that, quite specific areas are involved. But, far more deeply, it depends on the long preparation of human childhood. In scientific terms we are neotenous; that is, we come from the womb still as embryos. And perhaps this is why our civilization, our scientific civilization, adores above all else the symbol of the child: the Christ child painted by Raphael and re-enacted by Blaise

Pascal; the young Mozart and Gauss; the children in Jean-Jacques Rousseau and Charles Dickens.[24]

Now, the contradiction of the two philosophies is this: On the one hand they want to promote an infinitely plastic, growing, changing, neotenous personality. And on the other hand they want to revert to a primitive state where there is no long childhood and therefore no chance to develop plasticity; where instead children are plunged very quickly into adult responsibilities, and where identities and possibilities close up. In such societies there is no orientation to the future, fathers don't take responsibility for children, and the culture does not advance. There is no adoration of the child in such short-horizon cultures; neither is the cause of neoteny or fluidity served.

The transformationists may talk a great deal about keeping fluid, postponing choices, experiencing many life-styles—and all in the name of growth. Some may even call upon the principle of neoteny. But this whole growth philosophy depends on an even more prolonged period of childhood dependency than we now have. And that means that sometime, somewhere, someone has to grow up and make enough of an identity commitment to take care of growing children. But few will want to if a short-horizon philosophy of spontaneity becomes prevalent. In that case we will purchase our fluidity at the expense of the next generation. Instead of providing them a protective framework within which they can explore their individual possibilities, we will cast them into the sink-or-swim of our own impulsive and treacherous currents. They may swim and survive, but they will not be the flexible, open, and trusting children we desire. More likely they will be cautious, calculating, and mistrustful. Orphans of the flood cannot afford to be otherwise.

Constancy

The reason that traditional marriage, family, love, and friendship patterns are breaking down is not for lack of human relationship expertise. There is plenty of that around. Unfortunately, in all their concern with sensitivity and expressiveness, the experts fail to talk about the one thing that does make a relationship last: commitment. Commitment in turn requires a developed sense of identity; that is, a center of responsiveness that persists over time and is capable of sustained fidelity. The reason we are in such a quandary over relationships is that the individuals who enter into them are lacking in a sense of identity. And lacking it they want to keep all options open. Naturally their relationships will fail.

Some cultures—the mainland Chinese, for example—get along without cultivating in their citizens a sense of individual identity. There is always in such cultures either a tight web of community or else a strong sense of national purpose. But the lack of individual identity is disastrous in a culture which has no sense of community nor a sense of purpose. And ours does not. Where meaning is absent both on a national and an individual level, then there is indeed no reason to cultivate individual relationships or to tie oneself down to one person or one family, or any society. A meaningless vacuum inhabited by self-serving "actualizers" truly is a primitive condition, but it is not a noble or peaceful village.

Where does that leave us? Since the end of religion, and in a world that is fragmented and doesn't make sense as a whole anymore, a continuing sense of self and lasting individual commitment are all the meaning that we have left.

A hundred years ago Matthew Arnold described the world in which he lived as having

> . . . *neither joy, nor love, nor light,*
> *Nor certitude, nor peace, nor help for pain;*
> *And we are here as on a darkling plain*
> *Swept with confused alarms of struggle and flight,*
> *Where ignorant armies clash by night.*[25]

The lines have lost none of their relevance. Today there is considerably less certitude, and life seems even more meaningless. In describing the political and social atmosphere of the late sixties, Norman Mailer, despite his lavish imagination, merely paraphrased the last line of *Dover Beach*. And *Armies of the Night* is about as timely a title as anyone could have devised. For Matthew Arnold there was no longer anything to believe in:

> *The Sea of Faith*
> *Was once, too, at the full, and round earth's shore*
> *Lay like the folds of a bright girdle furled*
> *But now I only hear*
> *Its melancholy, long, withdrawing roar,*
> *Retreating, to the breath*
> *Of the night-wind, down the vast edges drear*
> *And naked shingles of the world.* [26]

The "Sea of Faith" that was receding in Arnold's time is now a dead sea. Religion is dead, and there is not much else to believe in. The new intimacy is, of course, a reaction to the salt marsh of loneliness and alienation that was left us after the death of religion, the death of community, and the death of the family. It is significant that the tendency today is to talk about intimacy rather than love. Perhaps it is easier to believe in intimacy than in love. If nothing else, there is the certainty of flesh against flesh, and that is something. For some it has become a whole new faith. Something of this new-time religion can be seen in *The New Intimacy: Open Ended Marriage and Alternative Life Styles* by Ronald Mazur, a Unitarian minister. "The encounter/sensitivity movement," he writes, ". . . is creating a new class of sensually adventurous persons; men and women who rejoice in their flesh-and-bloodness; who delight in mutual exchanges of being-with-you-in-the-flesh pleasure; who affirm their sensual condition without shame." [27] Mazur is talking about more than sex here; he is talking about affection, and warmth, and sharing and self-growth also. But it somehow sounds more like lovemaking than love, and it is still a love based on feelings alone. The new intimacy even has its own poet laureate—Kahlil Gibran. Mazur quotes Gibran's advice to lovers: "Love one another, but make not a bond of love. Rather let it be a moving sea between the shores of your souls."[28]

Those lines express very nicely the importance of fluidity and the limitations of possessiveness. Yet it is interesting that Gibran chose the sea as a metaphor for love; the sea may ebb and flow but it is constant. Poetically speaking, it has always been a symbol of timelessness. To Matthew Arnold, the roar of the waves on Dover Beach brought "the eternal note of sadness in," which "Sophocles long ago heard . . . on the Aegean." What is wrong with the "Movement for Alternative Lifestyles" (read Human Potential Movement), as Mazur calls it, is that it neglects this element of constancy in favor of fluidity and feelings. But where there is no constant sea to buoy us up, we drown in fluidity.

Although I like Gibran's ideas on love, I much prefer Matthew Arnold. His reply to the emptiness he felt around him was this: "Ah, love, let us be true to one another!"[29] If religion and the other institutions we counted on have failed us, we can at least believe in each other. We can at least be true to one another. But to do that we first have to be true to ourselves— and have a self to be true to, not one that melts away like ice on a hot stove. Fluid identity can only result in fluid relationships that are not very helpful in a world where all the other mooring posts have been torn away. A sense of persistent and permanent identity, on the other hand, is the only guarantee of solid and lasting relationship. Only those with a permanent sense of identity can afford to experiment with fluidity-in-identity; and only those with a strong sense of commitment can afford to experiment with fluidity in relationships, although they may have less need to (the marriage of Harold and Vita Nicolson, described by their son in *Portrait of a Marriage* is one illustration of this fluidity within commitment).[30]

There is no Ode to Identity. The subject does not inspire in poets the fine frenzy that the subject of love does; but both identity and love are a matter of constancy. "Love's not Time's fool," wrote Shakespeare; neither is identity. And without a constant identity, love cannot withstand the temptations of time. Shakespeare understood well the decaying power of time, against which "brass," "stone," "earth," and "gates of steel" could not prevail, and he asked what chance love, so seemingly frail, had against it. His most convincing answer is found in Sonnet 116:

> *Love's not Time's fool, though rosy lips and cheeks*
> *Within his bending sickle's compass come;*
> *Love alters not with his brief hours and weeks,*
> *But bears it out even to the edge of doom.*
> *If this be error and upon me proved,*
> *I never writ, nor no man ever loved.*[31]

What keeps love from altering? What makes it possible to bear it out "even to the edge of doom"? Feelings, warmth, closeness? Hardly. We have to go back to Kierkegaard's understanding of love as a choice—a choice, moreover, that is permanent, for, as de Rougemont observed, "the irrevocable alone is serious."[32] Serious love—love that "looks on tempests and is never shaken"—has to be based on an unalterable decision. Consider the marriage oath. It is a vow to "love, honor, and cherish for better or worse, for richer or poorer, in sickness and in health, till death do us part." But without the last phrase it is really an empty pledge. What secures all the rest is the promise to bear it out "till death do us part." That phrase clashes, of course, with all that is fashionable today in psychology. It should be no surprise, then, that many engaged couples now wish to dilute the marriage oath. One couple I know of were willing to take the oath up through "in sickness and in health," but requested that the remainder of the vow be left out. The priest involved, himself no slouch at innovation, nevertheless refused. He was disposed to join the couple in matrimony, but simply could not, since he understood well enough that the refusal of the clinching phrase would effectively negate the rest of the vow. The love that united the young couple in question did not lack for intensity, and it was certainly an honest love—but it was not a serious love. Serious love is a lifelong decision.

To this it will be objected: "You can't make decisions like that; you can't foresee how you will develop, or how your beloved will develop." That is a logical objection. No one can look into the future, it is true. And we do inevitably change. My answer to the objection is this: Love is simply a decision that in some essential ways we *will not* change; that, come what may, we *will* stick by certain commitments. I emphasize the word "will" because I wish to insist that the self creates its own directions; it does not merely bob around in the rivers of change. Such decisions are not out of our hands, though it would be foolish to think that they are easy—or that they are for everybody. If one's identity is still in an embryonic state, it is best not to make such decisions. For those, however, who are interested in a serious relationship, it is necessary to understand that such relationships are incompatible with a philosophy of tentativeness. Once again de Rougemont puts the matter succinctly when he writes, "the foundation of . . . fidelity is an initial refusal *on oath* 'to cultivate' the illusions of passion."[33] Constancy, in other words, is a decision that some doors will remain forever closed. To maintain fidelity is to decide in as many words: "Yes, someone better, someone more exciting, may very well come along—but that is an opportunity I will have to pass up." That is the price we pay for constancy.

13

Old Realities and New Myths

A FEW years ago, Philip Slater observed that the benefits that a sense of community would bring to our society would far outweigh the drawbacks. He wrote, "Communal, un-Oedipal children tend to be a little literal and uninteresting. An exaggerated swing of the pendulum in this direction, however, is not a problem we will have to worry about in *this* century."[1] A similar reasoning process is at work in the minds of those who seek a more fluid identity and an entanglement-free intimacy. It seems only yesterday that we began to break out of our character armor; only a moment ago that we began to experiment with a wider range of identities and relationships. Swings of the pendulum, however, take place rather rapidly these days. Already the smother-mother whom Slater castigated is a dying species. And already the pendulum of identity formation has taken an exaggerated swing toward fluidity and tentativeness and away from continuity and fidelity. When, for instance, in the spirit of the times, the Reverend Mr. Mazur can write, "We consider traditional monogamy, with its rigid requirements for exclusive devotion and affection, even though hallowed by the theological concept of fidelity, to be a culturally approved mass neurosis"[2]—that is an exaggerated swing of the pendulum.

My purpose in making these observations is not to encourage a swing of the pendulum back to the days of constricted emotions and stiff-upper-lip duty. There is a kind of sterile commitment that actually blocks love and about which Rollo May writes perceptively in *Love and Will.* This is commitment with the element of care gone out of it, based solely on concepts of duty, and held together by old-fashioned Victorian willpower. That is not fidelity to a person but to a code—a frozen duty made once and for all on oath, but unenlivened by a daily spirit of fidelity and renewal of fidelity. In previously juxtaposing love based on commitment to love based on feelings, I did not mean to imply that commitments are without feelings. A commitment of love *is* a feeling—perhaps the very deepest of all feelings—in which affection is inspired by fidelity. Rollo May astutely observes that mature love is love joined with will.

The turbulence and uprootedness of the present American experience does call for a redefinition of identity, and it does call for greater fluidity than we have in the past allowed ourselves. As much as anyone else, I believe that we must preserve in our lives a generous measure of fluidity if we are to survive these days of transition. This applies to our relationships as well as to our identities. Our commitments do not have to be so structured that they prevent self-growth or the growth of the ones we love; a loving commitment also has to be a realistic commitment, and that implies, as Eugene Kennedy has written, that in making our commitments "we appreciate and make room for the changes that will necessarily occur in ourselves and in those around us."[3] Or, to appropriate Kahlil Gibran's words, "Let there be spaces in your togetherness."[4]

What needs to be opposed is not fluidity per se, but fluidity removed from the context of commitment. As our society careens around ever sharper and more frequent turns in the road, it will be necessary to develop a quality which I would term "fluidity-within-commitment." That is a fine balance not easily preserved, but it seems the only sane approach to identity and intimacy. If the element of commitment is not preserved, then love will degenerate to feelings without fidelity, and Kahlil Gibran will be replaced as poet laureate of the Human Potential Movement by Sir John Suckling, who in the seventeenth century wrote:

> *Out upon it! I have loved*
> *Three whole days together;*
> *And am like to love three more,*
> *If it prove fair weather.*[5]

Along with commitment, continuity and fidelity are indispensable accompaniments of identity and love. Love is an act of will *and* an act of faith. Love requires that we believe in our beloved and that he or she believe in us; but such faith presupposes something to believe in: the inner coherence and reliability—even goodness—that is summed up in the term "identity." We fall in love in the first place because we see some goodness in another and experience that goodness directed toward us. Our love is based on the belief that the goodness will endure and will continue to be directed toward us. Fluidity —the self-in-process—with all its merits does not and never will inspire such faith.

The Human Potential emphasis on fluidity paves the way for easy acceptance of the doctrine that identity is altogether dispensable: the path advocated by McLuhan, Brown, and Laing. Whatever criticisms apply to the self-in-process, apply even more strongly to no-self. The doctrine of no-self means that we sacrifice personal responsibility, individual love, and perhaps a good bit of our cognitive and imaginative powers. And even if we were disposed to make those sacrifices there would be no profit in it, for the global consciousness which this brand of self-transcendence supposes is entirely nonexistent. The question that must be posed to advocates of this view is, What does it profit a man to lose both his soul and the world?

Nonetheless, the McLuhan/Brown philosophy does serve to remind us how important it is that our individual identity be confirmed and validated by the larger community; and it recalls us to the truth that beyond individual identity there lies a more inclusive human identity.

How do we achieve and maintain identity in a changing world? I have suggested several possibilities.

In general, it will become more and more important to develop the quality of fidelity and to concentrate on building lasting commitments and enduring relationships. This, in turn, requires that, both as individuals and in community, we strive to provide experiences of continuity to ourselves and to those about us. Perhaps this will entail a greater effort to stay in one place. Or at least to maintain contact with those from whom we have been separated either by time or distance, and perhaps it will require us to revive and cherish the many annual traditions—national, community, and family—that have fallen by the way. And there is much need to create new traditions as well—on the community and family level, but also on the more individualized level of friendships and love relationships. The turbulence and unconnectedness of modern society further demands that we look for guidance in places that might have once been thought most unlikely. From tribal societies we can learn about helping children to grow up to an unalienated adulthood. A Western equivalent of the rite of passage could help to support and ratify the adolescent during his lonely struggle to shape an identity. If properly structured, these rites or institutions of passage could benefit the whole society immeasurably; and beyond that they could call into play the Heroic sense which, tragically, lies untapped in the adolescent heart. Beyond identity it is necessary that we cultivate the quality of generativity, for it is the ultimate warrant that the cycle of development will go on. Last but not least is fluidity. It is fluidity that keeps the waters of life from freezing into cold duty and hardening into resignation. And within the framework of continuity, fidelity, and generativity there is more than enough space for it. But without those qualities, fluidity can be only a surface movement, for they form the deep and solid bed along which the true self flows.

We live in transitional times. New and changing realities confront us daily. The temptation is strong to do away with all the old and outworn myths, to file them away with the flat-earth theory and the Ptolemaic Universe.

But not all realities are new, and not all myths are old. And the danger always exists that new myths will replace old realities. One of these new myths is that we can get along without identity. Not only is the achievement of individual identity being neglected today in favor of the cultivation of spontaneity, but the very desirability of personal identity is called into question. Because of this new focus the elements out of which a personal identity might be fashioned are increasingly in short supply; and also in short supply are the capacities which emanate from identity: trust, fidelity, friendship, and love. The bonds which in the past tied individuals together have already been weakened by the forces of accelerating change; and the new myths of identity threaten to erode them even further.

The new myths have it that identity is expendable, or ought at best to be a moment-to-moment construct; the old and persistent reality is that we cannot do without a secure and continuous sense of identity. It is this older and plainer but increasingly elusive quality of abiding identity that we must work to recapture.

Notes

Introduction

1 Herman Hupfeld, "As Time Goes By," © 1931 by Harms Inc. Copyright renewed. All rights reserved. Reprinted by permission of Warner Bros. Music.
2 From the film *Black History: Lost, Stolen or Strayed*, CBS Television.
3 John Dos Passos quoted in Richard Hofstadter *The American Political Tradition* (New York: Vintage Books, 1959), p.v.
4 Joseph B. Fabry, *The Pursuit of Meaning* (Boston: Beacon Press, 1968), pp. 13–14.
5 Walt Whitman, "Native Moments" from *Leaves of Grass*.
6 Ernest Dowson. *"Non Sum Qualis Eram Bonae Sub Regno Cynarae"* from *Poems*.
7 Urie Bronfenbrenner quoted in *Time*, Dec. 24, 1973, p. 65.
8 *Esquire*, March 1974.
9 David Viscott, *Feel Free* (New York: Dell, 1971), p. 28.

Chapter 1

1 Robert Bolt, *A Man for All Seasons* (New York: Random House, 1962), p. 123.
2 Ibid., p. 140.
3 Ibid., p. xii.
4 Ibid., pp. 72, 75–76.
5 Ibid., p. 65.
6 Ibid., p. xiv.
7 Henrik Ibsen, *Peer Gynt* (New York: E. P. Dutton and Co., 1930), p. 202.
8 Erik H. Erikson, *Identity, Youth and Crisis* (New York: W. W. Norton and Co., 1968), p. 246.
9 Ibid., p. 50.
10 Alvin Toffler, *Future Shock* (New York: Bantam Books, 1970), p. 319.
11 Gilbert D. Bartell, *Group Sex* (New York: New American Library, 1973).

12 R. I. Evans, *Dialogue with Erik Erikson* (New York: E. P. Dutton, 1969), Erikson quoted, p. 39.

13 Kenneth Keniston, *The Uncommitted* (New York: Harcourt, Brace and World, 1965), pp. 239–40.

14 Evans, *Dialogue*, Erikson quoted, p. 30. Erikson, "Youth: Fidelity and Diversity," in *The Challenge of Youth*, E. H. Erikson, ed.(Garden City: Doubleday Anchor, 1965), p. 1.

15 Toffler, *Future Shock*, p. 122.

16 Kenneth Keniston, "Social Change and Youth in America" in *The Challenge of Youth*, p. 202.

17 F. M. Esfandiary, *Up-Wingers* (New York: The John Day Co., 1973), p. 116.

Chapter 2

1 Søren Kierkegaard, "The Journals," in *A Kierkegaard Anthology*, Robert Bretall, ed. (New York: Modern Library, 1946).

2 Sylvia Plath, *The Bell Jar* (New York: Harper and Row, 1971), p. 85.

3 Carl R. Rogers, *On Becoming a Person* (Boston: Houghton Mifflin Company, 1961), p. 27.

4 Ibid., p. 158.

5 A list of these institutions may be found in *Please Touch* by Jane Howard (New York: Dell Publishing Co., 1970), pp. 258–67.

6 Abraham Maslow, *Toward a Psychology of Being* (Princeton: D. Van Nostrand, 1962), p. 81.

7 Victor Frankl, *Psychotherapy and Existentialism* (New York: Simon and Schuster, 1968), p. 8.

8 Ibid., p. 9.

9 Ibid., p. 104.

10 Rollo May, *Love and Will* (New York: Dell Publishing Co., 1973).

11 Maslow, *Toward a Psychology of Being*, p. 192.

12 Robert Coles, *Erik H. Erikson: The Growth of His Work* (Boston: An Atlantic Monthly Press Book, 1970).

13 Erikson, *Identity, Youth and Crisis*, p. 94.

14 Arthur Miller, *Death of a Salesman* (New York: Viking Press, 1958), p. 23.

15 Ibid., p. 54.

16 Coles, *Erik H. Erikson*, p. 172.

17 William Shakespeare, *Hamlet*. Act II, Scene 2.

18 See Erikson, *Identity, Youth and Crisis*, pp. 236–40.

19 Erik H. Erikson, *Childhood and Society* (New York: W.W. Norton & Co., 1963), pp. 263–264.

20 Kenneth Keniston, *The Uncommitted*.

Chapter 3

1 Howard, *Please Touch*, p. 246.
2 Erikson, *Identity, Youth and Crisis*, p. 246.
3 Rogers, *On Becoming a Person*, p. 55.
4 Maslow, *Toward a Psychology of Being*, p. 102.
5 Morton Lieberman, Irving Yalom, and Matthew Miles, *Encounter Groups: First Facts* (New York: Basic Books, 1973). See also: Alan Mintz, "Encounter Groups and Other Panaceas," in *Commentary*, July 1973, pp. 42–49.
6 Pauline Kael, *Kiss Kiss Bang Bang* (Boston: Atlantic Monthly Press, 1968), p. 190.
7 Leo Tolstoy, "The Death of Ivan Ilyich."
8 May, *Love and Will*, p. 102.
9 C. S. Lewis, *The Four Loves* (New York: Harcourt Brace Jovanovich, 1960), p. 158.
10 Hesiod, *Theogony*, lines 120–22, trans. Richmond Lattimore (Ann Arbor: University of Michigan Press, 1961), quoted by Rollo May in *Love and Will*, p. 100.
11 Victor Frankl, *Man's Search for Meaning* (New York: Washington Square Press, 1969), p. 186.
12 Sonya Rudikoff, "O Pioneers! Reflections on the Whole Earth People" in *Commentary*, July 1972, p. 71. See also: Keith Melville, *Communes in the Counter Culture: Origins, Theories, Styles of Life*. See also: Ron Roberts, *The New Communes: Coming Together in America*.

Chapter 4

1 John Leonard, *This Pen for Hire* (Garden City: Doubleday, 1973), p. 75.
2 The poem of Ciro di Pers, "L'orologio da ruota," appears in Benedetto Croce, ed., *Lirici Marinisti*, Laterza, Bari, 1910. Quoted in Sebastian de Grazia, *Of Time, Work and Leisure* (New York: The Twentieth Century Fund, 1962), p. 311.
3 Marshall McLuhan, *Understanding Media: The Extensions of Man* (New York: McGraw-Hill, 1965), p. 153.
4 Lewis Mumford, *Technics and Civilization* (New York: Harcourt Brace, 1934), p. 14.
5 J. C. Carothers, "Culture, Psychiatry, and the Written Word." *Psychiatry*, 1959, 22, p. 308. Quoted in Marshall McLuhan, *The Gutenberg Galaxy* (New York: Signet Books, 1969), p. 27.
6 Rollo May, *Love and Will*, p. 243.
7 Marshall McLuhan and George Leonard, "The Future of Sex," *Look Magazine*, July 25, 1967, pp. 56–60.

8 Heroard, "Journal sur l'enfance et la jeunesse de Louis XIII." Quoted in Philip Aries, *Centuries of Childhood*, trans. Robert Baldick (New York: Alfred A. Knopf, 1962), pp. 100, 102.

9 David Hunt, *Parents and Children in History* (New York: Basic Books, 1970), pp. 159–79.

10 McLuhan, *Gutenberg Galaxy*, (New York: Signet Books, 1969), p. 9.

11 Ibid., p. 9.

12 Paul Goodman, "Today's Youth," *Chicago Tribune*, Sept. 14, 1969.

13 Baba Ram Dass, quoted in an interview with Jon Lipsky, "Meeting of the Masters," *Free Paper:* Boston, Nov. 14, 1973, p. 1.

14 Carlos Castaneda, *A Separate Reality* (New York: Pocket Books, 1972).

15 George Steiner, *In Bluebeard's Castle* (New Haven: Yale University Press, 1971), pp. 115–16.

16 Ibid., p. 116.

17 Ibid., p. 117.

18 David B. Wilson, "Digital Clocks and Machines Using Us," *Boston Globe*, Nov. 4, 1973, p. A-4.

19 George Steiner quoted in "The Freakish Passion: An Interview with George Steiner" by Elizabeth Hall, *Psychology Today*, Feb. 1973, p. 64.

20 Mark Gerzon, *The Whole World is Watching* (New York: Paperback Library, 1970), p. 67.

21 Howard, *Please Touch*, p. 245.

22 Pierre Teilhard de Chardin, *The Phenomenon of Man* (New York: Harper and Row, 1959).

23 George D. Spindler, "Education in a Transforming American Culture," in *Education and Culture—Anthropological Approaches*, G. D. Spindler, ed. (New York: Holt, Rinehart and Winston, 1963).

24 David Riesman, Nathan Glazer, and Reuel Denney, *The Lonely Crowd* (New Haven: Yale University Press, 1950).

25 Margaret Mead, *Culture and Commitment: A Study of the Generation Gap* (Garden City: Natural History Press, 1970).

Chapter 5

1 Edgar Friedenberg, *Coming of Age in America* (New York: Vintage Books, 1967), p. 211.

2 Edgar Friedenberg, *The Dignity of Youth and Other Atavisms* (Boston: Beacon Press, 1965), p. 5.

3 See, for example: Elizabeth Dovan and Joseph Adelson, "Orientation Toward the Future," in *Adolescents: Developments and Rela-*

tionships, M. S. Smart and R. Smart, eds. (New York: The Macmillan Company, 1973), p. 172.

Joseph Stone and Joseph Church, *Childhood and Adolescence* (New York: Random House, 1957), pp. 306, 316, 317.

4 Alexander A. Schneiders, *Personality Development and Adjustment in Adolescence* (Milwaukee: Bruce, 1960), p. 60.

5 Erikson, *Identity, Youth and Crisis*, pp. 24–25.

6 Erikson, *Childhood and Society*, p. 308.

7 Ibid., p. 308.

8 Ibid., p. 320.

9 A three-paragraph summary cannot, of course, do justice to the complexity of Erikson's observations on identity possibilities.

10 *Newsweek*, Dec. 29, 1969, p. 19.

11 Erikson, "The Dissent of Contemporary Youth" in *Youth and Culture*, Hazel V. Kraemer, ed. (Monterey: Brooks/Cole, 1974), p. 581.

12 Clifford Adelman, *Generations* (New York: Praeger, 1972).

13 Ivan Illich, *Deschooling Society* (New York: Harrow Books, 1971), p. 27.

14 Lawrence Kohlberg and Carol Gilligan, "The Adolescent as a Philosopher: The Discovery of Self in a Postconventional World," *Youth and Culture*, Hazel V. Kraemer, ed., p. 625.

15 Kohlberg, in Kraemer, *Youth and Culture*, p. 626.

16 Marshall McLuhan and Quentin Fiore, *The Medium Is the Massage* (New York: Bantam Books, 1967), p. 61.

17 See Ruth Benedict, *Patterns of Culture* (Boston: Houghton Mifflin, 1959), p. 126. See also: J. C. Carothers, "The African Mind in Health and Disease," *A Study in Ethnopsychiatry* (Geneva: World Health Organization, 1953, No. 17).

18 Kohlberg, in Kraemer, *Youth and Culture*, pp. 599–631.

19 Alan Harrington, *Psychopaths* (New York: Simon and Schuster, 1972).

20 *Uniform Crime Reports*. Federal Bureau of Investigation. United States Department of Justice, 1971.

21 Martin Pawley, *The Private Future* (New York: Random House, 1974), p. 207.

22 Kenneth Keniston, "Morals and Ethics," *The American Scholar*, 1965, Vol. 34, p. 628.

23 Ibid., p. 631.

24 John Gay and Michael Cole, *The New Mathematics and an Old Culture: A Study of Learning among the Kpelle of Liberia* (New York: Holt, Rinehart and Winston, 1967). Among the Kpelle, the question, What is a circle? or What is a triangle? is invariably answered by

pointing to objects that have those approximate shapes. A circle is "a pot, a pan, a frog, a sledge hammer, a tortoise, a water turtle, and a rice fanner." The Kpelle lack not only symbolic and abstract tendencies but also any semblance of the Western habit of grouping, ordering, and categorizing. When faced with an experiment in classifying objects into color, number, or shape—a task that is ridiculously easy for children raised in the Western tradition—Kpelle adults react with near-incomprehension, and even after careful explanation and demonstration the majority consistently fail to complete the task.

25 Kohlberg, in Kraemer, *Youth and Culture*, pp. 599–631.
26 This electronic erosion of the Western mind is, let me hasten to add, only a speculation on my part—one that runs counter to the prevailing notion that the youth of today are much brighter than previous generations. But one wonders. Apart from the fact that volume of information is often confused with intelligence, and aside from the fact that schools teach more for tests than ever before, there is another smoke screen that clouds the picture. In a TV society, language runs far ahead of conceptual abilities. Piaget, for example, has demonstrated that youngsters are capable of demonstrating verbal comprehension of concepts they actually do not understand at all. The television child picks up a wealth of knowledge and ready-made phrases from his TV set, but whether this reflects substantial conceptual gains or whether it is largely a case of imitation is not so easily discerned. In any event, there is one rather substantial statistical trend that indicates that all is not well with the brains of American youth. For the last ten years the mean scores on the Scholastic Aptitude Test (widely used as an admissions criterion by colleges) have dropped steadily, and no one has as yet come up with a redeeming explanation for the decline (see "Decline in the SATs," *Time*, Dec. 31, 1973, p. 45).
27 Kohlberg, in *Youth and Culture*, pp. 620–26.
28 Ibid., p. 625.
29 Adelman, *Generations*, pp. 113–25.

Chapter 6

1 Hermann Hesse, *Steppenwolf* (New York: Bantam Books, 1969), p. 187. Originally published in German. Copyright 1927, by S. Fischer Verlag AG, Berlin.
2 Norman O. Brown, *Love's Body* (New York: Vintage Books, 1966), p. 132.
3 William Blake, "Letter to Butts, 22 Nov., 1802." *The Complete*

Writings, ed. G. Keynes (London and New York, 1957). Quoted in Brown, p. 193. See also: McLuhan, *Gutenberg Galaxy,* p. 321.

4 Hesse, *Steppenwolf,* p. 201.

5 Brown, *Love's Body,* p. 98.

6 R. D. Laing, *The Politics of Experience* (New York: Ballantine Books, 1968), p. 74.

7 Brown, *Love's Body,* p. 11.

8 George Steiner, *In Bluebeard's Castle,* p. 41.

9 Ibid., p. 41.

10 Erich Fromm, *The Art of Loving* (New York: Harper Colophon Books, 1962), pp. 38–46.

11 Leslie Fiedler, *No! In Thunder* (Boston: Beacon Press, 1960), p. 287.

12 Brown, *Love's Body,* p. 250.

13 Sigmund Freud, "Dostoevsky and Parricide," p. 236. *Collected Papers V* (London, 1952). Quoted in Brown, p. 151.

14 Laing, *The Politics of Experience,* p. xii.

15 R. H. Tawney, *Religion and the Rise of Capitalism* (New York: Mentor Books, 1960), p. 114.

16 Acts 9:2–6.

17 Galatians 3:28–29.

18 Augustine, "Explanation of Psalm 30," S.1:3.

19 I Corinthians 12:21–27.

20 Tawney, *Religion and the Rise of Capitalism,* p. 211.

21 Brown, *Love's Body,* p. 85.

22 Ibid., p. 86.

23 Richard Kostelanetz, "Marshall McLuhan," in *The McLuhan Explosion,* Harry H. Crosby and George R. Bond, eds. (New York: American Book Co., 1968), p. 136.

24 Brown, *Love's Body,* p. 105.

25 Meher Baba, "Undoing the Ego" in *Sources,* Theodore Roszak, ed. (New York: Harper Colophon Books, 1972), p. 201.

26 George Leonard, *The Transformation* (New York: Delacorte Press, 1972), p. 201.

27 Roszak, *Sources,* pp. 112–13.

28 From a letter of Keats, quoted in Lionel Trilling, *Sincerity and Authenticity* (Cambridge: Harvard University Press, 1972), p. 166.

29 Edgar Friedenberg, *The Vanishing Adolescent* (New York: Delta Books, 1968), p. 13.

30 Victor Goertzel and Mildred Goertzel, *Cradles of Eminence* (Boston: Little, Brown, 1962), p. viii.

31 Herbert Marcuse, "Love Mystified: A Critique of Norman O.

Brown," in Roszak, ed., p. 447. Originally published in *Commentary*, Feb. 1967.

32 Stanley Coopersmith, *The Antecedents of Self-Esteem* (San Francisco: Freeman, 1967).

33 Julian B. Rotter, "Generalized Expectancies of Internal vs. External Control," *Psychological Monographs*, No. 209, 1966, p. 1–25.

34 Erikson, *Identity, Youth and Crisis*, p. 42.

Chapter 7

1 Andrew Weil, *The Natural Mind* (Boston: Houghton Mifflin, 1972).

2 Peter Marin, *"Greening of America:* A Critique," *The New York Times Book Review*, Nov. 8, 1970.

3 John W. M. Whiting, Richard Kluckhohn, and Albert Anthony, "The Function of Male Initiation Ceremonies at Puberty," in *Child Development and Behavior: Readings*, Freda Rebelsky and Lynn Dorman, eds. (New York: Alfred A. Knopf, 1970), pp. 132–43.

4 Francis J. Kelly and Daniel J. Baer, "Physical Challenge as a Treatment for Delinquency," *Crime and Delinquency*, Oct. 1971.

5 Ibid.

6 Karl Bednarik, *The Male in Crisis* (New York: Alfred A. Knopf, 1970).

7 Francis L. K. Hsu, Blanche G. Watrous, and Edith M. Lord, "Culture Patterns and Adolescent Behavior," *International Journal of Social Psychiatry*, 1961, 7, pp. 33–53.

Chapter 9

1 Leslie Fiedler, *Love and Death in the American Novel* (New York: Criterion Books, 1960).

2 Ibid., p. 332

3 George Gilder, *Sexual Suicide* (New York: Quadrangle/The New York Times Book Co., 1973).

4 Carl Rogers, *Becoming Partners: Marriage and Its Alternatives* (New York: Delacorte Press, 1972).

5 Ibid., pp. 162–63.

6 Ibid., p. 212.

7 Ibid., p. 212.

8 Rogers, "The Person of Tomorrow," in *Youth and Culture*, Hazel V. Kraemer, ed. (Monterey: Brooks/Cole, 1974), p. 668. First printed in *Colorado Journal of Educational Research*, 1972, 12 (1).

9 Nena O'Neill and George O'Neill, *Open Marriage: A New Life Style for Couples* (New York: M. Evans, 1972).

10 John Lobell and Mimi Lobell, *John and Mimi: A Free Marriage* (New York: Bantam Books, 1973).

11 Ibid., pp. 175–76.
12 Carl Rogers and Barry Stevens, *Person to Person* (New York: Pocket Books, 1971), p. 132.
13 F. M. Esfandiary, *Up-Wingers*, pp. 26, 31, 32, 36, 37–38.
14 Art Buchwald quoted in *Time*, Dec. 24, 1973, p. 60.
15 Urie Bronfenbrenner quoted in *Time*, Dec. 24, 1973, p. 65.
16 "The Woman's Touch," *Newsweek*, Jan. 6, 1975.
17 See David B. Lynn, *Parental and Sex-Role Identification: A Theoretical Formulation* (Berkeley: McCutchan, 1969).
18 David Gutmann, "Men, Women, and the Parental Imperative," *Commentary*, Dec. 1973, pp. 59–64.
19 Urie Bronfenbrenner, "The Changing American Child—A Speculative Analysis," in *Child Development and Behavior: Readings*, p. 149.
20 Gutmann, "Parental Imperative" p. 63.
21 See Gilder, *Sexual Suicide.*
22 Phyllis Chesler, *Women and Madness* (Garden City: Doubleday, 1972), p. 98.
23 Abraham Maslow, *Motivation and Personality* (New York: Harper and Row, 1954).
24 Erik H. Erikson, "The Roots of Virtue," in *The Humanist Frame*, Julian Huxley, ed. (New York: Harper and Bros., 1961), p. 160.
25 Ibid., pp. 160, 164.
26 Ibid., p. 159.

Chapter 10
1 Denis de Rougemont, *Love in the Western World* (New York: Fawcett World Library, 1969).
2 Ibid.
3 A more thorough discussion of *Lolita, The Man Without Qualities,* and The Romantic Myth can be found in Denis de Rougemont, *Love Declared: Essays on the Myths of Love* (Boston: Beacon Press, 1964), pp. 41–76.
4 de Rougemont, *Love in the Western World,* p. 300.
5 Philip Slater, *The Pursuit of Loneliness* (Boston: Beacon Press, 1970), p. 103.
6 Lionel Tiger and Robin Fox, *The Imperial Animal* (New York: Holt, Rinehart and Winston, 1971), p. 58.
7 See the sections on Don Juan in de Rougemont, *Love Declared.* See also Karl Stern, *The Flight from Women* (New York: The Noonday Press, 1966), pp. 212–26.
8 Søren Kierkegaard, "The Musical Erotic," *Either/Or.* Quoted in de Rougemont, *Love Declared,* p. 117.
9 de Rougemont, *Love Declared,* pp. 115, 117.

10 Tirso de Molina, *El Burlador de Sevilla.* Quoted in de Rougemont, ibid., p. 145.

11 From the opera *Don Giovanni* by Mozart. Quoted in de Rougemont, ibid., p. 156.

12 Robert Bolt, *A Man for All Seasons,* p. 65.

13 de Rougemont, *Love in the Western World,* p. 323.

14 Robert Herrick, "To the Virgins—" in *Sound and Sense,* Laurence Perrine, ed. (New York: Harcourt Brace and World, 1963), p. 76.

15 Andrew Marvell, "To His Coy Mistress," in Perrine, p. 64.

16 Alfred, Lord Tennyson, "Ulysses," in Perrine, p. 79.

17 Frederick Prokosch, "Sunburned Ulysses," in Perrine, p. 291.

18 de Rougemont, *Love in the Western World,* pp. 39, 39–43.

19 Ibid., p. 50.

20 Ibid., p. 55.

21 de Rougemont, *Love Declared,* p. 179.

Chapter 11

1 Richard Schickel, "Prurient Switch on a Sex Classic," *Life,* Feb. 16, 1968, p. 6.

2 Ibid.

3 C. S. Lewis, *The Four Loves,* p. 135.

4 Ibid., pp. 11–21, 163–92.

Chapter 12

1 Søren Kierkegaard, *The Works of Love.* In *A Kierkegaard Anthology,* Robert Bretall, ed. (New York: Modern Library, 1946).

2 Ibid., p. 293.

3 Joe K. Adams, "The Hidden Taboo on Love," *Love Today: A New Explanation,* Herbert A. Otto, ed., (New York: Association Press, 1972), p. 29.

4 Alexander Lowen, "The Spiral of Growth: Love, Sex and Pleasure," in Otto, *Love Today,* p. 19.

5 George B. Leonard, *The Transformation,* p. 15.

6 de Rougemont, *Love Declared,* p. 103.

7 Erikson, *Identity, Youth and Crisis,* p. 168.

8 Ibid.

9 Martin Buber, *I and Thou,* trans. Ronald Gregor Smith (New York: Charles Scribner's Sons, 1950), p. 28.

10 Ibid., p. 15.

11 Ibid., p. 14.

12 S. Freud, *Civilization and Its Discontents,* trans. and ed. by James Strachey (New York: W. W. Norton, 1962), p. 56.

13 Ibid., pp. 56–57.

14 Ibid., p. 90.

15 Kierkegaard in Bretall, ed., *A Kierkegaard Anthology*, pp. 288–289.
16 Buber, *I and Thou*, p. 32.
17 Harvey Cox, *The Secular City* (New York: The Macmillan Company, 1966), pp. 40–49.
18 McLuhan and Leonard, "The Future of Sex," *Look*, p. 56.
19 Ibid., pp. 58–59.
20 Ibid., p. 59.
21 Buber, *I and Thou*, p. 15.
22 John M. Darley and Bibb Latané, "Bystander Intervention in Emergencies: Diffusion of Responsibility," *Journal of Personality and Social Psychology*, 8 (4), 1968, pp. 377–83.
23 Adelman, *Generations*, p. 43.
24 J. Bronowski, "The Long Childhood," *The Nation*, Dec. 31, 1973, p. 714.
25 Matthew Arnold, "Dover Beach," in Perrine, p. 256–57.
26 Ibid.
27 Ronald Mazur, *The New Intimacy* (Boston: Beacon Press, 1973), p. 30.
28 Kahlil Gibran, *The Prophet* (New York: Alfred A. Knopf, 1923). Quoted in Mazur, p. 103. Also quoted in Carl R. Rogers, *Freedom to Learn* (Columbus: Charles E. Merrill, 1969), p. 231.
29 Matthew Arnold, "Dover Beach."
30 Nigel Nicolson, *Portrait of a Marriage* (New York: Atheneum, 1973).
31 Shakespeare, *Sonnets*, 116.
32 de Rougemont, *Love in the Western World*, p. 322.
33 Ibid., p. 327.

Chapter 13

1 Slater, *The Pursuit of Loneliness*, p. 149.
2 Mazur, *The New Intimacy*, p. 12.
3 Eugene C. Kennedy, *Believing* (Garden City: Doubleday, 1974), p. 81.
4 Gibran, from *The Prophet*.
5 Sir John Suckling, "The Constant Lover," in Perrine, p. 108.

Index